A Guide to the Teachings
of the
EARLY CHURCH FATHERS

A Guide to the Teachings of the Early Church Fathers

by

ROBERT R. WILLIAMS
B.A. (Wales), M.A. (Oxon.), S.T.D. (Temple)

WIPF & STOCK · Eugene, Oregon

Wipf and Stock Publishers
199 W 8th Ave, Suite 3
Eugene, OR 97401

A Guide to the Teachings of the Early Church Fathers
By Williams, Robert R.
Softcover ISBN-13: 978-1-7252-8064-9
Hardcover ISBN-13: 978-1-7252-8066-3
eBook ISBN-13: 978-1-7252-8065-6
Publication date 5/13/2020
Previously published by Eerdmans, 1960

To

DEAN THOMAS AND FACULTY
School of Theology
Temple University

ACKNOWLEDGMENTS

I am indebted to the following publishers for permission to use quoted material:

To the Wm. B. Eerdmans Publishing Co. for quotations from their reprint of *The Ante-Nicene Fathers*, edited by Roberts and Donaldson, and *The Nicene and Post-Nicene Fathers*, edited by Schaff and Wace;

To Thomas Nelson and Sons for quotations from the Revised Standard Version of the Bible.

The following works were of invaluable assistance in the understanding of doctrinal problems among the Church Fathers: *An Introduction to the Early History of Christian Doctrine* by Bethune-Baker and the writings of A. E. Burn on the Creeds. Other volumes which proved very helpful were: *A History of the Church* (Vol. I) by Philip Hughes and the translation of Eusebius' *Church History* by Roy J. Defarrari.

ABBREVIATIONS

ANF — Ante-Nicene Fathers
NPNF — Nicene and Post-Nicene Fathers
l.v. — longer version
s.v. — shorter version
1st ser. — first series
2nd ser. — second series

All quotations from the Church Fathers are from the editions reprinted by the Wm. B. Eerdmans Publishing Co. Volume and page numbers are taken from these editions; book and chapter numbers in the writings of the Fathers refer to those used in these editions. Words or phrases enclosed in brackets in the quotations were inserted by the editors of these editions; words or phrases enclosed in brackets together with parentheses are my insertions.

INTRODUCTION

A reader of the New Testament finds himself within a world entirely different from that of the Old Testament. The early followers of Christ lived under the Romans. Their contemporaries were influenced by Greek thought and speculation, not the divine revelation given to Moses and the Hebrew Prophets. Against Roman imperialism, the Church struggled for physical survival; against Greek intellectualism, she endeavored both to define and to vindicate her unique message.

The Fourth Gospel and the Epistle to the Hebrews had already suggested the possible doctrinal development of Christian thought within an empire saturated with pagan ideas. In his well-known Prologue, John had boldly identified the Savior with the Word, a cosmic concept long associated with Greek, especially Stoic, philosophy. The author of Hebrews similarly had drawn upon the platonic distinction between the world of sense impressions, which was a mere shadow, and the real world of the spirit.

The history of early Christianity may be divided into two stages. In the first, Church leaders were constrained to prove that Jesus of Nazareth was the Messiah of the Prophets and the Son of Man of the Apocalyptists. Paul, the chief protagonist of this period, sought to correct the many errors among Jewish converts of his day. Adherents of the subsequent Nazarene and Ebionite type failed to realize that the freedom in Christ released from a servile submission to the Mosaic Law, and thus they were guilty of the legalism condemned so severely in the Epistle to the Galatians. Such efforts by the Apostle and others determined both the catholic character of the Church as well as its line of defense, on a wider scale, in its phenomenal conflict with Graeco-Roman culture.

For the history of the second stage, we must turn principally to the Patristics, or Church Fathers. Their problems, as they were met, suggest certain chasms which had to be bridged if the truth as it is presented in the New Testament was to have relevance at the time.

One problem involved God in His relationship to all that exists. The unifying principle to the Greeks was the *Logos* or Word; to the Gnostics, *Pleroma* or Fullness; to the Church, Jesus Christ, the Son of God (Chapters II, III, IV).

In the matter of redemption, the Arians accepted Christ as a means of reconciliation and as a kind of Bridge constructed by God and to all appearances resembling Himself but which could not bear the whole strain of His Deity. The Church held the Bridge to be God Himself in His Son Jesus Christ, who was of the same essence or *ousia* as Himself (Chapter X).

The problem that eventually arose concerning the Trinity was solved by recognizing that God is both One and a Trinity of Persons or Expressions (Chapter VI).

In its Christology, after many attempts to relate the divine and the human natures, the Church affirmed that there was a real union of the two in Christ (Chapter X).

The chasm between reason and faith was bridged by the fusion of faith and reason, of philosophy and Christianity (Chapter V).

The ecclesiastical problem was solved by a stress on the One Faith and the uniform tradition handed down by the Apostles, which stabilized the early forms of the Christian ministry (Chapters I, IV, VII).

In the matter of discipline, the Church sought to protect its unity by calling on all offenders to repent and on all its members to be tolerant and charitable (Chapter VII).

The problem arising out of the disruption within the human soul was overcome by the stress on God's grace bringing man's will into harmony with the will of God (Chapter VIII).

The social problem concerning the relationship between Church and State was solved by the State's acceptance of the principle that a man's conscience is not of necessity a threat to its security (Chapter IX).

That any Christians were able to survive the intermittent persecutions of the Caesars is one of the wonders of history. That they not only survived, but even succeeded in making a patron of the emperor, and Christianity the official religion of his realm, is a greater wonder still!

Throughout this period of conflict the Fathers called themselves Catholics, the guardians of the true Faith and its tradition. But to call this Catholicism Roman is an anachronism. The Catholicism of the early Fathers was no more Roman than Antiochene, Alexandrian, or Carthaginian. Strictly speaking, the Christian Church today would be an enigma to an Ignatius, an Irenaeus, a Cyprian, or an Augustine. The Catholic Church of the first four centuries of our era was One, though world-wide; Apostolic, though universal; Holy, though functioning in a secular society; Ecclesiastical, though evangelical. The Holy Catholic Church of the Apostles' Creed was the Church of the early Fathers, not ours. When we repeat the Creed we affirm our belief in what was once a fact but which is now mainly an ideal. Insofar as Christ's presence is felt, every church has a right to the term Catholic whether its members are labelled Roman Catholic, Greek Orthodox, Lutheran, Episcopalian, Presbyterian, Congregational, or any other designation. The early Christians, however, called themselves Catholics because they were heirs to a tradition that made them witness *together* as did the Apostles, think or believe *together* as did the Apostles, and worship *together* as did the Apostles. This "togetherness" was essential to their idea of Catholicism. Heresies occurred when they did not believe the same things. Schisms divided them when they did not worship together in "the unity of the faith and of the knowledge of the Son of God."

CONTENTS

Introduction	9
I. Early Facets of the Faith	15
II. The Faith and Its Defenders	33
III. The Faith and Fantasy	51
IV. The Faith and Fact	71
V. The Faith and Fusion	89
VI. The Faith and Fallacy	113
VII. The Faith and Fellowship	131
VIII. The Faith and Freedom	153
IX. The Faith and Fetters	171
X. The Faith and Formula	193
Bibliography	211
General Index	219

I

Early Facets of the Faith

EARLY FACETS OF THE FAITH

By the end of the first century all of the New Testament books had been written, but no Church Council or ecclesiastical body up to that time had given them the authority conceded to the Old Testament. They were simply writings with a contemporary spiritual message, circulated among Christians as a permanent basis for faith and conduct. It was only later that the Church accepted these as Scripture or writings directly inspired, and the writers as "men moved by the Holy Spirit" and not by "the impulse of man" (II Peter 1:21).

What is known as the Apocrypha, usually inserted between the two Testaments, was regarded by both Jew and Christian as a work of men not moved by the Holy Spirit.

The Christian Church at the beginning was even more conservative than the Jewish. Only a few writings not in the New Testament as we now have it were included in some early manuscripts. For example, in what is known as Codex A, two writings described as the *Epistles of Clement* are added.

The Sinaitic Manuscript found by Count Tischendorf at the Convent of St. Catherine on Mount Sinai in 1859 contains, in addition to the books of the New Testament, the *Epistle of Barnabas* and *The Pastor of Hermas*. The *Codex Sinaiticus* embraces both the Old and the New Testaments and was written in the fourth century. In an early document on the New Testament called The Muratorium Fragment, the *Epistle of Barnabas* and *The Pastor of Hermas* are both excluded.

The mass of spurious Christian literature never received serious nor favorable consideration. None of these writings were canonized or accepted as inspired, although some of them had a special appeal, for they were supposed to be genuine.

The twenty-seven books which the Church finally accepted as authoritative served as its standard of belief and behavior. Anything contrary to the explicit teaching of these was considered heresy. Origen in his day wished there had been some instruction given about nonessentials. There seems to have been a certain amount of liberty concerning these. Take, for example, the reference to Jesus' descent into hell based on I Peter 3:16 and repeated by many Christians, Sunday after Sunday. In some of the early creeds, such as the Old Roman Creed (269-274), the Old Creed of Jerusalem (345), and the Creed of Antioch (375), the phrase is excluded.

We should have a few things before our minds as we seek to evaluate the contribution of the Apostolic Fathers. We should find out what kind of Gospel they presented and what form of a Christian ministry they upheld. It would be well also to stress those elements in their teaching which received greater emphasis or a fuller treatment by subsequent Christian thinkers.

The writers of the earliest period include Clement of Rome, Ignatius, Polycarp, Papias, Hegesippus, Hermas, the author of *Didache*, and the author of the *Epistle of Barnabas*.

I

Clement, Bishop of Rome, ministered at the end of the first century (95-97), perhaps earlier. In Clement of Rome's *Epistle to James*, a writing that is part of the doubtful literature attributed to him, known as *Pseudo-Clementina*, the bishop says that he was ordained by Peter on the eve of the Apostle's martyrdom in Rome (chap. 2).

Clement's *First Epistle to the Corinthians* is accepted as genuine. It is in the form of a letter sent by the Church of Rome to the Church of Corinth. In those days it was customary for churches to correspond with one another through their appointed leaders. The literary pattern and much of the contents of this Epistle recall Paul's First Epistle to the Corinthians. The Epistle opens with a salutation and ends with a benediction beginning with the words, "The grace of our Lord Jesus Christ be with you. . . ." As in Paul's time, dissensions still troubled the brethren at Corinth. Clement's stress on love reminds us of I Corinthians 13:

> Who can describe the [blessed] bond of the love of God? What man is able to tell the excellence of its beauty, as it ought to be told? The height to which love exalts is unspeakable. Love unites us to God. . . . Love beareth all things, is long-suffering in all things. There is nothing base, nothing arrogant in love. Love admits of no schisms: love gives rise to no seditions: love does all things in harmony (xlix, ANF, I, 19).

Wherever love dominates, good works follow. Though the Christian is justified by faith and though works wrought by him in holiness of heart can never be put to his credit, as regards his own salvation, many divine gifts, nevertheless, come to those who practice well-doing in the sight of God (xxxiii, xxxiv, pp. 13f.).

Early Facets of the Faith

In his treatment of the resurrection Clement has much in common with what is contained in the fifteenth chapter of First Corinthians, but he obviously parts company with Paul when he refers to the mythological Phoenix as an emblem of the resurrection (xxv, p. 12).

Of greater interest is his profound regard for the Christian ministry, formed, so he believes, after the high-priesthood in the Old Testament. He is as convinced as Irenaeus (125-202?) that the pastorate, with its bishops and presbyters, is in the Apostolic Succession and essential to the Church's witness and continuity. In these days, when we are so often reminded that Christianity at the outset was a lay movement, it is well to recall the emphasis laid by Clement and other early writers on clerical orders. To him the pastorate is a divine arrangement and as consecrated as the priesthood under the Hebrew system:

> The apostles have preached the Gospel to us from the Lord Jesus Christ; Jesus Christ [has done so] from God. Christ therefore was sent forth by God, and the apostles by Christ. . . . they went forth proclaiming that the kingdom of God was at hand. And thus preaching through countries and cities, they appointed the firstfruits [of their labours], having first proved them by the Spirit, to be bishops and deacons of those who should afterwards believe. . . . For thus saith the Scripture in a certain place, "I will appoint their bishops [(or overseers)] in righteousness, and their deacons [(or servants)] in faith" (xlii, p. 16).

Clement is the first to use the title "episcopate" for the office of bishop or overseer. He also refers to these overseers as presbyters. There was nothing regional about the episcopacy then. It would be misleading to regard his intervention in Corinthian affairs at this stage as anything but a friendly gesture on the part of a Christian leader. That he was bishop of Rome gave him no pre-eminence. Ignatius, Bishop of Antioch, as we shall presently see, wrote a number of letters to different churches. It would be reasonable to infer that these early ministers considered the welfare of the whole Church as their bounden duty, whether its members met in Rome, Corinth, Ephesus, or anywhere else.

As regards Apostolic Succession, he is "of the opinion" that "other eminent men," besides the first Apostles, could appoint worthy and blameless Christians to be overseers, bishops, and presbyters, provided that "the whole Church" is in agreement (xliv, p. 17). There is every reason to assume that by the "whole Church" he means in the context the local church, for it is unthinkable that he as Bishop of Rome would have anything to do with appointments at Corinth, for instance, unless he happened to be there as a visiting clergyman during the ordination service. Origen, as we shall see later, suffered severely at the hands of his bishop because the latter disapproved of his being ordained by bishops outside his own see of Alexandria.

II

Ignatius, Bishop of Antioch (c.110), wrote a number of letters while on his way to Rome to give his life for the Faith. Of the fifteen letters attributed to him, only seven are accepted as his. The other eight, three of which are written in Latin, show what later writers thought he should have written had he been as keen as they were about some theories concerning doctrine and polity or church government. What he did actually write has been left to posterity in his epistles to the Ephesians, the Magnesians, the Trallians, the Romans, the Philadelphians, the Smyrnaeans, and Polycarp.

These abound with wisdom, understanding, and an exceptional grasp of the Christian fundamentals. As he sets his face to go to Rome, the floodgates of his great heart are thrown open. What flows out in the form of advice, guidance, and inspiration is immense when we think that it all happened on a single journey under a terrible strain. The theologian, the preacher, and the historian could read these writings at random and without much scrutiny discover valuable material in them. Think of these sayings and metaphors: "Every kind of wound is not healed with the same plaster." "The times call for you as pilots for the winds." "Stand fast, as does an anvil which is beaten." Or this for a young people's message:

> Be sober as an athlete of God: the prize set before thee is immortality and eternal life, of which thou art also persuaded (*Ep. to Polycarp*, ii, s.v., ANF, I, 94).

On his eventful journey Ignatius passed through Philadelphia. On reaching Smyrna he was met by Polycarp, the bishop of the city. Many friends from the neighboring cities of Ephesus, Tralles, and Magnesia came to offer their moral support and prayers. While he tarried with them, he wrote a letter to each of the churches in these cities. From Smyrna he also wrote an epistle to the church in Rome, beseeching the brethren not to do anything to prevent his final sacrifice for Christ.

His words about martyrdom should be quoted here, as his attitude represented the ideal to many a Christian in the early Church:

> I write to all the Churches, and impress on them all, that I shall willingly die for God, unless ye hinder me. I beseech of you not to show an unseasonable goodwill towards me. Suffer me to become food for the wild beasts, through whose instrumentality it will be granted me to attain to God. I am the wheat of God, and am ground by the teeth of the wild beasts, that I may be found the pure bread of God. Rather entice the wild beasts, that they may become my tomb, and may leave nothing of my body. . . . Then shall I be a true disciple of Jesus Christ, when the world shall not see so much as my body. Entreat the Lord for me, that by these instruments I may be found a sacrifice to God (*Ep. to the Romans*, iv, l.v., p. 75).

Upon reaching Troas, where Paul once heard a call from Macedonia in a vision, Ignatius sent epistles to the churches in Philadelphia and Smyrna, and also to Polycarp. He was put to death on December 20, 107, when he was about eighty years of age.

The following excerpt is a fairly accurate summary of his teaching. I have italicized his special emphasis:

> *Stand fast*, brethren, *in the faith of Jesus Christ, and in His love, in His passion, and in His resurrection.* Do ye all *come together in common*, and *individually*, through grace, in *one faith of God the Father*, and *of Jesus Christ His only-begotten Son*, and the *"first-born of every creature,"* but of the *seed of David according to the flesh*, being under the *guidance of the Comforter*, in *obedience to the bishop and the presbytery with an undivided mind, breaking one and the same bread*, which is the medicine of immortality, and the antidote which prevents us from dying . . . *that we should live in God through Jesus Christ* (*Ep. to the Ephesians*, xx, l.v., p. 57).

Taking the epistles as a whole, we find that Ignatius' conception of Jesus Christ is typical of what theologians taught later and finally incorporated in the great creeds. Christ, or the Word (*Logos*), was "with the Father before the ages." There is one God, who became known through Jesus Christ, whose appearance in the flesh he describes as follows:

> For the Son of God, who was begotten before time began, and established all things according to the will of the Father, He was conceived in the womb of Mary, according to the appointment of God, of the seed of David, and by the Holy Ghost (*Ep. to the Ephesians*, xviii, l.v., p. 57).

Being incorporeal, He was in the body; being impassible, He was in a passible body (*ibid.*, vii, l.v., p. 52).

Leo uses the phrase "a passible nature" in his famous *Tome* of the fifth century. The phrase means that He had a body capable of suffering.

Ignatius tells Polycarp to "look for Christ, the Son of God, . . . who was impalpable, and could not be touched, as being without a body, but for our sakes became such, might be touched and handled in the body; who was impassible as God, but became passible for our sakes as man; and who in every kind of way suffered for our sakes" (*Ep. to Polycarp*, iii, l.v., p. 94).

The Magnesians are told that the "substance" of the Eternal Word was "begotten by divine power" (*Ep. to the Magnesians*, viii, l.v., p. 62).

With regard to common worship, another of his special emphases, he has this to say:

> Let every one of you keep the Sabbath after a spiritual manner, rejoicing in meditation on the law, not in relaxation of the body, admiring the workmanship of God, and not eating things prepared the day before, nor using lukewarm drinks, and walking within a prescribed space, nor finding a delight in dancing and plaudits which have no sense in them. And after the observance of the Sabbath, let every friend of Christ keep the Lord's Day as a festival, the resurrection-day, the queen and chief of all the days (*Ep. to the Magnesian*, ix, l.v., p. 63).

Within the one Church, so he tells us, there is but one faith, one preaching, one baptism, and one eucharist. In his *Epistle to the Smyrnaeans* (viii, s.v., pp. 89f.) he refers to the Christian fellowship as the "Catholic Church," and the Lord's Supper as the "Eucharist," which suggests that these names have come down from a very early time. There is no proof that he created these terms. He holds there is no proper Eucharist unless it is administered either by a bishop or by a representative of his (*ibid.*). He informs the Philadelphian Church:

> For there is one flesh of the Lord Jesus Christ; and His blood which was shed for us is one; one loaf also is broken to all . . . and one cup is distributed among them all: there is but one altar for the whole Church, and one bishop, with the presbytery and deacons, my fellow-servants (*Ep. to the Philadelphians*, iv, l.v., p. 81).

He is basically in agreement with Clement about the ministry, but he regards the bishop as a symbol of the unity of the whole

Church. Besides, the bishop is to be held in honor even if he were but a young man. By honoring him, God is also honored. All things should be done with the proper order in Christ. He goes on to explain:

> Let the laity be subject to the deacons; the deacons to the presbyters; the presbyters to the bishop; the bishop to Christ, even as He is to the Father (*Ep. to the Smyrnaeans*, ix, l.v., p. 90).

The presbyters as well as the bishops are regarded as apostles of Jesus Christ. The deacons, too, are ministers of His mysteries:

> And do ye reverence them [(viz. the deacons)] as Jesus Christ, of whose place they are the keepers, even as the bishop is the representative of the Father of all things, and the presbyters are the sanhedrin of God, and assembly of the apostles of Christ. Apart from these there is no elect Church, no congregation of holy ones, no assembly of saints (*Ep. to the Trallians*, iii, l.v., p. 67).

To Ignatius every church with which he corresponds is not only *a* church but *the* Church, provided that Christ is present and the orders in Him are truly honored. As Christ possesses two natures, the divine and the human, so has the Church both flesh and spirit. Its harmony and unity, whether in Ephesus or Rome, depend on the inspiration and guidance received by its leaders from Christ and the Comforter. The ministry, as it is composed of bishops, presbyters, and deacons, is an avenue of divine grace as it operates in each church. As he tells Polycarp, the work is God's and theirs. There is nothing hierarchical about this conception. It simply means that those who have been set aside by the Holy Spirit are supposed to function under His guidance. The ordination service of even the most evangelical of churches today must of necessity accept the truth that is taught here.

Both Clement and Ignatius are among the Congregationalists as far as the autonomy and the independence of the local church are concerned. Each church is complete in itself. Each has the same faith, the same sacraments, the same form of ministry, and the same Comforter to guide it. As far as the fundamentals in belief and polity are in question, Ignatius could have sent a circular letter, similar to the Epistle to the Ephesians by Paul, to be read in turn by all the six churches. It is the unity of the faith and the same church orders that make each church catholic. In the last analysis it is Christ's own presence: "Wherever Jesus Christ is, there is the Catholic Church" (*Ep. to the Smyrnaeans*, viii, s.v., p. 90). To say that he recognizes the "primacy of the Roman Church" is wishful thinking (cf. *A History of the Church,* I, 56, by Philip Hughes). In his salutation to that church in his *Epistle to the Romans* he lavishes the highest praise on the fellowship that had the honor of witnessing to the Master in the capital of the Empire because he is thinking of Caesar as well as Christ. Greater luster, so it seemed, was to be added to his own martyrdom by the fact that his end was to occur within the imperial city itself.

III

Polycarp, as we have seen, was Bishop of Smyrna, and he, too, was among the early martyrs. Historically, he is important. He remembered John and other Apostles with whom he often conversed, and later he himself became known to Irenaeus. Apart from being a link between two generations of Christians, a witness to the Faith, and a tutor of the greatest Catholic of the second century, his role as a leader of thought is of little consequence.

As a man and fellow worker he is held in high esteem by Ignatius, who writes of him as a devout Christian whose prayers preserved the peace of the church at Antioch, whose faith was unwavering, whose love of the truth was energetic, and whose mind was "established in God, as on a rock which is immoveable" (*Ep. to Polycarp*).

Irenaeus writes of him:

> Polycarp . . . was not only instructed by apostles, and conversed with many who had seen Christ, but was also, by apostles in Asia, appointed bishop of the Church in Smyrna, whom I also saw in my early youth, for he tarried [on earth] a very long time, and, when a very old man, gloriously and most nobly suffering martyrdom, departed this life, having always taught the things which he had learned from the apostles, and which the Church has handed down, and which alone are true (*Against Heresies*, Bk. III, iii, 4, ANF, I, 416).

The same writer narrates two incidents which occurred when Polycarp visited Rome while Anicetus was bishop. Each of these prelates represented a different custom in the observance of Easter, but in spite of their opposite views they joined together at the same Communion Table, maintaining thereby the peace of the Church (Irenaeus, *Fragments,* iii, ANF, I, 569). The other event concerned an unexpected meeting that Polycarp had with Marcion, the heretic, whom he knew in the East. On being asked by the heretic whether he knew him, the bishop replied, "I do know thee, the first-born of Satan" (*Against Heresies*, Bk. III, iii, 4, p. 416).

His *Epistle to the Philippians* is far from being equal to the letters of Ignatius, but it has a certain appeal on account of its practical wisdom and Scriptural references. In it he writes of Christ as the "Son of God, and our everlasting High Priest" (xii, ANF, I, 35). He, too, exhorts the saints to be "subject to the presbyters and deacons, as unto God and Christ" (v, p. 34). He tenderly reminds the Philippians:

> For neither I, nor any other such one, can come up to the wisdom of the blessed and glorified Paul. He, when among you, accurately . . . taught the word of truth in the presence of those who were then alive. And when absent from you, he wrote you a letter, which, if you carefully study, you will find to be the means of building you up in that faith which has been given you, and which, being followed by hope, and preceded by love towards God, and Christ, and our neighbor, "is the mother of us all" (iii, p. 33).

It is strange that in the only epistle now extant written by one who in early youth came under the influence of John, there are hardly any quotations from his works. Out of sixty New Testament quotations and references in his *Epistle to the Philippians*, only one is from the Apostle's writings. Matthew and Mark are mentioned, but not the Fourth Gospel. Peter's Epistles are drawn upon and half of the allusions are from Paul. In their Introductory Note to Polycarp's Epistle the American editors are aware of the difficulty, and although they assert that "he writes like the disciple of St. John," they too have to admit that as a writer he is "in perfect harmony with St. Paul's hymn-like eulogy of Christian love."

It may be that another explanation is possible. Is it not possible that the Philippians were better acquainted with Paul's teaching than with John's? If that were the case, then we are justified in inferring that at the time Polycarp wrote his Epistle there existed within the Church, which was both Catholic and Apostolic, two distinct traditions. The former would have its center of influence in Asia Minor, where John mainly ministered, and the latter would be followed by such European churches as Philippi, which were more conversant with Paul's teaching.

The story of Polycarp's martyrdom is found in an *Encyclical Letter* of the Church at Smyrna. On February 26, 156, the day of his martyrdom in Smyrna, the proconsul pleaded with him to recant and to "swear by the fortune of Caesar" (ix, ANF, I, 41) and join with an infuriated mob of both Jews and Gentiles in the mad cry, "Away with the Atheists!" When offered his freedom by blaspheming Christ, Polycarp courageously replied: "Eighty and six years have I served Him, and He never did me any injury: how then can I blaspheme my King and my Saviour?" (*ibid.*). As he was being led away to be burned, his final prayer ended with these words:

> I praise Thee for all things, I bless Thee, I glorify Thee, along with the everlasting and heavenly Jesus Christ, Thy beloved Son, with whom, to Thee, and the Holy Ghost, be glory both now and to all coming ages. Amen (xiv, p. 42).

IV

Papias, another of the Apostolic Fathers, was Bishop of Hierapolis in Phrygia in Asia Minor. Like Polycarp, his friend and contemporary, he knew John and some of the other Apostles. The little that is known of him has been handed down by Irenaeus and Eusebius, the church historian of the fourth century. Both were acquainted with the five books that he had written, of which only a few fragments remain. From what is extant, he stands out as a reporter of what he had received. He brings to mind in this respect the author of the Book of Revelation, for both testify to what they had heard. His source, however, was human and not divine. He mentions among his authorities certain presbyters or elders and also the daughters of Philip who lived in Hierapolis.

Of his records two are of special interest. One has reference to the millennium, a belief strongly held in that part of the Empire from early times. He lays particular stress on the abundant productivity of the earth under the reign of Christ and His saints. The other concerns the Gospels of Mark and Matthew:

> And the presbyter said this. Mark having become the interpreter of Peter, wrote down accurately whatsoever he remembered. It was not, however, in exact order that he related the sayings or deeds of Christ. For he neither heard the Lord nor accompanied Him. But afterwards, as I said, he accompanied Peter, who accommodated his instructions to the necessities [of his hearers], but with no intention of giving a regular narrative of the Lord's sayings. Wherefore Mark made no mistake in thus writing some things as he remembered them. For of one thing he took especial care, not to omit anything he had heard, and not to put anything fictitious into the statements. . . . Matthew put together the oracles [of the Lord] in the Hebrew language, and each one interpreted them as best he could (*Fragments*, vi, ANF, I, 154-55).

V

Hegesippus, a younger contemporary of Polycarp and Papias, was born in Palestine. He visited Rome in 150 during the reign of Antonius Pius, the foster father of Marcus Aurelius. This layman is known as the first Christian chronicler. His work, *Hypomnemata*, was in five books. The fragments of these *memoirs* preserved by Eusebius bear witness to the success of the Christian Church in Palestine under the leadership of James the Just, brother of our Lord, and Symeon, who followed him as Bishop of Jerusalem around the year 60. The subsequent activity of this church demonstrates its loyalty to the Catholic tradition as expressed by such churches as Corinth and Rome. His list of Roman bishops up to Anicetus, whose deacon was Eleutherus, and his account of what happened at Corinth as a result of Clement's letter have historical value. He relates how his soul was refreshed by the "true doctrine" preached at Corinth. In every city, so he states, the succession and preaching were as the Law, the Prophets, and the Lord proclaimed (Eusebius, *Church History,* Bk. IV, xxii, NPNF, 2nd ser., I, 198).

VI

Hermas, a brother of Pius, the ninth Bishop of Rome (c.140), wrote an allegory in Greek known as *The Shepherd,* or *The Pastor,* a form of literature made famous by Dante and Bunyan. In fact, *The Pastor* is regarded as the *Pilgrim's Progress* of the early Church. Dante is supposed to have been influenced by it — a reasonable deduction because it lasted in its popular appeal for many centuries. Besides, there is an unmistakable similarity between Rhoda, the woman Hermas knew, and Beatrice. The ideal in both instances was a living person. In the case of the former, it was the beautiful lady whom the author served as a slave in his youth.

This primitive allegory, so full of religious romance and instruction, was one of the most esteemed of all the Christian writings, especially in the East. Its literary form accounted to some degree for its fame, but there was another reason. It was considered by many as Scripture. As pointed out previously, it was included in the Sinaitic Manuscript of the fourth century. Irenaeus quotes it as Scripture (*Against Heresies,* Bk. IV, xx, 2, ANF, I, 488). Clement of Alexandria (180-202) seems to agree (*Stromata,* Bk. I, xxix, ANF, II, 341; Bk. II, i, p. 348). Origen (195-254) identifies the author with Hermas, a friend of Paul mentioned in Romans 16:14. This was the general belief. Portions of *The*

Pastor were read publicly in many churches as a befitting introduction to the Faith.

Even in the second century some, among whom was Tertullian (160-220), doubted its authorship. A fragment of manuscript belonging to this period, found by Muritori in Milan in the seventeenth century, says that

> The Pastor was written very lately in our times, in the city of Rome, by Hermas, while Bishop Pius, his brother, sat in the chair of the Church of the city of Rome (Introduction to *The Pastor*, ANF, II, 7).

By the time the New Testament Canon was decided on, *The Pastor* had been rejected on account of its late authorship and many a strange expression of Christian belief. Although there is every reason to infer that the author was a Trinitarian who accepted Christ as the eternal Son of God, yet his view of the Godhead is set forth in such a manner that he seems to assume there were only two Persons in the Deity, namely, the Father and the Holy Spirit, and not three. In his Parable of the Vineyard, God the Creator and Father is master, the Son of God the master's slave or servant, and the Holy Spirit the master's son (*Similitude Fifth*, v, ANF, II, 35).

This goes to show how precarious it is to deduce a doctrine from the descriptive or illustrative expressions of a work of this kind. To do so is no more logical than if someone were to measure a meadow from an artist's painting of it on a canvas. Similitudes and parables seek to tell what truth is like, not what it is. Even the likeness may have many facets, oftentimes paradoxical, never contradictory. The Kingdom of God which Jesus describes in His parables can be within and without. It can operate like a mustard seed and like leaven. A similitude, like a parable, is of service because man is a citizen of two worlds, the seen and the unseen. It is expedient for him, therefore, to suggest by the help of what is known what the unknown is like. Even his words, whether oral or written, are ambassadors from a realm that cannot be heard or seen. To understand *The Pastor*, an allowance should be made for this duality.

The work is in three books. The first contains Five Visions; the second, Twelve Commandments; the third, Ten Similitudes.

The *Book of Commandments* deals with religious and moral duties which can be performed only if the Spirit of God is in control of a man's life. Thus Hermas saves himself from being claimed by the legalists. Although he emphasizes the point that no one can be made perfect unless the commandments given to the author by a heavenly visitant in the form of a shepherd are piously kept, yet he holds that the power to do this comes from the Holy Spirit who dwells within the heart. Therefore he lays stress upon faith and prayer and warns against grieving the Holy Spirit (Bk. II, *Commandment Fifth*, ii, ANF, II, 23).

The *Book of Similitudes* portrays the Christian as a stranger whose citizenship is in heaven. Worldly possessions have a sacramental value. Earthly transactions become "sacred expenditure." Purchasing "afflicted souls" is more important than buying lands and houses. Wealth is considered a trust (Bk. III, *Similitude First*, pp. 31, 32). Hermas obviously believes in stewardship.

The *Book of Visions* resembles in some respects the Book of Revelation. The author relates that one day when he had fallen asleep, an Old Woman, his symbolic figure of the Church, began to unravel to him certain mysteries (cf. Rev. 1:10). Sitting on a chair of white wool, she held a book in her hand (Bk. I, *Vision First*, ii, p. 10). The author himself, to whom the messages are given, could be regarded as the angel of the church in Rome, or of the Church Universal, or Catholic (cf. the angels of the seven churches in Rev. 1-3). The standard by which the visible Church is judged is the invisible or ideal Church. The ideal, holy Church, by appearing as an Old Woman, sometimes weak, sometimes strong, whom the author addresses as "Lady," reflects its counterpart on earth with its varied experiences. Though old, she is ever young, powerful, and beautiful. It was on her account that the mountains and the hills were brought forth. The heavens and the earth declare her glory. Everything moves and has its being for her sake (*Vision Third*, pp. 12ff.). The earthly Church is also like a tower in process of building and nearing completion.

The Pastor as a whole may be viewed as a sermon full of symbols and similitudes and, like many of the parables of Jesus, a call to repentance because the Kingdom of God is at hand.

VII

The author of the *Didache*, or *Teaching of the Twelve Apostles*, is unknown. Some think he was a Christian Jew of Alexandria. *The Lord's Teaching through the Twelve Apostles to the Nations* is the longer title. The date of its composition is generally held to be around 120. Among the manuscripts discovered by Bryennios in 1873 in the library of the Jerusalem Monastery at Constantinople, it is inserted between the two Epistles of Clement and the Epistles of Ignatius. Clement of Alexandria, Athanasius (300-373), and other writers refer to it. Eusebius lists it with *The Pastor* and the *Epistle of Barnabas* as a spurious work (*Church History*, Bk. III, xxv, NPNF, 2nd ser., I, 156).

Its sixteen short chapters are full of Scriptural references, especially to the New Testament. The commandments concerning the Two Ways, namely, the Way of Life and the Way of Death, are repetitions of what was taught by Moses in the Moral Law and by Jesus in the Sermon on the Mount.

The contrast between the Two Ways brings out what is latent in Matthew 7:13, 14, a contrast which might have been included in the teaching of the first Apostles and in the generations that followed. This may account for the similarity between the Way of Death in the *Didache* and the Way of Darkness in the *Epistle of Barnabas* (xx, ANF, I, 149). See also Lactantius, *The Divine Institutes* (Bk. VI, iii, pp. 186f.); *The Epitome of the Divine Institutes* (lix, pp. 246f.). The author is considerate of those who fail to reach perfection on the Way of Life:

> For if thou art able to bear all the yoke of the Lord, thou wilt be perfect; but if thou art not able, what thou art able that do (*Didache*, vi, ANF, VII, 379).

This advice is typical of the writer's sane and practical approach in other matters. Take, for example, the question of deciding between false and true prophets. *The Pastor*, with probably the Montanists in view, makes what the author calls the "Spirit of Divinity" the criterion. If this Spirit is in control, the medium will prove by what he says and does that he is of God. The *Didache* has a simpler way still. If a prophet — many of them were traveling evangelists — overstayed his welcome and remained more than two days under the roof of his host, this was taken as sufficient evidence that he was not of God. Should he accept a recompense for his services, this again marked him as a false prophet. The same standards also applied to apostles (xi, p. 380).

These apostles, prophets, and teachers reveal the way in which they were regarded by the Church at the time. Bishops and deacons had a subordinate status, for they were *elected* by the Church to their respective offices. They, too, were considered capable of rendering the "service of prophets and teachers" (xv, p. 381). Ephesians 3:11 might throw some light on what the author had in mind. Paul thought of apostles, prophets, and teachers as the direct gifts of the ascended Christ to His Church. These were vital to the spiritual growth of the Church, just as bishops and deacons were necessary for its orderly functioning as a Christian fellowship.

Chapters vii-x, xiv (pp. 379ff.) of *Didache* present a Directory of

Early Facets of the Faith

Worship. Three prayers are given for use at the Eucharist, or the Lord's Supper: one to thank God for the Cup, one to thank God for the Broken Bread, one to thank Him after the elements are received. The Greek word translated "Eucharist" in English means "thanks" in the original. The Lord's Prayer is also added, with the reading, "And bring us not into temptation" (viii, p. 379). The Baptismal Formula, "Into the name of the Father, and of the Son, and of the Holy Spirit," is included. The outward sign of this rite was to be living (i.e., running) water, preferably cold. If this was not available, then any kind of water was suitable, even warm water. Pouring water on the head three times was also permissible. Only the baptized were to partake of the Holy Communion.

He instructs Christians to be conspicuous for their love toward God and man. They are enjoined to share with those in need. Their gifts of charity were to be given "without murmur." Idleness was not condoned. Idle Christians are called by the author "Christ-mongers" (xii, p. 381).

The book ends by stressing watchfulness because the Lord is at hand. Three signs are to accompany His appearance:

> First, the sign of an outspreading in heaven: then the sign of the sound of the trumpet; and the third, the resurrection of the dead; yet not of all, but as it is said: The Lord shall come and all His saints with Him. Then shall the world see the Lord coming upon the clouds of heaven (xvi, p. 382).

VIII

The *Epistle of Barnabas* was written about the same time as the *Didache*, by an Alexandrian Jew who had embraced Christianity. The name Barnabas led many in the early Church to identify the author with the Levite of Cyprus who was with Paul on his first missionary journey (Acts 13). Among these was Clement of Alexandria (*Stromata*, Bk. II, vi, ANF, II, 354). Origen accepted the Epistle as Scripture. It was in the *Codex Sinaiticus*. Eusebius called it a spurious writing (*Church History,* Bk. III, xxv, NPNF, 2nd ser., I, 156).

It is in two parts. The first deals with Christianity's superiority over Judaism. The second contrasts the Way of Darkness with the Way of Light (cf. *Didache*). The first part calls to mind the Epistle to the Hebrews. Both find types or symbols under the Old Covenant, the reality itself being made manifest through the New Covenant. Beyond this resemblance, there is hardly any affinity between the two writers. The author of the Epistle to the Hebrews is sympathetic and constructive in his treatment of the older religion. The author of the *Epistle of Barnabas* is apathetic and destructive. One reason for the Son of God to become incarnate was to bring judgment upon the Jews:

> The Son of God therefore came in the flesh with this view, that He might bring to a head the sum of their sins who had persecuted His prophets to the death (v, ANF, I, 140).

He apologizes at the end of the first part for not writing about "things future," on the ground that his readers could not fathom such knowledge because it is hid in parables. What he has written about the past needs both patience and ingenuity to interpret. His method of allegorizing facts and teachings of Old Testament writers makes strange reading. His Biblical quotations are so loosely and haphazardly used that the pattern of what is being discussed has the appearance of a crossword puzzle. The following is an example of the way he too often expresses himself:

> Attend carefully: "And let all the priests alone eat the inwards, unwashed with vinegar." Wherefore? Because to me, who am to offer my flesh for the sins of my new people, ye are to give gall with vinegar to drink; eat ye alone, while the people fast and mourn in sackcloth and ashes. [These things were done] that He might show that it was necessary for Him to suffer for them (vii, p. 141).

His main Gospel references and teaching are easy to follow, and they have a positive value. The Son of God became man and died for us men. He rose from the dead. He will be the "future Judge of the quick and the dead." "Through the blood of His sprinkling" He has "renewed us in the remission of sins, so that we should have the soul of children." The old sacrifices have been abolished, that man through the freedom that is in Christ might offer himself as an oblation (ii, pp. 137f.). His description of the new temple has a telling message:

> But it shall be built, observe ye, in the name of the Lord, in order that the temple of the Lord may be built in glory. How? ... Having received the forgiveness of sins, and placed our trust in the name of the Lord, we have become new creatures. ... Wherefore in our habitation God truly dwells in us. How? His word of faith ... He himself prophesying in us; He himself dwelling in us; opening to us who were enslaved by death the doors of the temple ... and by giving us repentance introduced us into the incorruptible temple (xvi, p. 147).

II

The Faith and Its Defenders

THE FAITH AND ITS DEFENDERS

These defenders of the faith are usually known as the Apologists. They wrote in the second century. Origen's work against Celsus, a heathen scholar, more voluminous than all the others taken together, is in a class by itself. Since it was written in the third century, a treatment of its contents will be given in the chapter entitled, "The Faith and Fusion." The shortest of the earlier complete compositions runs to only a few thousand words. The longest, Justin's *Dialogue with Trypho, a Jew,* exceeds in length all the New Testament Epistles.

The Apologists were the King's Counselors who defended His rights to the souls of men by the help of reason and argument in writing. Sometimes they turned prosecutors. Tatian attacked Greek culture. The author of the *Letter to Diognetus* was severe in his denunciation of the Jewish religion. The majority were converted laymen. Justin the Martyr paid for a transfer from Paganism to Christianity with his life. All these were known by their names, except one. They were not afraid of adverse criticism and the penalty which might have resulted from their courageous stand. In the case of the Apostolic Fathers, four of whom were bishops, what we have is a study in sainthood. The Apologists suggest a study in consecrated scholarship. The atmosphere is that of the lecture room, where such subjects as Comparative Religion, Theology, and the Philosophy of Religion are wont to be discussed. It would be well to regard these scholars as tutors in an introductory course preparatory to a more advanced study under Irenaeus, Clement, and Origen. For the sake of uniformity Tertullian's *Apology* will be considered along with the earlier works.

I

One may have a better grasp of their defense and its significance to later writers if the conditions prevailing at the time are understood. We have seen already that two of the Apostolic Fathers, Ignatius and Polycarp, were put to death by the Imperial Power because of their allegiance to Jesus Christ. While Nerva (96-98) was emperor, there were no persecutions. Trajan (98-117), his adopted son, is credited with a tolerant attitude toward Christianity. It was during his reign, however, that Ignatius suffered martyrdom at Rome. Tertullian's *Apology* gives an account of Pliny's request for a directive concerning Christians:

> For the younger Pliny . . . having condemned some Christians to death . . . being still annoyed by their great numbers, at last sought the advice of Trajan. . . . as to what he was to do with the rest, explaining to his master that, except an obstinate disinclination to offer sacrifices, he found in the religious services nothing but meetings at early morning for singing hymns to Christ and God and sealing home their way of life by a united pledge to be faithful to their religion, forbidding murder, adultery, dishonesty, and other crimes. . . . Trajan wrote back that Christians were by no means to be sought after; but if they were brought before him, they should be punished (ii, ANF, III, 18).

Under Hadrian (117-138), false accusers were punished, but in many a locality there was much suffering caused by the people's fear and hatred of Christians. In a letter written to a friend while visiting Alexandria, the emperor identified Christ with Serapis and the religions of both Jew and Christian with financial success.

Antonius Pius (138-161) also followed a tolerant attitude, and Christians, on the whole, were safe from illegal attacks. Nevertheless, Polycarp suffered death at the hands of the proconsul in Smyrna.

Marcus Aurelius (161-180), the most outstanding of the Antonies, was a philosopher well versed in the Stoic tradition, which was famous for its wider sympathies, its liberal consideration, its spirit of brotherhood, and its moral ideal of living in conformity with the divine order as expressed by reason. Under him, Christians were hunted out and punished for not sacrificing to the gods. It was while this idealist was in power that Justin, a man who had found an affinity between the ideals of the Stoics and of Christ, was martyred.

Commodus (180-190) seemed a better Stoic than his illustrious father. Under him, Christians were generally protected. He lacked, nevertheless, the moral goodness of Marcus. In spite of the claim that Commodus was a friend of the Church, Mardaura suffered martyrdom in Numidia in 180, and Apollonius, a Roman senator, was beheaded. Marcia, the emperor's mistress, inclined toward the Faith, and Callistus, a slave, later became a bishop.

The persecution instigated by the people, under Hadrian, for instance, when the *vox populi* was positively not the voice of God, has its significance, for it reveals how loyal they were to the old customs and what a tremendous task the Christian evangelist had taken in hand. According to the Apologists, they had but the faintest idea of what Christianity stood for. There was a general belief that Christians were guilty of the vilest practices. Even the intellectuals maintained that at the ceremony of initiation of young novices, a child was sacrificed and eaten (Minucius Felix, *The Octavius*, ix, ANF, IV, 177, 178).

The thinkers of the day as represented by Caecilius the Gnostic, whom Felix has in mind in his apology, and Celsus the Philosopher, who inspired Origen's comprehensive defense, found the Faith contrary to reason, and its basic principles not valid. Jewish intellectuals like Trypho maintained that Christianity was incompatible with the older revelation as given in the Old Testament. Celsus attacked both the Old and the New Testaments. Marcion, a native of Pontus who settled in Rome about 140, agreed with Celsus in rejecting the Old Testament, and with Trypho that the Old and the New Testament are antithetical and cannot be harmonized. He disagreed with both as regards the New Testament, for he accepted certain parts of it as being inspired and as conveying the truth.

Marcion was a great admirer of Paul but was led astray by a wrong interpretation of what the Apostle taught about the Law. He is commonly included among the Gnostics, yet he never indulged in their fanciful theories concerning existence nor in their allegorizing methods. To him, faith and not knowledge is the ideal. His stress on grace as against works would have made him a good Protestant had he lived later. The Cross was central to him. His fundamentalism regarding certain doctrines is praiseworthy. His attack on the older Scripture as containing a conception of God far inferior to that of the Gospel shows how a fine intellect can become inconsistent by overemphasizing one aspect of the truth. He lacked a historical perspective of what Tennyson, in his poem "Locksley Hall," conceived as an unfolding purpose moving from stage to stage until the dawn breaks in its full splendor:

> *I doubt not thro' the ages one increasing purpose runs*
> *And the thoughts of man are widen'd with the progress of the suns.*

There was a feeling among Christian writers that something should be done to bring the Old Testament up to date. To overcome their opponents' argument that it was inconsistent with the ideas of their day, they resorted to what is called the Allegorical Method. In the hands of the author of the *Epistle of Barnabas* it produced strange results. Others, like Justin Martyr, were more successful with it. At best it is a tantalizing process. To the shrewd it becomes a device to disrobe facts for the sake of fads and fancies. It was Philo, a brilliant Jew of Alexandria living in the time of Paul, a man with a strong religious bias, who brought this method into prominence. The creation stories and incidents in the lives of Moses and the Patriarchs were so allegorized by him that they became spiritual truths to reconcile revelation as given to the Jew with reason as followed by the Greek. This novel way of detouring around facts avoids many pitfalls, but who is to tell what incident is a symbol and what situation is a sign? It takes for granted that man is a poet by nature and that there is enough mysticism in his make-up to find every experience a signpost pointing the way to the City of God. Even Paul found it useful (cf. Gal. 4:21-26). Modern commentators apply it to the Fourth Gospel, whose facts are fast becoming signs and allegorical wonders. For example, the water in the miracle at Cana is the Old Dispensation which was turned into the new wine of the Gospel (2:1-11). The five husbands of the woman by the well (4:18) stand for the five senses or the five books of the Law or the five gods worshipped by the Samaritans when they settled in the central part of Palestine (II Kings 17:29-31).

II

It was within a pagan atmosphere steeped in misunderstanding, slander, and hostility, that the Apologists took up the defense of the Faith. Their writings were addressed to the highest authorities and leading intellects of the day.

Quadratus and Aristides, the Athenians, handed their *Apologies* to Hadrian when on a visit to Athens. Justin addressed one of his *Apologies* to Antonius Pius about 150. Around the same time he sent another to the Roman Senate. A third work of his is in the form of a dialogue with Trypho, a Jew. Melito, Bishop of Sardis, around 170, sent his to Marcus Aurelius, whom he greets as a "person of liberal mind and familiar with the truth." The *Apology* of Tertullian (160-220) is addressed to the Rulers of the Roman Empire. Theophilus, Bishop of Antioch (170), addressed his to Autolycus, a pagan thinker and a scorner of Christians. An unknown Apologist years earlier had sent his to Diognetus, who in the opinion of some was a Stoic philosopher. Tatian, an Assyrian (170), the author of the *Diatessaron*, a harmony of the Four Gospels, the standard Church lectionary till the fourth century, addressed his *Apology* to the Greeks. Athenagoras, an Athenian philosopher, sent his *Plea for the Christians* to Marcus Aurelius and his son Commodus, whom he praises as great conquerors and philosophers. His *On the Resurrection of the Dead* was delivered in the form of a discourse at Athens, with a better result than that which followed Paul's sermon on the same subject before the Athenians of his day (Acts 17).

Only fragments of the *Apology* of Quadratus are now extant. A Syriac version of the *Apology* of Aristides was found in the Convent of St. Catherine on Mount Sinai in 1889 by J. Rendal Harris, an Englishman. Thirty years earlier Tischendorf, a German, had discovered the *Codex Sinaiticus* there. The original Greek text of Aristides' *Apology* was found embedded in a Christian romance of the Middle Ages called *Barlaam and Joasaph*.

Many of the Apologists were as well acquainted with Greek philosophy as with the Scriptures. Some of them were philosophers before their conversion. Justin wore his philosopher's cloak to the end. They were thus trained to meet the leading intellects on their own ground. Tatian, in his *Address* to the Greeks, ridicules Greek mythology and thought and points out the vices and the fallacies of the philosophers. Aristippus was a profligate; Plato, a glutton; Aristotle, a flatterer. Both the Stoics and the Cynics lacked wisdom. Greek philosophy made a man neither wise nor good. In art the Greeks were imitators. Astronomy, geometry, music, and alphabetic writing originated in other lands (Tatian, *Address*, i, ii, iii, ANF, II, 65, 66). Tertullian was a debtor to Greek culture, and his thinking reveals Stoic influence (cf. also Lactantius, *The Divine Institutes*, Bk. III, ANF, VII).

Justin, born in Samaria about 114, was in all probability of Roman descent. He suffered martyrdom at Rome in 165. Before his conversion he had studied in the schools of various philosophers. He was led to Christ, being profoundly impressed by the heroism of the martyrs and the loftiness of Old Testament teaching. Of the many works attributed to him three, his two *Apologies* and *Dialogue with Trypho, a Jew,* are accepted as genuine. The *Dialogue* lists numerous reasons for identifying Jesus with the Messiah. This work is regarded as the first systematic attempt to show how false the Jewish position is concerning Christianity. He is more sympathetic with the pagan's quest after truth than his disciple Tatian. Like Augustine two centuries later, he had tried many avenues to truth until he finally found the Way which is also the Truth and the Life. He recognized, none the less, much that is of value on the avenues he had traveled. Contemplating Plato's ideas furnished his mind with wings, and he expected at any moment to find himself gazing on God (*Trypho*, ii, ANF, I,

195). Those who followed reason before Christ's Advent, such as Socrates and Heraclitus among the Greeks, and Abraham and Elias among the barbarians (*First Apology*, xlvi, ANF, I, 178), were Christians. In comparing the Greeks with the Hebrew barbarians, he asserts that Plato was indebted to Moses for some of his teaching (lix, pp. 182f.). The words of Jesus are superior to those of Socrates, for they have in them a power to change men's lives (*Second Apology*, x, ANF, I, 191). He maintained that whatever was rightly said among all men, pagan or otherwise, belongs to Christians (xiii, pp. 192f.).

Minucius Felix, a lawyer and the author of *The Octavius*, is in full agreement with Justin that all truth is one, that neither Jew nor Gentile has an exclusive right to it. Both hold with the Epistle to the Hebrews that God had "spoken in divers manners in time past" (1:1), and only differ in that they include Greek philosophy and thought within the divine guidance. Much that was taught by Socrates, Plato, and Aristotle, and the Stoics, so he argues, is in harmony with the Christian's conception of God (*The Octavius*, xix, ANF, IV, 183f.). His work is unique among the Apologies, for it is supposed to be an argument between Caecilius, a heathen, and Octavius, a Christian, the writer himself acting as a kind of umpire or judge in the contest. Many of the arguments and solutions suggest an acquaintance with Tertullian's *Apology*. Both of these were written in Latin, *The Octavius* being the first Christian document in that language, a fact which can be used as an argument that it is the more original of the two.

There appears a critical attitude to the Jewish religion in the earliest of the Apologies, *The Epistle to Diognetus*, written by an unknown author who refers to himself as a "disciple of the Apostles" (xi, ANF, I, 29). He found Jewish ritual less impressive and less significant than the author of the Epistle to the Hebrews did. What is regarded by the latter as the shadows of the real, the former considers nothing but a "manifestation of folly" (iv, p. 26). Christianity to him is superior and different from anything that either Jew or pagan could boast of.

The defense of the Apologists could be summed up in the well-known words of Glover: "They [that is, Christians] out-thought, out-lived, and out-died their generation." They presented the Faith as a form of wisdom which transformed believers into holy men whose moral integrity was without question and whose loyalty to all commitments, whether they involved Christ or Caesar, never faltered. The *Epistle to Diognetus* alludes to Christians as the "soul of the world" and its "preservers," just as the soul preserves the body (vi, ANF, I, 27). To the author of this letter, the fact that a Christian sealed his faith with his blood was the strongest of all arguments in support of what he stood for. He tells Diognetus,

> Do you not see them exposed to wild beasts, that they may be persuaded to deny the Lord, and yet not overcome? Do you not see that the more of them are punished, the greater becomes the number of the rest? This does not seem to be the work of man: this is the power of God; these are the evidences of His manifestation (vii, pp. 27f.).

Tertullian was in agreement: "The oftener we are mown down by you, the more in number we grow; the blood of Christians is seed" (*Apology*, l, ANF, III, 55; see Lactantius, *The Divine Institutes*, Bk. 5, xiii, ANF, VII, 148f.).

The Apologies are instructive in many other respects. Take, first of all, Justin's telling description of his spiritual pilgrimage, which is typical of what other thinkers of those days experienced before finally entering the Christian fold. The first stage in his quest for truth ended in a stalemate, for the Stoic whom he had consulted did not include God in his instruction. His next guide was a Peripatetic, that is, a graduate of the Aristotelian School of Philosophy. He again was no better. The third tutor, a Pythagorean, tried to make a mystic out of him through a study of the mystery of numbers, music, geometry, and astronomy, which were supposed "to wean the soul from sensible objects and render it fitted for objects that appertain to the mind." The fourth instructor, a Platonist, did succeed in creating a response to the Sublime. On further reflection, his tuition also seemed "folly." The fifth, a Christian teacher, who knew what was basically wrong with his pupil, led him with the help of the Scriptures to the great Master of all, Jesus Christ (*Trypho*, iiff., ANF, I, 195ff.).

Consider again the light Justin's *First Apology* to Antonius Pius throws on the manner in which a church service was conducted at the time:

> And on the day called Sunday, all who live in cities or in the country gather together to one place, and the memoirs of the apostles or the writings of the prophets are read, as long as time permits; then, when the reader has ceased, the president verbally instructs, and exhorts to the imitation of good things. Then we all rise together and pray, and . . . when our prayer is ended, bread and wine and water are brought, and the president in like manner offers prayers and thanksgivings,

according to his ability, and the people assent, saying Amen; and there is a distribution to each . . . and to those who are absent a portion is sent by the deacons. [(The offering was for the poor)] (lxvii, ANF, I, 185f.).

III

An understanding of how the Apologists thought of God and especially His revelation in Jesus Christ is extremely important. Whatever ideas they had were bound to affect other Greek thinkers in their approach to the Faith. As Paul was inspired in his day to bring about a reconciliation between Moses and Jesus in the thinking of his own people, so were Justin and other Apologists of the second century used by the Spirit of God to bridge the chasm between Christianity and Greek thought. One cannot but be amazed at their masterly handling of the doctrines of the Church.

The lay Apologists, Justin, Tatian, Athenagoras, Felix, and Tertullian, had been reared in the world of Greek thought. Their primary interest was in ideas, not in a way of life. Even a way of life meant, to the Stoic, conformity with Reason regarded as the controlling principle of the Universe. Before these men could be converted and subsequently become defenders of Christianity, the way of life offered by the Church had to be proved consistent with their way of thinking about reality as a whole. Justin, for example, discovered that B.C. was as much Christ's as A.D.

The link which made possible this spiritual union composed of patriarchs, prophets, philosophers, saints, and scholars was a conception known to the Greek thinker as the Logos, translated "Word" in English. As it came out of the soul of Greece, especially by way of the Stoics, it was purely an abstraction. It was never a person, nothing but an idea. This conception was so central to their thinking that the inner meaning of reality was interpreted by it. If someone could ever conceive of this impersonal concept becoming a person, then the widest chasm in men's thinking could be bridged. If such a bridge was ever constructed, the Supreme Being would cease to be a mere idea. It would eventually become a Person and a Father, and the Logos His Son.

Philo, the Jewish philosopher of Alexandria, following the Stoics, gave much thought to this idea of the Logos. He clothed it with power and beauty. He found it operating as Light within the Universe and as a living spark within the souls of men. The Wisdom of Proverbs 8 and the Logos were to him one and the same, both conceived as an agent to bring the world into being. But he stopped short of regarding the Logos as a person.

The first to proclaim that the Logos was a Person was the Christian prophet and evangelist who wrote the Fourth Gospel. He also believed, with Justin later, that the Spirit of God had influenced and guided the Greek thinker as well as the Hebrew saint. In the case of the latter, a direct revelation is implied; in the case of the former, an indirect. The Jews are regarded as God's own people (John 1:11). John the Baptist followed others who had been sent by God to His people. As regards the Greeks, they were guided by Him who is the light of men (1:4). The One that Peter called the Messiah is spoken of by the author of the Fourth Gospel as the Logos or the Word, the loftiest conception that the Greek thinker arrived at as he thought of the Eternal reaching out so as to create a world and all that is.

The I AM THAT I AM or I WILL BECOME WHAT I WILL BECOME in the burning bush set Moses and Aaron ablaze and made of them His agents and prophets. The Greek had a similar idea. He distinguished between the Logos as a principle within the Eternal and the Logos that became active in the souls of men and which, in its modern form, makes all men divine. Christianity, however, does not stand for such scattered sparks of divinity. It claims but one Logos, whose personality is as eternal as God Himself: Very God of Very God, as the Church states in its great creeds.

The problem facing the Apologists, the pioneers of doctrinal expressions that were developed more fully later, concerned the relationship existing between the Logos and God. We shall see to what extent they agreed with the opening verses of the Fourth Gospel:

> In the beginning was the Word, and the Word was with God, and the Word was God. He was in the beginning with God; all things were made through him; and without him was not anything made that was made. In him was life; and the life was the light of men. . . . And the Word became flesh and dwelt among us, full of grace and truth; we have beheld his glory, glory as of the only Son from the Father (John 1:1-4, 14).

It would be of help to point out here that the Prologue to the Fourth Gospel is not a summary of what the Greeks held concerning the Logos, nor did John *prefix* it to the Gospel in order to make it more appealing to his readers. It is rather a summing up of the whole Gospel message, presented in an environment saturated with pagan ideas. The author begins, not in the beginning with God, but in Galilee of long ago. It was there he first met Jesus of Nazareth, who came to mean for him what God Himself stood for. What God was, Jesus was. In analyzing what was a fact in his own experience, he found that the Logos conception, so well-known to his readers, both Greek and Roman, was the very thing that would enable them to discover for themselves the reality that was Jesus Christ. By making use of this concept they, too, would find that a belief in the Deity of Christ did not conflict with belief in the unity of the Godhead.

Furthermore, the Prologue could be regarded not only as a summing up of what the whole Gospel maintains, but also as the author's own confession of faith similar to that of Nathanael, Peter, and Thomas. He simply stated what he believed. There is no attempt to explain or interpret after the manner of theologians. The statement as contained in the Prologue is there expressed as a matter of belief. There is nothing that can be done about it but to take it or leave it. If accepted, it could be turned as easily into a hymn as into a doctrine.

The Apologists felt they were under a constraint to explain in what manner the Word was in the beginning with God. In their effort to do so, some of them fell short of giving a satisfactory interpretation, such as did finally satisfy those who formulated the Nicene Creed in the fourth century. They can be divided, therefore, into two classes: those who held that the Word is a distinct Person within the Godhead, and those who thought that the Word was only a potentiality in the beginning, like reason within a man's mind, until it is bodied forth as word or action. This distinction will be further discussed in Chapter 6, "The Faith and Fallacy."

(i)

The first group among the earlier Apologists includes the author of the *Epistle to Diognetus*, Athenagoras, Melito, and Tertullian. These four are practically orthodox in their expressions concerning the way the Word or Logos is related to God and the Son to the Father.

According to the *Epistle to Diognetus*, the Word is Himself
> the very Creator and Fashioner of all things — by whom He [(God)] made the heavens — by whom He enclosed the sea within its proper bounds. . . . As a king sends his son, who is also a king, so sent He Him; as God He sent Him; as to men He sent Him; as a Saviour He sent Him, and as seek-

ing to persuade, not to compel us; for violence has no place in the character of God. . . . He will yet send Him to judge us, and who shall endure His appearing? (vii, ANF, I, 27).

In Christ God took upon Himself the burden of our iniquities:

> He gave His own Son as a ransom for us, the holy One for transgressors . . . the righteous One for the unrighteous . . . the immortal One for them that are mortal. For what other thing was capable of covering our sins than His righteousness? By what other one was it possible that we, the wicked and ungodly, could be justified, than by the only Son of God? (ix, p. 28).

Athenagoras in his *Plea for the Christians* states,

> Our doctrine acknowledges one God, the Maker of this universe, who is Himself uncreated . . . but has made all things by the Logos which is from Him (iv, ANF, II, 131). . . . But the Son of God is the Logos of the Father, in idea and operation; for after the pattern of Him and by Him were all things made, the Father and the Son being one. And, the Son being in the Father and the Father in the Son, in oneness and power of spirit, the understanding and reason [(*nous kai logos*)] of the Father is the Son of God (x, p. 133).

The Athenian philosopher is also positive in his thinking about the Holy Trinity:

> The Holy Spirit Himself also, which operates in the prophets, we assert to be an effluence of God, flowing from Him, and returning back again like a beam of the sun. Who, then, would not be astonished to hear men who speak of God the Father, and of God the Son, and of the Holy Spirit, and who declare both their power in union and their distinction in order, called atheists? (x, p. 133).

Melito, Bishop of Sardis, who was martyred probably during the reign of Marcus Aurelius, has left a discourse "which was given in the presence of Antonius Caesar." Also, among the fragments attributed to him there are excerpts from an *Apology* addressed to Marcus Aurelius, around 170. He assigns real existence to God, by whose power everything subsists:

> [(He was)] in no sense made, nor did He ever come into being; but He has existed from eternity, and will continue to exist for ever and ever. He changeth not, while everything else changes. No eye can see Him, nor thought apprehend Him, nor language describe Him [(cf. I Cor. 2:9)]; and those who love Him speak of Him thus: "Father, and God

of Truth" (*Fragments* I, ANF, VIII, 751).
He points out to the Emperor that Christians paid homage to the only God who is before all and over all and that they worshipped Christ who is in truth God the Word existing before all time. He teaches, according to the fragments, that the Eternal appeared in time enshrined in a vesture of flesh.

The deeds done by Christ after His baptism, and especially His miracles, gave indication and assurance to the world of the Deity hidden in His flesh. For, being at once both God and perfect man likewise, He gave us sure indications of His two natures . . . [(in His humanity)]. He concealed the signs of His Deity although He was the true God existing before all ages (*Fragments* VII, p. 760).

The following is typical of the manner in which second-century Christians expressed themselves as they thought of Jesus Christ (cf. Chapter IV, "The Faith and Fact," section "God the Son"):

The Word of God; He who was begotten before the light;
He who is Creator together with the Father; He the Fashioner of man; He who is all in all;
He who among the patriarchs is Patriarch;
He who in the law is the Law;
among the priests, Chief Priest;
among kings, the Ruler;
among prophets, the Prophet;
among the angels, Archangel;
in the voice of the preacher, the Word;
among spirits, the Spirit;
in the Father, the Son;
in God, God . . . .
. . . .
God who is from God;
the Son who is from the Father;
Jesus Christ the King for evermore. Amen (Melito, *Fragments* IV, ANF, VIII, 756f.).

Tertullian's *Apology* is considered by many to be the most famous of his numerous writings. Since we shall have reason to stress later his teaching about the Trinity in Chapter 6, "The Faith and Fallacy," only a very brief summary is given here of his view of God and the Word. Chapter 21, the longest in Tertullian's work, deals directly with what is of interest at this juncture.

As regards God, both Christians and Jews agree and believe

in the unity of the Godhead. Concerning the Logos, Christians are in agreement with Greek thinkers, for to both "God made the world, and all which it contains, by His Word, and Reason, and Power." Zeno, the Stoic philosopher, held that the Word was the agent in creation, bringing all into being according to a definite plan. Cleanthes, another Stoic, refers to the Word as the Spirit pervading the universe. Christians maintain that "the Word, and Reason, and Power, by which . . . God made all, have spirit as their proper and essential *substratum*"; this Spirit being Word "to give forth utterances," Reason "to dispose and arrange," and Power "to execute."

The Christian tradition according to him is that

> He proceeds forth from God, and in that procession He is generated; so that He is the Son of God, and is called God from unity of substance with God. For God, too, is a Spirit. Even when the ray is shot from the sun, it is still part of the parent mass; the sun will still be in the ray, because it is the ray of the sun — there is no division of substance, but merely an extension. Thus Christ is Spirit of Spirit, and God of God, as light of light is kindled . . . that which has come forth out of God is at once God and the Son of God, and the two are one. In this way also, as He is Spirit of Spirit and God of God, He is made second in manner of existence — in position, not in nature; and He did not withdraw from the original source, but went forth (xxi, ANF, III, 34).

(ii)

Before we consider the second group of early Apologists, we may be able to suggest what the Apologists were up against by the help of a modern concept such as "Force," which in itself implies activity. It would be reasonable to assume a Source from which it draws its vitality and also a Law governing its operation. Source, Force, Law, all have Power as something shared in common by the three. Source is Power, Force is Power, and Law is Power; Law being regarded here as a power of controlling and directing energy. As creative Power, Force can be identified with the Source and differentiated from it. As regards Power itself, both Source and Force are identical. In operation, Force can be distinguished from the Source. Law, again, as Power is one with the Source and with Force. In operation it is different from the other two. They are one because each is Power. They are three because each has a distinctive function of its own.

Both groups among the Apologists would not have much difficulty in identifying the Logos as Force, the Father as Source, and the

Holy Spirit as Law governing the operation of the Logos. The first group in terms of the above analogy found Force and Law to be one with the Source, though distinct from it. The distinctions were inherent in their concept of Power. That is, the Father and the Son and the Holy Spirit are distinct, though one, as God. The second group found Power to be one, with distinctions as a *potential* within it, until it became active in one way or another. The moment it begins to operate, we have to think of it in terms of Source, Force, and Law. That is, the Father and the Son and the Holy Spirit only became distinct forms or expressions of the Deity when God began to function as Creator or Savior.

Tatian's *Address to the Greeks* clearly regards the Logos as a potentiality or Logos-Power which was finally brought forth by the Will of God. It was only then that it became a distinct personality from the Father for the purpose of creation and redemption:

> God was in the beginning; but the beginning, we have been taught, is the power of the Logos. For the Lord of the universe, who is Himself the necessary ground [(*hypostasis*)] of all being . . . inasmuch as He was all power, Himself the necessary ground of things visible and invisible, with Him were all things; with Him, by Logos-power [(*dia logikes dunameos*)], the Logos Himself also, who was in Him, subsists. And by His simple will the Logos springs forth; and the Logos, not coming forth in vain, becomes the first-begotten work of the Father. Him (the Logos) we know to be the beginning of the world (v, ANF, II, 67).

Theophilus is virtually in agreement that the Logos dwelt within the Godhead. The Logos, however, was part of a continuous process of begetting whenever the Father wills to bring Him forth as an expression of Himself (cf. Origen in Chapter 5, "The Faith and Fusion"). Before anything was created, the Word resided "within the heart of God." He had been as "a counsellor, being His own mind and thought. But when God wished to make all that He determined on, He begot His Word, uttered the first-born of all creation, not Himself being emptied of the Word, but having begotten Reason [(or Word)], and always conversing with His Reason" (*Theophilus to Autolycus*, x, xxii, ANF, II, 97f., 103).

Minucius Felix has nothing to say of the Logos. His nearest approach to the conception is his reference to God ordering all things by a word, arranging all things by His wisdom, and perfecting all things by His power. Throughout *The Octavius*, God is in direct contact with the world which was created by Him,

The Faith and Its Defenders

sustained by Him, and controlled by Him. There seems to be a unique relationship between God and Christians. No mention is made of a Mediator. Christ is not even named. He writes of a future resurrection, but there is no word about the resurrection of Jesus. He argues that the sign of the cross is a universal symbol. God is alone. God is sufficient within Himself, invisible, independent of everything He brought forth. The Christians are brethren by being born of one God and Parent. They are companions in faith and fellow heirs in hope (xviii, xx, ANF, IV, 182ff.).

Justin is included among the second group because he is not as exact or as scientific in his thinking as Tertullian. Allowance should be made for his poetic imagination, which is put to good use as he allegorizes the past. Besides, his interest is mainly evangelical and not doctrinal or theoretical. He is pleading with a hostile world. His authority for what he claims in defense of Christianity is the Word whom he calls Teacher, "the light which lights every man, that comes into the world" (John 1:9). In his appeal to the Old Testament for support, the Word becomes an Apostle, and an Angel, revealing and guiding toward the Advent of Jesus Christ. Beyond all this there is the Apologist's conception of God, which is basic to his whole message, for out of God came the Word, who is Teacher, Apostle, and Angel.

In his interpretation of the scheme of salvation there appears between the "beginning" of John's Gospel (v. 1) and what happened at Bethlehem, the Word, the first-born of God. He does not seem to be too concerned with what is claimed by verse 1, though he also says that the Word was in the beginning with God. It is verse 14 that has the greater attraction for him. There the firstborn of God was born of a virgin that He might through His death become our Saviour and "the chief of another race regenerated by Himself through water, and faith, and wood, containing the mystery of the cross" (*Trypho*, cxxxviii, ANF, I, 268). His realistic way of expressing the third means of the new life in Christ brings to mind the book of Jonah, which begins with God and ends with cattle. There is no danger of Justin falling among the mystics, for he found the faith lying between water and wood. He discovered the mystery of redemption operating in a deluge of water and of blood (*ibid.*).

To his way of thinking, there had to be a "before and after." The Son of God came forth to be the medium of God in order to save us. It was by the Will and Power of God that the Word was begotten. It was by the same Will and Power that the Incarnation was made possible. Even within a philosophic setting, he was first of all an evangelist and not a theologian.

Years later, Arius gave an undue prominence to some of the expressions coined by him in the hope of confirming his own theory that the Son was inferior to the Father and His existence conditioned by the Father's Will. That is, there was a time when the Father was on His own, as Tatian maintained, and a time when the Son came forth by the power of His Will, the way all creation came into being. This seems logical on the surface. Every father exists before his son is born. But the question is, Are human expressions and analogies adequate to explain the mystery of the Godhead?

As Justin holds, in his attack on Greek mythology, the higher cannot be explained in terms of the lower. Here are a few relevant quotations: "Christ, who appeared for our sakes, became the whole rational being, both body, and reason, and soul" (*Second Apology*, x, ANF, I, 191). "For next to God, we worship and love the Word who is from the unbegotten and ineffable God, since also He became man for our sakes, that, being partaker of our sufferings, He might also bring us healing" (xiii, p. 193). "His Son, who alone is properly called Son, the Word, who was also with Him [(God the Father)] and was begotten before the works, when at first He created and arranged all things by Him" (vi, p. 190).

The following recalls Tertullian's metaphor of the ray:

> God begat before all creatures a Beginning, a certain rational power [proceeding] from Himself, who is called by the Holy Spirit, now the Glory of the Lord, now the Son, again Wisdom, again an Angel, then God, and then Lord and Logos. . . . For He can be called by all these names, since He ministers to the Father's Will, and since He was begotten of the Father by an act of the will; just as we see happening among ourselves: for when we give out some word, we beget the word; yet not by abscission, so as to lessen the word in us, when we give it out: and just as we see happening in the case of a fire, which is not lessened when it has kindled [another], but remains the same; and that which has been kindled by it likewise appears to exist by itself, not diminishing that from which it was kindled (*Trypho*, lxi, ANF, I, 227).

III

The Faith and Fantasy

THE FAITH AND FANTASY

I

The Gnostics

In our study of the Apologists we found a sympathetic attitude toward Greek culture and thought. The Word was recognized as a light shining everywhere and at all times, never confined to any particular era or area. The twilight preceding the full dawn of Christ's Advent was long and widespread. It was the reflection of the true light.

The Gnostics, who also came into prominence in the second century, regarded Christ as a light, but not *the* Light. The Redeemer was only one among a graded series of what we might call, for the moment, "reflectors." The Eternal Fount of Light was solely reflected by what they termed the *Pleroma*, the Greek word for "fullness." This Fullness consisted of Aeons and Emanations, each losing some of its radiance the farther it receded. The farthest of all had lost so much of its original power of reflection that within its orbit a world of complete darkness, where evil and corruption lurked, came into being.

Gnosticism, in its effort to bridge the chasm between Spirit and Matter, between Light and Darkness, became a convenient halfway house where both the Christian and pagan discovered something appealing. Its oriental antiques, draped in the most fantastic fashion by the vagaries of Ophites, Sethians, and Cainites, made a pagan feel at home. Many a Christian was no less comfortable. Both the Syriac and Alexandrian mystic, both the Graeco-Roman and Christian thinker, were attracted by its alluring atmosphere.

Fantasy has an entrancing appeal. The Wonderland of Alice and many of Walt Disney's creations are as real as our capacity for enchantment. We are free to roam within them as if reason has fallen asleep until it is all over.

By the help of reason, combined with imagination, the Gnostics turned the universe into an enigmatic wonderland, partly fanciful, partly grotesque, partly stimulating. But they were also realists.

Their method, especially in the case of the most advanced systems, had the precision of mathematics. When one thinks of it, there is a certain charm in the way figures on being added, subtracted, multiplied, or divided, arrive at the desired results. These systems were out to find a common denominator for the Gnostic conceptions of Spirit and Matter, the former being regarded as inherently good, the latter, inherently evil. This formula, x:y, represents their problem: x standing for Spirit, and y for Matter. Their solution could be symbolized by x:y=p: the p standing for the *Pleroma*. Paul uses the word in Ephesians 1:23: the Church is the fullness or *Pleroma* of Christ. This *Pleroma*, to the Gnostics, is filled with various beings or types of existences, and it is through the *Pleroma* that they discovered a common denominator to the problem represented by x:y. Part of the common denominator was closely related to x and part to y.

In an effort to save God, the Source of all goodness, from being directly responsible for the existence of Matter, the seat of all evil, Gnosticism held He was only indirectly responsible. Matter came into being through the medium of emanations and angelic beings called Aeons. The most perfect of these had no direct contact with God. The least perfect was so far removed from the Source of all goodness that the creation of Matter with the evil therein was ascribed to it. This theory assumes that the power of God, but not His goodness, was transmitted from Aeon to Aeon. In trying to overcome one form of dualism, they presupposed another, because they separated the goodness of God from His power.

To what extent Gnosticism had developed in Paul's day is difficult to determine. It is obvious from the Epistle to the Colossians that he was aware of one of its basic ideas. As a Jew, he was heir to a literature which filled the heavens with "thrones, dominions, principalities, and authorities." The writers of this particular literature, popular in the time of Jesus, indulge in a grand and speculative description of heavenly hierarchies and angelic orders.

The Apostle's answer to the heretics of his day who maintained that such celestial beings had a part in the creation of the world and in man's salvation is found in Colossians 1:15, 16, 19:

> He is the image of the invisible God, the first-born of all creation; for in him all things were created, in heaven and on earth, things visible and invisible, whether thrones or dominions or principalities or authorities — all things were created through him and for him. . . . For in him all the fullness [*pleroma*] of God was pleased to dwell.

The Faith and Fantasy

Moreover, the supposed chasm separating Spirit and Matter is not really bridged by the *Pleroma*, as the Gnostics conceived it, because the ends are left unconnected. At best, it is simply a hanging ladder. The most perfect of the Aeons is not completely divine and spiritual, that is, in the sense that God is Spirit; nor is the Aeon at the lower end of the scale entirely material. The highest cannot be identified with God, nor the lowest with man. It is a fullness, as Irenaeus held, within a more comprehensive fullness.

The Roman Catholic chain of intermediary Saints as presented in our day is open to a similar criticism. Peter and the Saints are on the human side of the chasm that lies between man and God. That they are canonized and called Saints does not mean that they are divine. They still remain men, and we are no nearer God because of their intercession. The divinity ascribed to Mary, again, makes no better contact, for she has only *become* divine by being the Mother of God. All that deification can do to humans is to elevate them among the Aeons, whose status is no higher than that of the angels.

The Wonderland that is Gnosticism was not constructed as a counterattraction to Christianity. In its second-century form it was a means to popularize the Gospel and make it more appealing to certain minds. Gnosticism had been in existence for a long time. In its primitive form its Oriental character was very much in evidence. With the passing of the years it became more intellectual through the introduction of Greek thought. On the appearance of Christianity, it tried to adjust itself to the new religion by adopting some of its tenets and its form of worship. Its attitude in general was friendly, and although it gave the Saviour a unique place in some of its systems, it retained, despite all apparent changes and adaptations, the basic elements of its first environment.

What was easily absorbed was gnosticized, whether it was Oriental mysticism, Greek philosophy, or the Hebrew and Christian religions. In this Wonderland, personalities, ideas, and incidents, peculiar to all these and others, were transformed to fit a common mold of fantasy. The disciples of Moses and Christ, of Zoroaster and Socrates, of Pythagoras and Plato, upon visiting this land of enchantment, were thrilled by the resemblances to their own beliefs. People of all faiths were lured toward the entrance, but only those in possession of *Gnosis* or Knowledge discovered the secret passage that led to bliss and perfection. The majority who entered, satisfied with what caught the eye, simply wandered about and finally became lost. The few alone found. The many missed the means of salvation. Those who were led by Faith and not Knowledge preferred the simple way of the Gospel to the secret access that could but lead to a complex and confusing labyrinth.

The movement within the Church against this bewildering syncretism and hodgepodge of ingredients pleasing to all was not initiated by the criticism of Irenaeus and other Christian thinkers of the second and third century, but by Paul and the Apostles. The rank and file, by following their lead, kept clear of Gnosticism with its fantasies, and thus saved the Gospel from any compromise with Paganism, before the mass of anti-Gnostic literature was ever produced. As a threat to Christian belief and morality, the worst was over by the end of the second century, when the great writings against Gnosticism first appeared. In the literary conflict that ensued, which was, by the way, entirely one-sided, convictions were clarified, beliefs reaffirmed. By the help of reason and Scripture, the Catholic faith in the Christian fundamentals was proved to be invincible.

It is important to bear the following two facts in mind. First, the Gnostics are seen through the eyes of Christian writers, such as Justin Martyr, Irenaeus, Tertullian (whose work against Marcion alone runs into five books), Hippolytus, Clement of Alexandria, and Origen. The second fact is that the leading systems had a number of exponents, who differed from one another in their interpretation of the basic principles. What follows is meant to be a *general* description of Gnosticism. References to the original written material will be given as we visit the chief wonders in Gnosticland.

WONDER ONE

(*Simon Magus and His Votaries*)

By the time of Justin Martyr and Irenaeus, a shrine had been built to Simon within Gnosticland. Its teaching in this particular instance was a challenge to Christianity. Near the river Tiber stood a statue with the inscription, *Simoni Deo Sancto* (To Simon the Holy God). His followers, the Simonians, worshipped him as god. They had an image of him fashioned after the likeness of Jupiter, and another of Helen, whom he claimed to be his first Principle or Logos.

The Gnosticism that developed into full bloom in the second century is traced by the early Fathers to Simon, the man whom the Samaritans acclaimed as "that power of God which is called Great," who thought he could buy the gift of the Holy Spirit with money from Peter and John (Acts 8). Justin, who was himself a Samaritan, connects him with a village named Gitto in Samaria. He is denounced by the Apologist as a magician possessed of demons. Some think he was the author of the *Great Announcement*, fragments of which remain.

Simon, as a Gnostic, was aware of the struggle between Good and Evil. His solution to the problem set the pattern which was developed more fully later. His system had in it both Christian and pagan elements. He adopted the Trinitarian formula. He claimed to be the Son among the Jews. He appeared as the Father to the Samaritans and as the Holy Ghost to other nations. His conception of Helen recalls the Logos idea among the Greeks. She is referred to as the first conception or principle of his mind: the mother of all. This *Ennoea*, the Greek word for thought, intent, design, descended to the lower regions of space and generated Angels and Powers who, after creating this world, abused their prerogative and held men captive. Following her initial act of creating, she herself was shut up in a human body and for ages passed in succession from one female body to another, as from vessel to vessel (Irenaeus, *Against Heresies*, Bk. I, xxiii, 2, ANF, I, 348). One of these was Helen of Troy. She ended her descent as a common prostitute, the lost sheep spoken of in the Gospels (Matt. 18:12).

Like Hosea, the jilted Hebrew prophet who redeemed Gomer his estranged wife from slavery, Simon, the divine father of Helen, saved her too, and at the same time emancipated mankind from the power of the Angels. He himself appeared among men in the guise of man and went through what was supposed to be real suffering in Judea. All this was an act of grace, the redeemed having no claim to any merit of their own. The final result of his appearing meant the complete destruction of angelic domination and man's release forever.

At his shrine in Gnosticland, ingredients to master the magic art and sorcery, such as charms and love potions, were on sale. Knowledge, or *Gnosis*, the guaranteed key to all mysteries, could also be acquired.

Menander, another Samaritan, and Simon's successor, disagreed with his master concerning the Primary Power, for to him it was unknown. Neither did he agree about the mediator. It was he and not Simon who was sent by the invisible beings to be the savior of men. As a magician, he claimed that he alone possessed the Knowledge which could overcome the angels and bring immortal youth to all baptized in his name (Justin's *First Apology*, xxvi, ANF, I, 171; Irenaeus, *Against Heresies*, Bk. I, xxiii, 5, p. 348). He held that there was a Mother among the heavenly orders, but creation itself was the work of Seven Archons, or Chiefs.

WONDER TWO
(*Cerdo and Marcion*)

These two are included among the wonders of Gnosticland as intellectuals and Christian thinkers who tried to overcome the conflict which is basic to Gnosticism by maintaining the existence of two Gods. Marcion was a member of the Church of Rome at the time Eleutherus was bishop. He was excommunicated. This severance from the Catholic tradition led to the creation of a sect of his own which lasted for several centuries. Tertullian poignantly remarks, "Even wasps make combs; so also these Marcionites make churches." Neither he nor Cerdo succumbed to the magic art of Simon and his followers. Their forte was argument supported by theories, many of which were contradictory to what Christians accepted at the time.

Some of the Apologists were critical of the Jewish religion, and by comparison with it Christianity was considered far superior (cf. *The Epistle to Diognetus*). Cerdo, a Syrian, who came to Rome during the episcopacy of Hyginus, carried the contrast to the wildest possible conclusion. He held that the God of the Jews was not the God revealed in Jesus Christ, who is by His very nature invisible. He regarded the God of the Old Testament as righteous, but the God of the New as benevolent.

Marcion, a native of Sinope in Pontus, who arrived in Rome around 140, stressed with telling ingenuity the implications of what Cerdo believed. Judaism and Christianity, he asserted, are irreconcilable. He agreed with Cerdo that the God manifested by the Law and the Prophets is entirely different from Him who was made known through the Gospel, the former being a God who is just, the latter a God who is good. But he went a step farther. The former God sanctioned theft and delighted in war, whereas the latter is a God of righteousness and love. He identified the former with the Creator, or Demiurge, a being absolutely inferior to Him who sent His Son to redeem the world. In one respect, the superior Deity of Marcion resembles the Invisible Power of Menander. Hippolytus, however, finds an affinity between his

The Faith and Fantasy

two Gods, with the conceptions of Discord and Friendship, in the teaching of Empedocles, the pagan philosopher (*The Refutation of All Heresies*, Bk. VII, xvii, ANF, V, 110ff.) Tertullian argues that if the heretic considered the logical ramifications of his theory, he would arrive at nine gods and not two (*Against Marcion*, Bk. I, xv, ANF, III, 367).

On the positive side of Marcion's teaching the main stress was on the Gospel as opposed to the Law of Moses; on grace, and not works. In this respect he was one with Paul, whom he claimed to follow. In his emphasis on grace he was also in agreement with Simon, more by accident than by intention. Concerning Knowledge, he disagreed with both Simon and Menander, maintaining that Faith, and not Gnosis, is the way to perfection. Nor did he indulge, with the Gnostics in general, in the allegorical method and in reading into facts his own meaning of the Faith.

As in the case of many of the Gnostics, his point of view led to extremes. His Scripture was merely a selection of passages from the New Testament. Only the Epistles of Paul and a mutilated version of Luke's Gospel, which he assigned to his favorite Apostle, were accepted as inspired. The record of Christ's nativity was rejected from the Third Gospel because an Incarnation meant that the Word was made flesh, and flesh, like all other forms of matter, was the work of the inferior Demiurge, the God of the Jews. As Tertullian points out, such a Christ would be incarnate without being flesh, and human without being a man. In fact, both Christ and the God revealed by Him are mere phantoms. And as this able critic maintains, there cannot be any merit in the suffering and death of a phantom. Nor is there much point in believing in the resurrection of one who did not have a real body. In his denial of the unity of the Bible, his Christ is cast into the human scene like a bolt from the blue. There is no Patriarch or Psalmist, no Law or Prophets, to prepare the world for His coming. His sense of moral judgment, although he is a strict moralist as compared with some of the Gnostics, seems to be perverted by his theory of existence. Cain and other reprobates are saved by Jesus on His descent into hell. Abel, Enoch, Noah, Abraham, and the saints that sprang from his loins, are left in the lower regions forever because they gave Him a cold shoulder when He visited there. A chilly reception did not go with the climate (Justin's *First Apology*, xxvi, ANF, I, 171; Irenaeus, *Against Heresies*, Bk. I, xxvii, pp. 352f.; Tertullian, *Against Marcion*).

WONDER THREE

(*Carpocrates*)

In this particular section of Gnosticland, the followers of Carpocrates referred to themselves as "Gnostics" (The Knowing Ones). They, too, delighted in magic, spells, incantations, and images. These images were not of the founder, but of Greek philosophers, such as Pythagoras, Plato, and Aristotle. There was one of Christ, claimed to be the work of Pilate. These they honored "after the manner of the Gentiles." Hippolytus writes of their voluptuous feasts, a perversion of the Christians' *Agape*, or Love Feast, as Clement tells us. Each of these Gnostics had the inside of the lobe of the right ear branded with a special mark.

Carpocrates and his followers referred to the Supreme Being of Marcion and the Primary Power of Menander as the Unbegotten Father. Creation was the work of an inferior order of Angels or Archons, chief among whom was the devil, the "adversary" of the Gospels (Matt. 5:25; Luke 12:58).

The most peculiar thing in their teaching was their conception of the human soul, held to be fashioned after that of Christ's, who while here on earth still remembered what He had seen and heard in His pre-incarnate state. The soul of Jesus, essentially more firm and hardy than all others, was delivered from the tyranny of angelic control by a baptism of divine power which descended on Him from the Father. In addition, He was endowed with faculties which saved Him from the passions and practices that would have been naturally His as a Jew and a man.

Every other soul goes through a similar experience, divine help being given to resist the domination of a man's material body. So strongly did they believe in this theory that some of them declared that they were like Jesus, and better than Peter and Paul and other Apostles. A certain group among them boasted that they were even ahead of Jesus.

As compared with Him who had become incarnate but once, the Carpocratians held that other souls might migrate from body to body, after the manner of Helen, until a state of perfection was attained, when the transfer automatically ceased. This changing from body to body was deemed necessary in order to fill a man's cup to the full. Only on rare occasions could the soul get the best out of existence through the medium of a single body. It was necessary, therefore, for it to change its abode, in the belief that what one body could not furnish, another would. Souls were

The Faith and Fantasy

created to have "experience of every kind of life as well as every kind of action." This, however, could never be complete or fully comprehensive, for the soul was said to be *shut up* in the body, just as Helen was. Final redemption meant a release of the soul from this material bondage, after it had received all that this world could offer and paid "the utmost farthing" (Matt. 5:26) for any crimes committed. The theoretical subtlety of the Carpocratians led to moral degradation. Many led a life of depravity, which was condoned by a way of thinking that had within it no moral imperative, whether conscience or anything else.

The devil, who had a leading part in the creation of the world, also assisted in the final redemption of men. He was depicted as playing the role of a good shepherd in the service of God to seek lost souls and bring them back to the Supreme Ruler (Irenaeus, *Against Heresies*, Bk. I, xxv, ANF, I, 350f.; Hippolytus, *Refutation of All Heresies*, Bk. VII, xx, ANF, V, 113f.; Clement, *Stromata*, Bk. III, ii, ANF, II, 382f.; Tertullian, *A Treatise on the Soul*, xxv, ANF, III, 205f.).

WONDER FOUR
(*Saturnilus or Saturninus*)

Saturnilus of Antioch in Syria thought of God as the One Father unknown to all (see Menander). The act of creating was relegated to lower beings. His teaching could be summarized thus:

GOD THE UNKNOWN FATHER

Angels: Seven of these made
Archangels   the world and man
Principalities
Powers

        In his primitive form man resembles a writhing worm unable to stand erect

God of the Jews, one of the Angels

        Man assumed an erect posture when the Father, whose likeness he was, filled him with the spark of life which returns to God on the dissolution of the body

Christ is a Spiritual Being without birth, body, or figure. In Jesus He looked like a man though He had no physical substance.

God of the Jews is to be destroyed by Christ, who will save all of those in possession of the divine spark.

Other peculiar ideas:
> The Angels made some men good, others bad. Christ came to destroy the bad and save the good.
> Like Marcion, Saturnilus renounced marriage and animal food. Natural birth was Satan's work.
> Some prophesies are the work of the Seven Angels; others, the work of Satan.
> Satan hated the Seven Angels, and especially the God of the Jews.
>> (Irenaeus, *Against Heresies*, Bk. I, xxiv, 1, 2, ANF, I, 348f.; Hippolytus, *Refutation*, Bk. VII, xvi, ANF, V, 109f.).

WONDER FIVE
(Basilides)

This Alexandrian Gnostic produced the first well-developed Gnostic system. In important respects it resembles that of Saturnilus. He wrote twenty-four books on the Gospel (Eusebius, *Church History*, Bk. IV, vii, NPNF, 2nd ser., I, 178ff.). One requires imagination, mathematical precision, and much patience to follow the ingenious way the different spheres, with the leading Archons and Sons, are related to one another, and the manner in which the secrets of the higher region are always transmitted to the lower in the descent toward Formlessness, his particular term for our quarter of creation.

Before an attempt is made to sketch Basilides' theory of existence, certain of his ideas about Christ and man's upward climb should be mentioned. Since God is regarded as the Ineffable, Unnamable, and the Non-existent One, Christ descends from the loftier realms to be united with the man Jesus, who at Calvary so changed Simon of Cyrene to look like Himself that the unfortunate benefactor was crucified in His place. While all this was going on, without the Jews having an inkling of what was happening, Christ stood by and laughed at their ignorance:

> For since He was an incorporeal power and the Nous (mind) of the unborn father, he transfigured himself as he pleased, and thus ascended to him who had sent him, deriding them, inasmuch as he could not be laid hold of, and was invisible to all (Irenaeus, *Against Heresies*, Bk. I, xxiv, 4, ANF, I, 349).

As regards man, his soul alone is immortal. His body, like that of Christ, is subject to decay. This system implies a kind of evolution through the light of knowledge and purification, from a lower scale of existence to a higher. *Gnosis*, to Basilides, is not primarily concerned with the truth as it is in Jesus, but with the intricate mysteries that make up his scheme of things. Many of them came from Matthias, a man he knew, to whom Jesus had entrusted these secrets. Only the few knew of this special instruction and guidance. The many were held captive through ignorance, without hope of ever ascending to the higher realms.

We might have some idea of the theory of being which is the basis of his religious conceptions if we were to bear in mind the modern way of relating the earth to the stratosphere and the other layers above it. God exists in a vacuum, away from any contact with even the highest forms of existence. The first assembly of beings came forth from a particular Seed of supernatural essence, which contained within itself the potentiality of all things, in accordance with the plan of the Non-existent Deity. This combination of existences is referred to as celestial creation. It embraces the Great Archon, the Son who is his Adviser, and Aether.

The Great Archon considered himself to be Lord and Governor and a wise Master Builder. Nevertheless, he felt lonely. To overcome his loneliness a Son, far wiser than he and superior to himself, was generated. He caused him to sit on his right hand within the glory of the Ogdoad. Other great Archons in time came into being, and they in turn created Principalities and Powers and Rulers. One of these Archons was called Abraxas, who controlled 365 heavens.

Among the descending planes or spheres of existence is found what is called the Hebdomad, with its Archon and his Son. As in the case of the Ogdoad, it is the Son of the Archon of the Hebdomad who does the greater service, as the light from above descends toward the lower regions. It is always the Son that enlightens the Ruler of each sphere. These Sons, in their own peculiar way, are evangelists. The Son of one sphere tells the Gospel-secret to the Son of another. So the good news is passed down from plane to plane until finally,

> The light (therefore) which came down from the Ogdoad above to the Son of the Hebdomad, descended . . . upon Jesus the son of Mary, and he had radiance imparted to him by being illuminated with the light that shone upon him (Hippolytus, *The Refutation of All Heresies*, Bk. VII, xiv, ANF, V, 107f.).

With regard to the existence of material things, Basilides argues that we cannot think of God, who is non-existent, constructing a world as "the spider its web." The reason for this form of being must be found in the cosmic Seed out of which evolved the Archons and other lofty types of existences. The cosmic Seed is responsible for both celestial and terrestial beings. It has within itself a trinity of substances. The highest is so refined that it can become celestial beings. The second is not so refined, but it is capable of being purified. The third is so gross that it can never ascend. It was from this lowest potentiality within the cosmic Seed that the world and all it contains came into being (Hippolytus, *The Refutation of All Heresies*, Bk. VII, x, pp. 104ff.).

WONDER SIX

(*Valentinus*)

Justin Martyr, describing his quest after truth, mentions Pythagoras as one of the guides whom he had abandoned. Valentinus, however, tried to harmonize some of the basic ideas of the Greek philosopher with the teaching of Paul, from whom he had derived certain secrets about Christ through Theodas his own master.

The system of this Gnostic, the most comprehensive and the most influential of all, is obviously constructed after the pattern of Pythagoras, as Irenaeus and Hippolytus point out. The Greek thinker insisted that reality consists in *number*. Definiteness and regularity, so he held, are symbolic of all existence. There is nothing capricious or haphazard about it, otherwise reason would be unable to explain it. Everything has its own definite number. More basic for the purpose of interpreting Valentinus and the various theories of his followers, are the following ideas of Pythagoras: The Cosmos, the world of order and form, is the result of combining the Unlimited and the Limit. Marriage (represented by the number five), the first harmony of male (odd) and female (even), is typical of all forms of existence. "The originating principle of the universe was the unbegotten monad and the generated duad, and the rest of the numbers." The monad is the father of the duad; and the duad the mother of all things that are begotten (Hippolytus, *Refutation*, Bk. VI, xviii, p. 82).

The system of Valentinus begins with the Monad or Father, unbegotten, imperishable, inconceivable, unlimited, and subsisting in a state of undisturbed silence. Since he is Love, other beings were brought forth to be objects of his affection. The first to be projected were Bythus (male) and Ennoea (female),

The Faith and Fantasy

the Duad whose conjugal union generated all other Aeons within the *Pleroma*. This pair projected Nous and Aletheia. From Nous and Aletheia came Logos and Zoe. From Logos and Zoe came Anthropos and Ecclesia. Twenty-four more Aeons were generated by four of the above; Sophia being the last female Aeon among these, all the others appearing in pairs of opposite sexes. Christ and the Holy Spirit and the Saviour are not included among these Thirty Aeons of the *Pleroma*.

The big occasion occurs when Sophia, who had no male partner, left the *Pleroma* on her own. This adventure called for special measures to protect the *Pleroma* from within. In order to bring this about, the Father produced another Aeon named Horos, whose mission was to defend the frontiers of the *Pleroma*. Under his protection, nothing could pass from what was below to the higher plane. Hence Horos is also called the Limit and the Ogdoad. In his interpretation of Ephesians 3:14, 18, Valentinus says that the "depth" of knowledge is the Father of the universe; the "breadth" is Horos, the Limit of the *Pleroma*; and the "length" is the *Pleroma* of Aeons.

The immediate result of Sophia's experiment on her own away from the *Pleroma* was Formlessness, or Amorphous Substance, that is, substance without form. The Gnostics believed that the female produced substance; and the male, form. Since Sophia had no partner, what she produced was without form. This female Aeon cried her heart out when she saw what had happened. The thirty Aeons of the *Pleroma* took pity on her. In order to allay her sadness they generated together another Aeon, a male partner, called the First Fruit of the *Pleroma* or Jesus. With his help Formlessness began to take shape:

> Then, out of gratitude for the great benefit conferred upon them, the whole Pleroma of the Aeons, with one design and desire, and with the concurrence of Christ and the Holy Spirit, their Father also setting the seal of His approval on their conduct, brought together whatever each one had in himself of the greatest beauty and preciousness; and uniting all these contributions so as skilfully to blend the whole, they produced, to the honor and glory of Bythus, a being of most perfect beauty, the very star of the Pleroma, and the perfect fruit [of it], namely Jesus. Him they also speak of under the name Saviour, and Christ and . . . Logos, and . . . Everything . . . [and] angels of the same nature as Himself were . . . produced, to act as His body-guard (Irenaeus, *Against Heresies*, Bk. I, ii, 6, p. 318).

Sophia is the most romantic of all the Aeons. Sometimes she is called the Ogdoad and the Mother of All. With the exception of the Aeon Jesus, she is of greater interest to us who are born of the flesh, a material substance, than the others. Out of her tears came our trials; out of her agony, our bodies and souls. The Demiurge, in Valentinus' system, is just a passive and ignorant servant through whom her creative energies are put into action. Of all the Aeons she alone was acquainted with sorrow and grief, but she also found a recompense for her travail and suffering. Within the *Pleroma* itself there is nothing to affect its harmony. There is no passion or despondency, only compassion and pity. Agony and despair are without, never within. It was by the assistance of the Aeon Jesus, the First Fruit of the Thirty Aeons, that she recovered again what Pythagoras calls "the music of the spheres."

The souls that came into being through her intervention have a divine spark within them. In their creation they are of the Logos type, visitants from above in a mortal garb that perishes at death. Redemption is concerned with the recovery of the spark and its development, until it finally returns whence it came. It is through Knowledge that this is accomplished, and this special *Gnosis* is in possession of a few only. In the case of the rest the divine spark becomes completely extinguished.

Valentinus' chief disciples differed in their interpretation of the body of Christ. Heracleon and Ptolemais, the Italian followers of Valentinus, held that His body was like ours and that the Holy Spirit came on Him at His baptism. The Orientals, Axionicus and Bardesanes, maintained that His body was spiritual, made such when the Holy Spirit came upon Mary.

By their theory of numbers they arrived at strange conclusions. They believed that knowledge of God could be attained by help of numbers, syllables, and letters. The Twelve Apostles were held to be Twelve Aeons. The Thirty Aeons typified the fact that Christ was baptized in His thirtieth year. The woman who suffered from an issue of blood, whose story is told in the Gospels, was a type of the suffering Aeon (Irenaeus, *Against Heresies*, Bk. I, ii, p. 317f.; Hippolytus, *Refutation*, Bk. VI, xvi, xxxii, ANF, V, 81f., 90f.).

Our *immediate* reaction to this hurried visit to the Gnostics' Wonderland is a feeling of frustration, for we cannot find within it anything that looks like a unifying principle. The best the most advanced systems could give us is unrelated spheres, and not a universe. When we try to reach God, the earth seems to fall from under our feet. When the earth seems too real, spiritual substances flit away. We are never in possession of both heaven and earth, for owning one means losing the other. If we prefer the earth, there is but one result, "earth to earth." If we prefer heaven, we become mere phantoms. The choice between a worm and a ghost cannot be very alluring.

In their effort to interpret the Person of Jesus Christ the Gnostics were compelled by their dualism to presuppose the existence of two natures. In respect of one, He is Spirit, and therefore essentially good. His human body, which was made of Matter, was essentially evil. As Orientals, the Gnostics found no difficulty in believing in the existence of two natures since reality is accepted as being dualistic in form. As Greeks, they had no problem in identifying Christ with the Logos, who was an expression of Deity in human form. Difficulties arose when they looked at Him through the eyes of a Christian whose thinking was based on the New Testament. Their dualism led them to deny the reality of His body. Within their Wonderland Christ appears as a ghost, a Guest from the Unseen, whose physical aspect was a mere illusion. Hence, within Gnosticland there is no Bethlehem, no Calvary, no Empty Tomb, as we know them; no Virgin Birth, no Atonement, no Resurrection. He came and departed without leaving His footprints within the world of our experiences. He looked at human tragedy through the eyes of an observer, and, according to some of the Gnostics, He turned the tragedy into a comedy, instead of facing the trials of our common humanity with tears and suffering.

Their novel conclusion concerning the two natures in Christ recalls the heresy known as Docetism, which some of the New Testament writers denounced in their day. John calls certain men deceivers and antichrists because they did not "acknowledge the coming of Jesus Christ in the flesh" (II John 7). Cerinthus was one of these. His view of Christ and of the universe as the work of an inferior power is in agreement with what many of the Gnostics taught, and also with the main ideas of a Jewish sect called Ebionites, who looked at Paul as an apostate from the Law.

The Gnostics are no more consistent in their conception of Knowledge, or *Gnosis*, as the sole way to spiritual perfection. Those among them who used magic and incantations to hypnotize their followers left them wandering within a dreamland. The most advanced among them, with the help of worthier methods, seem to put one of their basic ideas in reverse, as they tried to reach their goal. They admit that the impact upon life comes from above. The soul is a visitant here. In considering its release from the shackles of the flesh, the main stress is on Knowledge as a way of escape. That is to say, man can of himself return to the realms above. If Gnosticism had started with man, this form of Humanism would not have been too bad. Had the Gnostic constructed his *Pleroma* in the form of a pyramid, and not as a hanging ladder, then the stress on *Gnosis* as the secret of man's ascent would have been feasible enough. To the Christian, who accepts the Incarnation as an entrance of the Divine upon the human scene, to live by a faith in the continuous effect of that fact seems the only reasonable thing to do. The claim of Knowledge as against Faith, or vice versa, depends upon where we begin. If we begin with God, then Faith alone has the secret to our ascent.

As we take our final leave of Gnosticland, we cannot but be impressed by the immense scope of its scenery. This earth is a mere side line compared with the *Pleroma*. The earth is earth, a substance that can never be mixed with anything belonging to the regions above. The soul of man is a stranger here; his body a prison. His citizenship is in heaven, with Principalities and Dominions and Powers; akin to Angels, not animals, high or low. Christ is of the vastnesses where heavens exist in countless numbers and where the many mansions of the Father's House increase ad infinitum. He passed through Bethlehem as if it were not there, and left Calvary to suffering humanity. His abode was of the spheres, among the Archons, the Aeons, and the Incorruptibles. His Gospel was the talk of the universe. They started with One whose perfection is within Himself, at home within the eternal solitudes, independent of the limitations of space and time. They tried to save Christianity from its parochialism by placing it within its original pleromatic setting.

II

THE MONTANISTS

These could very well be described as the Latter Day Saints of the early Church. They were found in Asia Minor, Rome, Africa, and Gaul. They were known as Phrygians, Montanists, Pepuzians and, in the West, Cataphrygians. All of their writings, with the exception of fragments here and there, are lost. What they stood for and accomplished is found in the works of Tertullian, Epiphanes, Jerome, and Eusebius. Eusebius quotes from the writings of some of their critics, Miltiades, Alcibiades, and Apollonius (*Church History*, Bk. V, xiv, xvi, NPNF, 2nd ser., I, 229ff.).

Montanus, the founder, was an ex-priest of Cybele. The strange religious revival inaugurated by him in Asia Minor around 150 was condemned by the Church because of the fantastic claims involved. Two women, Prisca and Maximilla, accompanied him from the beginning and did as much as he to popularize the movement. Eusebius referred to them as heretics, crawling like reptiles full of poison. Victor, Bishop of Rome, on the other hand, acknowledged their claim to prophetic gifts. It is doubtful whether Eleutherus, his predecessor, went as far. They were finally excommunicated by the Church and expelled. Eusebius writes of a widespread report that both Montanus and Maximilla committed suicide by hanging. Tertullian, the greatest of their defenders among Catholic writers, joined their ranks. In the end he left the Apostolic Church and became the head of the Montanists in Africa.

On the credit side, these facts stand out: Their stress on a Church within the Church, created by the Paraclete and not by bishops or any clerical order, is a conception not too distinct from the idea of the Remnant in the Hebrew Prophets. In this respect, they were in a way precursors of the Protestant Reformers. Their Puritanism was a welcome antidote to the rationalism of the Gnostics and the moral laxity on the part of some Christians. Their strict discipline could not but appeal to a man of Tertullian's temperament. Their championing of lay leadership was a challenge to those who might be inclined to relegate undue authority to the ecclesiastics. At its best it was a recognition of the priesthood of all believers.

On the debit side, they are one with the Gnostics, as far as certain fantastic claims are concerned. In one respect, Montanism was less Christocentric than Gnosticism, though orthodox in many of its beliefs. Both Basilides and Valentinus, in their own way, recognized the importance of Jesus Christ to any plan of salvation. Montanus resembled those Gnostics who thought themselves superior to Him. For this reason Eusebius is justified in calling him and his two companions heretics. Their conception of prophecy was also a heresy. It was so entirely different from the teaching of the New Testament that the Church was bound to protest. Their particular form of this special gift of the Holy Spirit was an anachronism. It had more in common with the First Book of Samuel than the Books of Acts. Montanists exercised their gift of prophecy in a state of ecstasy and frenzy in a manner reminiscent of the seers of Israel before the great prophets of the eighth century came on the scene. Moreover, the inflated ego of the founder led to the fantastic assertion that he was the medium of the Paraclete, a Being or Power that was even superior to the Holy Spirit. This particular Power had become incarnate in him, with the result that he could have told Jesus of Nazareth many things that He did not know. Montanus was another Simon Magus. With his incarnation a new era of the Paraclete had begun, soon to end with the reappearance of Jesus. This reign of selective inspiration made the Church in general more of a hindrance than a help. At the Second Coming the New Jerusalem was to have its earthly abode in Pepuz and Tymon, in Phrygia.

IV

The Faith and Fact

THE FAITH AND FACT

Irenaeus' five books *Against Heresies* could be used to advantage as textbooks of the Church of the second century on Gnosticism, Church Catholicism and Unity, Apostolic Tradition, the New Testament Canon, and Christian Doctrine. None ever gave a more minute account of the Gnostic systems. There was no greater Catholic and exponent of the Unity of the Faith in early times. The Church, whose foundation is one and whose faith is worldwide, is designated by him as "the Catholic Church." His answer to the dualism of the Gnostics and their novel device of segregation was the Unity of the Faith and the Universality of the Christian Church. Eusebius refers to him as "one from whom the sound and orthodox form of the apostolic tradition has come to us in writing" (*Church History*, Bk. IV, xxi, NPNF, 2nd ser., I, 237f.).

Within this unity there was room for diversity and disagreement concerning nonessentials. In recalling a Holy Communion Service administered in his church by Anicetus, Bishop of Rome, at which Polycarp, Bishop of Smyrna, offered the Prayer of Thanksgiving, Irenaeus points out that their differences on how to keep Easter did not prevent their being one in the Faith (*Fragments*, iii, ANF, I, 568f.).

This famous Catholic, who hailed from Asia Minor, became Bishop of Lyons in Southern Gaul in 177, soon after the martyrdom of Pothinus, his predecessor. Some time earlier, as a presbyter, he had visited Rome to consult Eleutherus, the bishop, about Montanism. He was acquainted with Polycarp, who knew the Apostle John. He knew Christian life and thought in Asia Minor, Rome, and Gaul, so his evidence as to the tradition of the Church rests on experience in widely separated parts of the Empire.

Of his many works, his *Against Heresies* is the most important. Hippolytus used a Greek version which has disappeared. The Latin translation used by Tertullian is still extant. The first book gives a description of the Gnostic systems. The second gives his refutation of these. Books three, four, and five, set forth the doctrines of the Christian Faith. The Scriptures are freely quoted, and much light is cast on both Catholic belief and practice at the time.

Details concerning his early life are wanting, and there is no certainty when he died. It is very probable that he visited Rome with Polycarp. Lyons, which he first served as presbyter and then as bishop, had its ecclesiastical antecedents in Asia Minor and not in Rome. Asia Minor, where Ephesus was situated, assumed the spiritual leadership of the Church for some time following the death of Timothy. Irenaeus' belief in an early return of Christ reflects the influence of this section upon him.

As a champion of Catholicism, he lays stress on a Rule of Faith, the New Testament Canon, and the Primacy of the Episcopate, or government of the Church by bishops. He is no pioneer of what we may call an ecumenical movement, for the unity of the Christian Church and its world-wide scope was a *fait accompli*. This fact is basic to his arguments against the Gnostics. As a thinker he is more of a theologian than a philosopher, more like Paul than Plato, and therefore different from the Apologists. Nor does he represent any particular school of thought. He is more of a free lance, guided by New Testament thinking and blessed with an uncanny intuition at getting to the heart of what was true, and what was heretical.

As compared with the two Alexandrians, Clement and Origen, whom we shall discuss in the next chapter, he is more conservative in his conception of the Gospel and less concerned with its power to change the world. To him it was more of a fixed testimony to the spiritual forces already in operation. He was more interested in the Parable of the Vineyard than in the Parables of the Leaven and Mustard Seed, especially if we think of the last two as referring only to the future. His primary concern was not the fusion of Faith and Reason, or Christianity and Philosophy. His mission was to interpret to his day a Gospel which had been handed down from Christ to the Apostles, and by them to their successors. It was this Gospel that gave the Church both its unity and universality. The Christian fellowship, by being true to its message, remained one and catholic.

This Gospel contained the Gospels and other New Testament writings, that which the Book of Acts calls "the doctrine of the apostles." If Irenaeus had been pressed to give one word covering all, it would have been "Apostolic." Once Christ was accepted as the final answer, then the men whom He first commissioned are the vital link between Him and those who followed them. Among the latter were men like Polycarp and others whom the Church of the second century knew. It is to the Apostles that he appeals when seeking a criterion to determine what the Church is. The Christian and Catholic tradition, so he maintains, is characterized by a book that is apostolic, by a faith that is apostolic, and by a succession of Church leaders that is apostolic.

The Church, therefore, stands out as the guardian of what was handed down from the days of the Apostles. Wherever it is, whether in the far East or far West, there is a uniform loyalty to this tradition:

> For, although the languages of the world are dissimilar, yet the import of the tradition is one and the same. For the Churches which have been planted in Germany do not believe or hand down anything different, nor do those in Spain, nor those in Gaul, nor those in the East, nor those in Egypt, nor those in Lybia. . . . But as the sun, that creature of God, is one and the same throughout the whole world, so also the preaching of the truth shineth everywhere, and enlightens all men that are willing to come to a knowledge of the truth (*Against Heresies,* Bk. I, x, 2, ANF, I, 331).

Tertullian, too, traces all the churches of his day to their apostolic foundation. He tells us how the first messengers, filled with the Holy Spirit, witnessed to the faith in Christ Jesus in Palestine, and then, proceeding to the world at large,

> founded churches in every city, from which all the other churches, one after another, derived the tradition of the faith, and the seeds of doctrine, and are every day deriving them, that they may become churches. Indeed, it is on this account only that they will be able to deem themselves apostolic, as being the offspring of apostolic churches (*Prescription against Heresies,* xx, ANF, III, 252).

Irenaeus, in his Preface to Book III, expresses his general point of view:

> For the Lord of all gave to His apostles the power of the Gospel, through whom also we have known the truth, that is, the doctrine of the Son of God; to whom also did the Lord declare: "He that heareth you, heareth Me, and he that despiseth you, despiseth Me and Him that sent Me" (ANF, I, 414).

In dealing with the churches in general, despite the fact that he recognizes the importance of Smyrna and Ephesus as influential apostolic centers, he holds "that every Church should agree with this Church [in Rome] on account of its pre-eminent authority," "founded and organized" as it was "by the two most glorious apostles, Peter and Paul" (Bk. III, iii, 2, p. 415).

Regarding this stress on the pre-eminence of the Roman Church, he is obviously thinking of its apostolic origin, and not of any inspiration that its bishops could have claimed because they were the successors of Peter and Paul. Apart from its exceptional foundation and its allegiance to the apostolic tradition, the Church in Rome did not have any more claim to pre-eminence than any of the others. If it had, how is it that down to the time of Irenaeus none of its bishops or presbyters could be compared with the Bishop of Lyons or Tertullian of Carthage as defenders of the Faith, in its struggle against Gnosticism or any of the other heresies? There was no Roman bishop among the Apologists. Hippolytus, who joined Irenaeus and Tertullian against the heretics, was not a bishop of Rome. If the Roman Church had any pre-eminence in the Apostolic Succession, one would expect to find the champions of the Apostolic Faith among its leaders. As we shall see later, Antioch and Alexandria and Carthage had more to do with directing Christian thinking than Rome. A stress on Apostolic Succession, without an equal stress on inspiration or the spiritual endowment that should go with it, invalidates any argument based on it. There is no more to Apostolic Succession in itself than there is in following Christ without the baptism of the Holy Spirit. In both instances it is simply a pattern sequence without the power. Moreover, there is a theoretical issue involved. Irenaeus' argument against the Gnostics would have no validity if he were to base his conception of Catholicity on the pre-eminence of one Christian center only. If there is but one Church that is truly and pre-eminently Catholic, then his idea of the Church as one and true to the Faith, wherever it was, is either superfluous or pointless.

I

IRENAEUS THE GREAT CATHOLIC

(i) *The Apostolic Writings*

The teaching of the Apostles, so he informs the heretics, are found in certain Apostolic Writings. The whole plan of salvation is made plain in these. They constitute the foundation and the superstructure of the true Faith. With regard to the Gospels, he has this to say:

> For, after our Lord rose from the dead, [the apostles] were invested with power from on high when the Holy Spirit came down [upon them], were filled with all [his gifts], and had perfect knowledge: they departed to the ends of the earth, preaching the glad tidings. . . . Matthew . . . issued a written

Gospel among the Hebrews in their own dialect, while Peter and Paul were preaching at Rome, and laying the foundations of the Church. After their departure, Mark, the disciple and interpreter of Peter, did also hand down to us in writing what had been preached by Peter. Luke, also, the companion of Paul, recorded in a book the Gospel preached by him. Afterward, John, the disciple of the Lord . . . did himself publish a Gospel during his residence at Ephesus in Asia (Bk. III, i, 1, p. 414). (Tertullian is also in agreement. See *Against Marcion*, Bk. IV, ii, ANF, III, 347f.).

The aim of this stress by both Irenaeus and Tertullian on the apostolic origin of these writings was to refute those heretics who had mutilated the New Testament. It was also important to prove what was apostolic and what was not, for some of the Gnostics claimed possession of secret formulas and teaching supposed to have been handed down to them from the Apostles through masters of their own. An instance of the mutilators is Marcion, who had made a New Testament Canon of his own, which seemed to him to incorporate the heart of the Gospel, that men are saved by grace and grace alone. Those Epistles of Paul which brought this fact to the forefront were accepted in an expurgated form. The Gospels were rejected, except Luke's, which he also expurgated.

Irenaeus stood for a more extended Canon, and so did Tertullian. His New Testament contained the Gospels, Acts, twelve Epistles of Paul, I Peter, I and II Epistles of John, and Revelation. Philemon is not mentioned. He shows an acquaintance with James and Hebrews. It was many years later that the Church as a whole included Hebrews and Revelation in the Canon. The East, in general, doubted the authenticity of the Apocalypse; the West, that of the Epistle to the Hebrews.

Reasons are given why the Gospels can be neither more nor less than four in number:

> For, since there are four zones of the world in which we live, and four principal winds, while the Church is scattered throughout all the world, and the "pillar and ground" of the Church is the Gospel and the spirit of life; it is fitting that she should have four pillars, breathing out immortality on every side, and vivifying men afresh (Bk. III, xi, 8, p. 428).

He goes on to explain that each Gospel has its own peculiar stress concerning the Person of Jesus Christ. John's Gospel, so full of confidence, is concerned with His "original, effectual, and glorious generation from the Father." Luke has His priestly character in mind. Matthew's is "the Gospel of His humanity," for the emphasis is on His becoming man. Mark's Gospel presents Him as a Prophet.

(ii) *The Apostolic Faith*

Irenaeus did not confine himself to the Apostolic Writings alone. He appealed also to tradition, that is, to a definite set of truths handed down, so he maintained, from the Apostles. This tradition is summarized in a form of words, or Rule of Faith, something in substance similar to the Apostles' Creed, which belongs to a later period. His Rule of Faith is a confession or statement with the Person of Jesus Christ as its main theme, as will be seen from the following. Similarities to the Apostles' Creed are italicized for the sake of comparison:

> The Church, though dispersed throughout the whole world, even to the ends of the earth, has received from the apostles and their disciples this faith: [She believes] in *one God, the Father Almighty, Maker of heaven and earth,* and the sea, and all things that are in them; and in *one Christ Jesus,* the Son of God, who became incarnate for our salvation; and in the *Holy Spirit,* who proclaimed through the prophets the dispensations of God, and the advents, and *the birth from a virgin, and the passion,* and *the resurrection from the dead, and the ascension into heaven* in the flesh of the beloved Christ Jesus, our Lord, and *His [future] manifestation from heaven* in the glory of the Father "to gather all things in one," and *to raise up anew all flesh* of the whole human race, in order that to Christ Jesus, our Lord, and God, and Saviour, and King, according to the will of the invisible Father, "every knee should bow, of things in heaven, and things in earth, and things under the earth, and that every tongue should confess" to Him, and that *He should execute judgment towards all* . . . (Bk. I, x, 1, p. 330).

As in the preaching of the Apostles immediately after Pentecost, nothing is said about the ministry of Jesus, with its miracles of healing and His emphasis on the Kingdom of God. This Rule of Faith was obviously not meant to be a general summary of what the Church preached at the time. It was more of an answer to the heretics, whose quaint theories challenged the basic truths of the Faith, especially the beliefs that the universe was the work of one God, the Father Almighty; that the Word, the Agent of all His activity in creation and redemption, became man in Jesus Christ; and that His death proved how good and righteous and benevolent the Creator and the Ruler of the world is.

(iii) *The Apostolic Succession*

In addition to the Scriptures and the tradition contained in a Rule of Faith, there was the living voice of those who presided over the Catholic churches and who had received their appointment in a regular succession from the Apostles. These officers are called both bishops and presbyters:

> It is within the power of all, therefore, in every Church, who may wish to see the truth, to contemplate clearly the tradition of the apostles manifested throughout the whole world; and we are in a position to reckon up those who were by the apostles instituted bishops in the Churches, and [to demonstrate] the succession of these men in our own times; those who neither taught nor knew anything like what these [heretics] rave about (Bk. III, iii, 1, p. 415).

The worthiness of those in the Apostolic Succession is stressed:

> For they [(the Apostles)] were desirous that these men should be very perfect and blameless in all things, whom also they were leaving behind as their successors, delivering up their own place of government to these men; which men, if they discharged their functions honestly, would be a great boon [to the church] but if they should fall away, the direst calamity (Bk. III, iii, 1, p. 415).

He enumerates the twelve bishops of Rome, from Linus, whom Peter and Paul appointed, down to Eleutherus, his own contemporary, as witnesses to the continuity of the true Catholic tradition at Rome. This evidence of loyalty to the apostolic Faith is hypothetical, for Victor, the successor of Eleutherus, acknowledged the prophetic gifts of the Montanists, whom Irenaeus condemns in the following quotation:

> Others, again (the Montanists), that they may set at nought the gift of the Spirit . . . do not admit that [(truth)] presented by John's Gospel, in which the Lord promised that He would send the Paraclete; but set aside at once both the Gospel and the prophetic Spirit. Wretched men indeed! who wish to be pseudo-prophets . . . who set aside the gift of prophecy from the Church (Bk. III, xi, 9, p. 429).

II

IRENAEUS THE THEOLOGIAN

Although details are wanting to write a biography of the Bishop of Lyons, it is safe to assume that his time would be fully occupied with the strenuous tasks of his office. A bishop in those days, in addition to being the official head of his congregation in control of its government, would also be primarily responsible for the spiritual and material welfare of his people. Not only would he be the pastor of their souls and their leader in public worship, whose duty it was to be the preacher at the main services, but also their counselor and defender in persecution. The Christian ministry and evangelism would be his basic concern. He had been called not to defend the truth but to testify to it even with his life. A Rule of Faith had been handed down from apostolic times and all that was asked of him was to present it to the world. If he were to change this form of confession or add to it, the very thing that made him a Christian would be in danger.

Irenaeus was a writer and theologian by necessity, and in this respect he was in the Pauline succession. Any theological writings that can be assigned to the Apostle, he wrote by compulsion and not by choice. He had been called to preach Jesus Christ and Him crucified, and not in the first place to write epistles. He was forced by external circumstances and unexpected events to think through and to interpret to the churches founded by him, or to individuals saved by him, how the fundamental principles of the Faith were applicable to the whole of life. That beautiful chapter on love in First Corinthians is ours because certain members of the Church in Corinth vied with one another concerning gifts of the Spirit. Had some of them not doubted the resurrection, we would never have had the 15th chapter of the same epistle. The Letter to Philemon is ours because a slave who had robbed his master became a Christian. The Cross seems very practical when it comes to reconciling people.

It was the Gnostics and other heretics that compelled the bishop to use his pen, in addition to the pulpit. In his denunciation and condemnation of these heresies he both confirmed and clarified the beliefs of the Christian Faith. Not only was Christ the Saviour of men's souls, but also the Truth which set men free.

(i) *God the Father*

Since the Gnostics, and especially Marcion, are to be refuted, Irenaeus is bound to tell us something about God as being near or far, and whether He Himself is responsible for the world we live in. The Gnostics created a distance between us and Him and filled it with Aeons as the sole means of contact. These heretics never asked themselves whether this line of communication could stand the strain of our sins, for sin to them was merely ignorance. Marcion had two worlds, one material, the other spiritual, with two distinct creators. In the former all were irreparably lost. In

The Faith and Fact

the other, there was a way of escape through one whose suffering body had nothing in common with ours, for in His case what appeared to be real was only a phantasm.

In his general refutation of these heresies, he appeals to both reason and revelation, to man's common sense and Scripture. Judging from what we have in his *Against Heresies*, he would not qualify as a Gifford Lecturer, for neither reason nor what is known as Natural Theology seems to be his strong point in his attack on heresy. He appeals to reason to show the *absurdity* of the theories involved. He appeals to revelation, as given mainly in the Bible, to prove their *fallacy*. It is in the light of Scripture, whose final revelation in Christ is implemented by Christian tradition, that he finds how false they are. As compared with the Apologists, his references to Greek philosophy are very few. Plato is mentioned as being more religious than Marcion and others (Bk. III, xxv, 5, p. 459). He assigns to him also the theory of the Transmutation of Souls (Bk. II, xxxiii, 2, p. 410). Democritus and Plato are referred to as being responsible for the idea that things below are images of things above, which alone are real, an idea accepted by some of the Gnostics (Bk. II, xiv, 3, p. 377). He relates the Gnostic theory of Numbers to that of the Pythagoreans. There is a reference to Anaxagoras, Empedocles, and Plato, who taught that the Creator formed the world out of previously existing matter (Bk. II, xiv, 4, p. 377). With the exception of these, his sole book of reference and proofs is the Bible, or what Christian tradition maintained. The reason for his confining himself to these is the fact that the heretics had perverted the Scriptures or mutilated them to support their own beliefs. In his Preface to Book I he denounces the heresies as "an abyss of madness and of blasphemy against Christ." He used reason to expose the "madness," and the Scriptures to condemn the "blasphemy."

By the help of reason alone, Irenaeus points out how absurd the Gnostics were in their conception of the *Pleroma*. They had a *Pleroma* and a Beyond. If there is a Beyond, the *Pleroma* is short of the fullness which comprises the All in All. The *Pleroma* of the Gnostics must be embraced within another, more comprehensive, or else the universe is broken up into segments. Their *Pleroma* must be related to some *Pleroma* that is final, without anything beyond itself. Thus he explains:

> How can there be any other Fulness, or Principle, or Power, or God above Him, since it is a matter of necessity that God, the *Pleroma* (Fulness) of all these, should contain all things

in His immensity, and should be contained by no one? (Bk. II, i, 2, p. 359f.).

With regard to the belief that creation was the work of Angels, we are driven to the absurd conclusion, so he argues, that God is inferior to these in power or that He is at least too careless to heed what is happening within His possessions for good or evil (Bk. II, ii, 1), or that perhaps He appears unconcerned so that He might, after all is finished, give His approval to what pleases Him or reject what He does not like (ibid.).

Marcion's distinction between a God that is just and a God that is good is treated in a similar manner, for this, too, is madness. He even claims that the heretic put an end to Deity by assuming the existence of two Gods:

> For he that is the judicial one, if he be not good, is not God, because He from whom goodness is absent is no God at all; and again, he who is good, if he has no judicial power, suffers the same [loss] as the former, by being deprived of the character of deity (Bk. III, xxv, 3, p. 459).
>
> Nor does goodness desert Him in the exercise of justice nor is His wisdom lessened; for He saves those whom He should save, and judges those worthy of judgment. Neither does He show Himself unmercifully just; for His goodness, no doubt, goes on before, and takes precedency (ibid.).

The Scriptures are quoted time and again in confirmation of the Christian belief that only one God exists, whose almighty power, operating through the Word, as the Apologists held, created the world. There is but one Lord and Father and Creator of all things, who revealed Himself to Moses and finally in His Son. His providential wisdom, goodness, and love were as real under the Old Dispensation as they are under the New. The prophets were sent by Him who finally sent His Son. Both the Law and the Gospel are from Him.

In his answer to both the Gnostics and Marcion he concludes:

> These eternal things He did not make by angels, or by any powers separated from His Ennoea. For God needs none of all these things, but is He who, by His Word and Spirit, makes, and disposes, and governs all things, and commands all things into existence, — He who formed the world ... — He who fashioned man, — He [who] is the God of Abraham, and the God of Isaac, and the God of Jacob, above whom there is no other God, nor initial principle, nor power, nor pleroma. — He is the Father of our Lord Jesus Christ ... (Bk. I, xxii, 1, p. 347).

The Faith and Fact

Having thus removed the *Pleroma* and established a direct contact between God and man through creation, revelation, and redemption, he says that man's upward climb is not through Knowledge, as the Gnostics held, but through a response to the divine impact in terms of faith and action and in what we might call "the experience of God." As a moral being, he is capable of distinguishing between good and evil, and this kind of knowledge is essential to the development of his character (Bk. IV, xxxix, 3, p. 523). As a work being fashioned and beautified by the great Master, he must through faith subject himself to Him, confident that he shall in the end become "the perfect work of God" (*ibid.*, 2). As a child of God, for him the goal is an unclouded vision of the Father. This ultimate experience makes him immortal, for he shall behold Him forever (Bk. IV, xxxviii, 3, p. 521f.). He refutes the Gnostic division of men into spiritual, material, and animal, represented by Seth, Abel, and Cain, with their contention that the second class is capable of improvement, whereas the third is beyond redemption (Bk. I, vii, 5, p. 326). On the contrary, he holds that God is revealed through men, "just as the physician is proved by his patients" (Bk. III, xx, 2, p. 450).

(ii) *God the Son*

The chasm between God and man is filled by Jesus Christ, known also as the Son, the *Logos*, or Word, who is both God and man. Before any peculiarities in his conception of Christ are noted, the following fragment from his lost writings, taken from the Armenian MS in the Mechitarist Library at Venice, will serve as a summary of his teaching in general.

> The law and the prophets and evangelists have declared that Christ was born of a virgin and suffered on the cross; was raised also from the dead, and taken up to heaven; that He was glorified, and reigns for ever. He is Himself termed the Perfect Intellect, the Word of God. He is the First-begotten, after a transcendent manner, the Creator of man; All in All; Patriarch among the patriarchs; . . . the Angel among angels; the Man among men; Son in the Father; God in God, King to all eternity. . . . He is the Salvation of the lost, the Light of those dwelling in darkness . . . the Shepherd of the saved; the Bridegroom of the Church; . . . God of God; Jesus Christ our Saviour (*Fragments*, liv, ANF, I, 577).

As we shall point out later, in explaining his view of the Atonement, his conception of the solidarity of the human race is of importance. In Adam all are lost. In Christ we are all one through the redemption that is in and through Him.

Irenaeus seems to have recovered for the early Church what Paul told the Ephesians: "That in the dispensation of the fulness of time he might gather together in one all things in Christ" (1:10). This idea of "gathering together all things in Christ" is emphasized by him, a stress that was peculiar to him among the Fathers. In Christ, so he maintains, the whole plan of existence in heaven and earth is realized and fulfilled. His coming in the flesh was a culmination of what was begun in the creation of the world. His appearance as Man among men brought about the fulfillment of all the divine purposes; first of all, by the act of becoming incarnate; secondly, by the Church which is His spiritual Body. He "recapitulated in Himself the things that constitute our humanity by uniting man to the Spirit, and causing the Spirit to dwell in man" (Bk. V, xx, 2, p. 548):

> There is . . . one God the Father, and one Christ Jesus, who came by means of the whole dispensational arrangements . . . and gathered together all things in Himself. But in every respect, too, He is man, the formation of God; and thus He took up man into Himself, the invisible becoming visible . . . and the Word being made man, thus summing up all things in Himself: so that as in super-celestial, spiritual, and invisible things, the Word of God is supreme, so also in things visible and corporeal He might possess supremacy, and, taking to Himself the pre-eminence, as well as constituting Himself Head of the Church, He might draw all things to Himself at the proper time (Bk. III, xvi, 6, p. 443). . . . For all these things were foreknown by the Father; but the Son works them out at the proper time in perfect order and sequence (*ibid.*, 7).

(iii) *The Atonement*

What Irenaeus has to say about the death of Jesus recalls Justin Martyr and the idea prevalent in his time among Christian thinkers, that Satan for some reason had a right to a man's soul. The Cross meant deliverance from this claim. Divine justice required that man be freed from the tyrant's hold, but justice also demanded that this should be done in an honorable manner. Even the archenemy deserved a square deal. Both Irenaeus and Augustine were pacifists as far as Satan was concerned. Neither believed in the application of force in his case. According to the former, God released Satan's captives by consent and persuasion, and not by compulsion, by an action considered just and reasonable (Bk. V, i, 1, p. 526f.). The latter tells us that Christ overcame Satan by justice and not by might, so that we could likewise triumph.

The Lord, not desiring to use "violent means" to recover what was originally His,

> has thus redeemed us through His own blood, giving His soul for our souls, and His flesh for our flesh, and has also poured out the Spirit of the Father for the union and communion of God and man, imparting indeed God to men by means of the Spirit, and, on the other hand, attaching man to God by His own incarnation, and bestowing upon us at His coming immortality durably and truly, by means of communion with God (*ibid.*, i, 1).

The foregoing passage implies a redemption and a restoration, an atonement and an attachment. There is the breaking of a chain that holds man captive; there is also the forging of another to link him to God. The first is broken by the death of Christ; the second is formed by His becoming man. So these two conceptions are so closely connected in Irenaeus that his view of the Atonement includes both. As a doctrine, it is basically Christocentric. That is, it is what he thinks of Christ that determines his view of His death.

To begin with, in Christ there is a "togetherness," a gathering together, or summing up, of all things in heaven and earth. There is a solidarity within the universe through Him. He is in agreement with Paul that "just as we have borne the image of the man of dust, we shall also bear the image of the man of heaven" (I Cor. 15:49, R.S.V.). We are all one in our relationship to both Adam and Christ.

The Gnostics, as we have seen, used a massive canvas to illustrate their idea of the universe. Irenaeus also regards Christ in a comprehensive manner. Through Christ's Incarnation, the whole scheme of existence found its fulfillment. At our end of things, Bethlehem is not a point on a map, it is the whole map. It is in the light of what happened there that we interpret all being. To Irenaeus the Cross was hidden in the manger. It is through His birth that we recover our perspective of the universe and our contact with God.

In his treatment of the result of the Incarnation, his thinking can be compared to what Paul says about the Resurrection of Jesus and what followed. To the Apostle (I Cor. 15), His Resurrection is the beginning of a process, Christ being the first-fruits of an abundant harvest of incorruptibility. To Irenaeus, the Incarnation is also the beginning of a process, the final results of which are incorruption and a vision of God that embraces both life and service. Compare with this Paul's instruction to "abound in the work of the Lord." In his conception there is no room for a cemetery. A graveyard is No *Man's* Land. Through the Incarnation the corruptible puts on incorruption and the mortal puts on immortality. Then shall come to pass, through the restoration of man, a universe all throbbing with life as originally made. At Bethlehem we are brought into a holy communion. We find no broken body there: we find the Son of God, through our body "attaching us to God and bestowing upon us at His coming immortality durably and truly by means of communion with God."

(iv) *God the Spirit*

All the functions attributed to the Holy Spirit in the New Testament are recognized and stressed. He is God, existing eternally with the Father and the Son. "The Spirit [is eternal and] peculiar to God" (Bk. V, xii, 2, p. 538). "I have also largely demonstrated," so he tells us, "that the Word, namely the Son, was always with the Father; and that Wisdom also, which is the Holy Spirit, was present with Him, anterior to all creation" (Bk. IV, xx, 3, p. 488). In his explanation of Isaiah 61:1, "The Spirit of the Lord is upon me," he refers to the Father as the One who anoints, to the Son as the Anointed, and to the Holy Spirit as the Unction.

According to his Rule of Faith, the Church believes in the Holy Spirit. In Book IV, xxxiii, 7, p. 508, he describes the "spiritual man" as one who has "a firm belief in the Spirit of God, who furnishes us with knowledge of the truth, and has set forth the dispensations of the Father and the Son, in virtue of which He dwells with every generation of men, according to the will of the Father."

In creation, both the Son and the Holy Spirit were co-workers. "For with Him were always present the Word and Wisdom, the Son and the Spirit, by whom and in whom, freely and spontaneously, He made all things" (Bk. IV, xx, 1, pp. 487f.). He identifies the Holy Spirit with Wisdom, the Creative Agent mentioned in Proverbs 8:22-25. It is in this connection that he refers to the Son and the Holy Spirit as the two hands of God, when God created man in His image (Preface to Book IV). "For His *offspring* and His *similitude* [(the early Fathers often spoke of the Spirit as the similitude of the Son)] do minister to Him in every respect; that is, the Son and the Holy Spirit, the Word and Wisdom; whom all the angels serve, and to whom they are subject" (Bk. IV, vii, 4, p. 470).

If we were to interpret the work of the Spirit among men in the light of what he has to say, the idea of permeation would clarify his teaching. In the past, the Spirit pervaded the Jewish Church as a Spirit of Prophecy. Within the Christian Church He is a Spirit of Grace and of Spiritual Gifts. In the life of the world at large He resembles the "still small voice" of Mount Horeb (I Kings 19:12) (Bk. IV, xx, 10, pp. 490f.).

It was by being filled with His guiding light and direction that the Hebrew prophets predicted what was to come. The Church performs its tasks as the Body of Christ through the Spirit's presence. "Where the Church is, there is the Spirit of God; and where the Spirit of God is, there is the Church, and every kind of grace" (Bk. III, xxiv, 1, p. 458). Within the Church, "the Spirit is the earnest of incorruption, the means of confirming our faith, and the ladder of ascent to God." In the end, through His pervading influence within the hearts of those who are saved, they will become possessors of spiritual bodies and heirs to a perpetual life. Through His fellowship they will cease to be carnal and become spiritual. Where the Spirit of God is, there is a living man. "The Spirit will render us to the Father, and accomplish His will, for He shall make man after the image and likeness of God" (Bk. V, vi, 1; vii, 2; viii, 1; ix, 2, 3, pp. 531ff.).

(v) *The Eucharist*

Since the Eucharist is interpreted by Irenaeus as both a symbol and something more than a symbol, it is important to understand why he stresses the latter in his *Against Heresies*. Both the Protestant and the Roman Catholic could quote him in support of their opposite theories.

It could be argued that his normal position was that of the Protestant, who accepts the elements as symbols of spiritual realities, the bread representing His body and the wine His blood. In one of the fragments assigned to him, found in Oecumenius' writings, which is believed to be a summary of a longer passage now lost, Irenaeus refers to certain slaves. These Christians while being tortured made a confession of what was not true. To save themselves from further punishment, they gave an entirely false interpretation of the facts at issue. They admitted, in order to please their tormentors, "that they had heard that the divine Communion was the body and blood of Christ, and imagining that it was actually flesh and blood, gave the inquisitors an answer to that effect." It would be reasonable to infer from this quotation that this was not the view of Irenaeus.

Another extract of his, discovered in 1715 in the Library of Tunin, also gives the spiritual explanation of the Sacrament: "The oblation of the Eucharist is not a carnal one, but a spiritual. . . . Those persons, then, who perform these oblations in remembrance of the Lord, do not fall in with Jewish views, but performing the service after a spiritual manner, they shall be called sons of wisdom."

In his *Against Heresies*, the Sacrament is something more than a symbol for two reasons. The heretics held that the body of Jesus was not real. They taught also that the Demiurge was the creator of substances like bread and wine. He used the elements in the Eucharist to refute both these contentions. Our Lord, so he argues, would never have referred to the bread as His body and the wine as His blood if His body and blood were not as real as our own: The wine, a gift of creation, which He acknowledges as His own blood, bedews our blood; and the bread, also a part of creation, which is His own body, gives increase to our own bodies. Moreover, it would be unthinkable that He would consecrate bread and wine, one as His body, and the other as His blood, if these elements were not part of the benevolent bounty created by God the Father Almighty. His concern, however, is not with any theory, such as Transubstantiation, which seeks to explain how the bread becomes His body and the wine His blood. All we have is an ingenious device on his part to identify the bread of the Communion Table with the body of the Lord and the wine with His blood, in order to show how absurd the heretics were in denying God's direct intervention as Creator and the reality of the body of Jesus Christ (Bk. V, ii, 1, 2, pp. 527f.).

V

The Faith and Fusion

THE FAITH AND FUSION

With the appearance of Clement and Origen, Alexandria plays an important role in the development of Christian thought for over two centuries. Up to this point the Church that was one, apostolic, and catholic, had been appealed to in matters of belief and conduct. From now on, certain intellectual and spiritual centers direct men's thinking concerning the Faith. At times, these schools of thought appeared so contrary in their approach and stress, that the Church as a whole had to intervene. Synods and councils were held to determine what was really catholic and apostolic. Among these were the Schools of Alexandria in Egypt, where the Old Testament had been translated into Greek, and Antioch in Syria, the starting-point of Christian expansion among the Gentiles.

Alexandria was the Athens of early Christianity. Its atmosphere was as intellectual as that of the famous Greek city in the time of Socrates and the Stoics. Judaism, Gnosticism, and Christianity had no hope of survival within it unless supported by the intellect. Whenever a conflict became apparent between belief and reason, Jews, Gnostics, and Christians fell back on the allegorical method, a convenient device to win reason over to the side of religion. When Mark the Evangelist founded the first Christian fellowship in the city, the two greatest influences were the Jewish religion and Greek philosophy. It was about this time in the first century of our era that Philo, a brilliant Jew, tried to fuse the best within the two cultures into a single system. The very atmosphere was conducive to any kind of syncretism. Every cult and religion took to itself what it could easily absorb from others without abandoning its basic ideas and principles. The Gnostic systems connected with the city illustrate how such an absorbing and blending was brought about.

Antioch also exerted great influence on the development of Christian thought, but along more theological lines. Its leaders were opposed to the popular Alexandrian method of interpreting the Bible. By a further comparison, the Alexandrian School positively reflects its environment. Generally speaking, what Plato said, carried. His conception of God as a Being that is indefinable and unknowable is reflected in its thinking. As regards the Person of Christ there is a tendency to overemphasize His divinity. The Antiochene School, on the other hand, brings His humanity to the fore. The Alexandrian School sought to protect the unity of His Person at all costs. Antioch stressed the two natures that are united in the one Person. Later we shall see what all this meant and the reason for the opposite emphases. The Alexandrians wanted to make sure that Christ was God; the Antiochenes, that He was man. There is also an obvious difference in their attitude to what is to happen at the end of time, the doctrine usually referred to as Eschatology. The Antiochene School gave a literal meaning to what the Book of Revelation has to say about the last days and the Second Coming. Clement and Origen, among the Alexandrians, were inclined to spiritualize the resurrection completely. Dionysius, Bishop of Alexandria, even denied the apostolic origin of the Apocalypse and wrote a treatise entitled, *On the Promises,* against Millenarianism so strongly believed in by Irenaeus, for example.

At the end of the second century there was in Alexandria a Church school or seminary for the purpose of training catechumens, or converts, in need of tuition before entering the Church through baptism. Its founder was Pantaenus, who had been a Stoic philosopher before his own conversion. Upon becoming a Christian he took the Gospel to India and the far East. During his mission he discovered the Gospel of Matthew among the people of India, entrusted to them by Bartholomew, one of the Apostles (Eusebius, *Church History,* Bk. V, x, 3, NPNF, 2nd ser., I, 225). Under Clement and Origen, his successors, the school came to be a bulwark against Gnosticism. As a counteraction to its appeal, Clement, in particular, stressed a kind of Christian Gnosticism entirely free of any wild pagan fantasies. This form of knowledge was based on the best in Greek philosophy and the Jewish religion, and it realized its perfection in Christ, God's own divine Instructor.

This famous seminary continued the work of Justin Martyr and other Apologists, combining in its teaching an acquaintance with Moses and Plato. Both the scholar and the saint met within its sympathetic atmosphere. It was abreast of the movements of those days in fusing into one system what was appealing in the various cults and religions. It also took advantage of the popular intellectual approach to Reality. Both Clement and Origen, following the lead given by Pantaenus, welded Christianity with the best in Greek culture. To these teachers, truth was not a one-way thoroughfare. It was a combination of many roads; all

The Faith and Fusion

narrow until the broad way was found in Christ. Gnosticism, as we have seen, was a halfway house, a compromise between Paganism and Christianity. The Alexandrians took what was of value in Greek culture and pagan philosophy all the way to Christ, where Jew and Gentile, Greek and barbarian, finally met; the Jew being led to Him by faith, and the Greek by reason. Wisdom, the queen of philosophy, became a handmaid to theology, with the maid and her new mistress existing in harmony. Clement even recognized the value of philosophic culture as a means of attaining true Christian knowledge.

The school agreed with Irenaeus and Tertullian in emphasizing the contents of a Rule of Faith, which had been handed down by the Apostles. The Scriptures were regarded as the supreme revelation in writing. Both Clement and Origen quote from it extensively. The former claims that he "could adduce ten thousand Scriptures of which not 'one tittle shall pass away' without being fulfilled" (*Exhortation to the Heathen*, ix, ANF, II, 195). He tells us that even the letters and syllables are inspired of God, all profitable in the instruction to make man perfect.

The emphasis of the school was on both theory and practice, but of the two the practical aspect of its instruction had the greater import. Its purpose was to turn out Christians who not only knew what the Faith was all about, but could also testify in their own lives to its spiritual power and high moral standards. Perfection included both piety and a pattern of behavior worthy of a Christian.

When Clement became head of the school, in 190, the Empire was prosperous. As in the days of Jeroboam II in Israel, there was a keen interest in religion, with the exception that during the reign of Emperor Commodus many cults were in the field. Practically all of these offered checks to be cashed in the future in the form of immortality. The old Babylonian cult of Isis, with its promise of a new life through death, attracted many. Besides, there was Neo-Platonism, a fusion of Oriental ideas and Greek philosophy, which catered to a man's sentiment and intellect. Its mysticism tried to meet the longing for contact with the Eternal; its philosophy, the demands of reason along the lines suggested by Plato. Its lofty idea of God, though abstract and impersonal, lifted the mind to a realm where its power to analyze or to define ceased to function.

Septimius Severus (193-211), the African who followed Commodus as emperor, introduced something new as an imperial persecutor. His predecessors from the time of Nero made Church leaders such as Peter, Paul, Ignatius, Polycarp, and Justin their main targets. (See Lactantius, *The Deaths of Persecutors,* 2.) An attempt was made to destroy the Faith at its important sources. This emperor directed his attack on the newly born seminary in Alexandria, in the hope of preventing any more converts from being trained for the Church. During the persecution which occurred in 202, Clement was driven into exile after serving as head of the school for about thirteen years. In 203 the school was reorganized by Origen, the ablest of Clement's pupils, in his eighteenth year, under the patronage of Demetrius, Bishop of Alexandria. It gained a world-wide fame under this outstanding scholar and his successors, Heracles and Dionysius, two of his pupils. Alexandria, because of the seminary, became the best educated city in the Empire.

Until Septimius made his attack, Clement had been able to dedicate his time and talent to his duties as head of the school, without any apparent hostility from the State. Upon leaving the city, he visited Syria and Asia Minor and, as far as we know, died in peace. Origen's life, on the other hand, was full of tragedy. He was harassed by both his patron and his foes. Leonidas, his father, lost his life in the persecution of 202 and the son would have suffered martyrdom also had his mother not concealed his clothes. At the end of his eventful career, forty-five years later, his death was the result of tortures at the hands of Decius. Origen was born in a Christian home. Clement, like Justin Martyr, had sought the truth here and there until he finally found what he was after in Christ. He was of the scholarly type. In his teaching and writings he shows how naturally everything leads to Christ and how every reasonable argument confirms the ultimate answer. Origen, a greater scholar still, and less academic, not only presented the Gospel as the final goal of man's quest, but also defended it in the manner of the Apologists against calumny and vicious attacks.

I

Little is known of the early life of Clement. He was probably born in Athens. Before he was saved he, too, had been a pagan philosopher, like Pantaenus, his master. In his search for greater knowledge of the truth, many a guide came to his assistance:

> I was privileged to hear ⋅ . . truly remarkable men. Of these the one, in Greece, an Ionic; the other in Magna Graecia: the first of these from Coele-Syria, the second from Egypt, and others in the East. The one was born in the land of

The Faith and Fusion

Assyria, and the other a Hebrew in Palestine. When I came upon the last (he was the first in power), having tracked him out concealed in Egypt, I found rest (*Stromata*, Bk. I, i, ANF, II, 301).

That he was a scholar and a saint is attested first of all by his own students, among whom were Origen and Alexander, Bishop of Jerusalem, who refers to him as "the holy Clement my teacher." Later, others speak of his sainthood and scholarship. According to Cyril, Bishop of Alexandria (412-444), "he was a man admirably learned and skillful, and one that searched to the depths all the learning of the Greeks with an exactness rarely attained before." Jerome (340-420) refers to him as "the most learned of all the ancients." To Eusebius, the historian, "he was an incomparable master of Christian philosophy."

Of the many books he wrote three are usually mentioned as furnishing the basis of his teaching. These are, *The Exhortation*, or *Cohortatio*; *The Instructor*, or *Paedagogos*, in three books; and *The Miscellanies*, or *Stromata*, in eight books. Taken together, they present a continuity of teaching, with the conception of the *Logos* or Word as the theme. In the first of the books the *Logos* attracts. In the second He directs. In the third He perfects. He is the Spiritual Magnet that draws all men who have any affinity with Him, whether Jew or Gentile. He is the Spiritual Star that guides the faithful amid the darkness and uncertainties of life. He is the Spiritual Goal which, once reached, fills the soul with the knowledge and love that ultimately guarantee fellowship with God. The culture that is attained through Christ, the Instructor, is spiritual, moral, and intellectual. It pervades the heart, fills the mind, and directs the will. The pupil under His tuition feels the best, thinks the best, and does the best. Man's heart and mind and will are affected by this soul culture. Through Christ all the faculties function in harmonious unity. To Clement, music and harmony accompany the oneness that is in Him.

Man, the pupil, is like a musical instrument which produces the most beautiful strains under the masterly touch of the "celestial Word who is all harmonious, melodious, holy instrument of God" (*Exhort.*, i, pp. 171f.). The pupil also resembles a patient to whom many treatments are applied. In order to cure the diseased part, or member, the Good Physician sometimes opens with a lancet, or cauterizes, or amputates. In some instances, His treatment includes cataplasm, rubbing, or fomentations (*ibid.*). Man is a lost sinner in dire need of the Saviour's pity and salvation (*ibid.*). There is still a closer and a more intimate relationship involved:

> O surpassing love for man! Not as a teacher speaking to his pupils, not as a master to his domestics . . . but as a father, does the Lord gently admonish his children (*Exhort.*, ix, pp. 195f.).

Man, the pupil, through regeneration becomes a member of the first-born Church, composed of the first-born enrolled in heaven, who hold high festival with so many myriads of angels (*ibid.*).

(i)

One may have a fairly concise idea of Clement's main message by keeping in mind that the Christ he sees is looked at through a tutor's eyes. He was a great teacher, and his Christ is also a Teacher, far greater than any among the Hebrews or the Greeks. Christ the *Logos*, or Word Incarnate, who is both God and man, is in truth an Educator, or One who brings to the surface what is latent in the soul of man. Greek philosophy, like the Law of the Hebrews, so Clement maintains, is "the humble tutor to bring us to Christ." Every spark within the human soul is a reflection of Him who is the Light of the World. The reflection was as real in Socrates as in Abraham, in Plato as in Moses. The light, in its fullness and perfect radiance, however, appeared in Christ alone. Each man is held to have been created in the image of God, and this image was never completely obliterated. Man is endowed with freedom of will. With the help of the *Instructor's* guidance, working through the Holy Spirit, the pupil will favorably react to the processes of grace, until he is finally assimilated to the *Logos* and to God Himself. This idea of "assimilation" is stressed time and again, and man is made like God, but never God. There is an assimilation, but no deification, in the sense of becoming divine, as God and Christ are.

The Deity of Christ is conceived as something distinct and eternal. Clement's teaching, in this respect, is typical of the stress laid by the Alexandrians on the divinity of the *Logos*, who in His incarnation was still God. There was never a time when the Word did not exist with the Father. He is the First Principle and the Interpreter of the Father's attributes. He is the manifestation of the Truth in His own Person. "He is the image of God and the archetypal light of light" (*Exhort.*, x, pp. 197f.). "He . . . is made equal to the Lord of the Universe" (x, p. 202). "He enacted the drama of human salvation: for He was a true champion and a fellow-champion with the creature" (*ibid.*).

He [(manifested)] Himself as the Herald of the Covenant, the Reconciler, our Saviour, the Word, the Fount of life, the Giver of peace, diffused over the whole face of the earth; by whom, so to speak, the universe has already become an ocean of blessings (*ibid.*).

(ii)

In the instruction given by Christ the stages of growth are clearly traced until perfection is reached. First of all, we have the step from heathenism to faith; then that from faith to knowledge, which at last becomes love, "which gives the loving to the loved and that which knows to that which is known" (*Stromata*, Bk. VII, x, pp. 538f.). He distinguishes between knowledge and wisdom. Wisdom is the result of teaching. His conception of knowledge resembles that of John 17:3, "And this is eternal life, that they know Thee the only true God, and Jesus Christ whom thou hast sent." This kind of knowledge is akin to that which we have through loving another person. It is acquired through the heart, not the mind.

Clement finds that the knowledge which is acquired by spiritual affinity purifies the soul. It conveys man "through the mystic stages of advancement; till it restores the pure in heart to the crowning place of rest; teaching to gaze, on God, face to face" (p. 539). To both John and Clement perfection is attained through an apocalypse, or vision. As man gazes upon the face of God he finds his eternal rest.

It should be understood that the contemplation he writes about has nothing in common with the ecstatic and mystic experience so appealing to the Neo-Platonists. To them the final stage is something that has no reference to anything at all, not even to one's own consciousness. All thought, all desire, all activity, all that makes man a man is lost as he is being absorbed within the great Beyond. To Clement Christ is now and forever: Christ is both foundation and the superstructure. By Him are both the beginning and the end — faith, the beginning, and love, the end, become part of our experience in Him who is the Alpha and the Omega.

(iii)

God is no Beyond, as the Neo-Platonists and the Gnostics taught. To Clement He does not absorb but assimilates. To be like God is the goal of existence. This assimilation is so complete and intimate that at times he seems to suggest that man will finally become God. He is thinking then, however, of man's moral and spiritual perfection, and not of being one with God as the Father and the Word are one: "Godliness . . . makes man as far as can be like God . . . who alone can worthily assimilate man to God" (*Exhort.*, ix, p. 196). After the process of assimilation is complete, man's perfection will still consist of his beholding the Father in the Son, "through whom alone God is beheld" (*Exhort.*, i, p. 174).

He claims that God is by nature a Revealer and Instructor who, because of the goodness of His being, unfolds Himself. "Nothing exists, the cause of whose existence is not supplied by God" (*Instructor*, Bk. I, viii, p. 225). There are not two divine powers, the one just, the other, good, working in opposition, as the Marcionites held. The very being of God makes that impossible. The whole of existence is the result of "His bare volition," which is inherently good (*Exhort.*, iv, pp. 184ff.). As "General, the Word, the Commander-in-Chief of the universe," He has power to judge and to do good. As the Source of all goodness, He treats the just and the unjust alike (*Instructor*, Bk. I, viii, p. 226). As the Savior of man, He is "the living God, who suffered" (*Exhort.*, x, p. 201).

(iv)

As regards man's growth toward perfection, "assimilation" is in the forefront. When he considers man's duty as a moral being, the word Clement uses is "adjustment." He interprets virtue as "a will in conformity to God and Christ, rightly adjusted to life everlasting" (*Instructor*, I, XIII, p. 235). Christians in this world are "trained in a system of reasonable actions," that is, actions that are adjusted to the claims of eternity, performed by an "unfailing energy . . . called faith." This system is revealed in the commandments of the Lord, which are "divine statutes and spiritual counsels . . . being adapted for ourselves and our neighbors" (*ibid.*).

Within the pagan world of his day, man's divine estate had been exchanged for husks and swine. Gaudiness was preferred to godliness, vice to virtue, superficiality to spirituality. Success meant excess, wealth, and wantonness. In the *Instructor* Clement writes of mixed bathing in public baths, where modesty had been washed away. The people's houses were richly furnished and decorated. The men dressed in showy apparel, and the women had their hair dyed, their faces painted, and their sandals covered with jewels. They ate and drank to excess. Luxury and gluttony and all kinds of superfluities showed how superficial the social life had become. Their habits were without decorum or restraint.

Their lack of moral balance was exhibited by the way they walked, their shallowness by their empty and uncontrollable laughter.

It is in the light of these facts that his instructions to his fellow Christians must be studied. Both he, and Amos centuries earlier, might appear to us extremely critical and uncompromising killjoys. In their own day, however, there was too much at stake to tolerate any laxity in the lives of those whose religious beliefs determined their moral behavior. Their strict attitude reflects their well-balanced convictions. Clement was promoting, at the time, a way of life, Christian in nature, puritanical in its moral pattern, and universal in its redeeming and transforming power. God's ideal man, so he asserted, is not fashioned by glittering gold and gaudy garments, but by well-doing and by a minimum of worldly goods. There is no beauty comparable to that of character: "The man with whom the Word dwells does not alter himself . . . he is made like to God; he is beautiful, he does not ornament himself: his is beauty, the true beauty, for it is God" (*Instructor*, Bk. III, i, p. 271).

His criterion is the Master's saying in Luke 12:22, 23, "Therefore I tell you, do not be anxious about your life, what you shall eat, nor about your body, what you shall put on. For life is more than food, and the body more than clothing."

> If, then, He takes away anxious care for clothes and food, and superfluities in general, as unnecessary; what are we to imagine ought to be said of love of ornament . . . and fastidiousness about gems, and exquisite working of gold, and still more, of artificial hair and wreathed curls; and furthermore, of staining the eyes, and plucking out hairs, and painting with rouge and white lead, and dyeing of the hair, and the wicked arts that are employed in such deceptions? (*Instructor*, Bk. II, xi, p. 264).

II

Origen surpassed his master in activity, originality, and in the scope of his work. Persistency, perseverance, and patience characterized the man, surnamed Adamantinus, or Indefatigable. It took him twenty-eight years to complete the *Hexapla*. As a Christian theologian he is ranked with Augustine, Aquinas, and Calvin. The chief sources of information concerning his life and work are found in Eusebius' *Church History* (Book VI) and in *The Defence of Origen*, in six books, written by Eusebius and Pamphilus. Only the first of these is extant. Eusebius lived in Caesarea, where Origen's library was preserved. What is recorded about

Origen by Jerome, Rufinus, and Photius, is mainly based on the record of the above-mentioned sources. Gregory Thaumaturgus, or Wonder Worker, of Neo-Caesarea, a pupil of Origen, describes his master's method of teaching in a work called *Panegyric*.

His life was strenuous and exacting, beginning and ending in tragic circumstances. In early adolescence he was the mainstay of the family. Not yet eighteen, he was entrusted by Demetrius, Bishop of Alexandria, with the reorganization of the Christian seminary, after its suspension by Severus. He was master from 203 to 215, during which time he visited Rome, Greece, Asia Minor, and Palestine. In 215, when the city once more became a danger zone for educated Christian leaders, he retired to Caesarea in Palestine for a stay of four years. While there, he was invited to preach by Theoctitus, the Bishop, and Alexander, Bishop of Jerusalem. Demetrius immediately protested against extending such a privilege to a layman. Origen was recalled. On his return, he again served the school as head, from 219 to 230, being financially supported by Ambrose, a friend and admirer whom he had converted from the Valentinian form of Gnosticism. In 230 he paid another visit to Caesarea, and this time was ordained priest by his two Palestinian friends. This made Demetrius furious. On his return to Alexandria he was deposed from the priesthood and expelled from the city by two synods convened by the bishop. From 231 to the end of his life he was settled in Palestine, wielding great influence as teacher, writer, and counselor.

At different times he acted, by request, as consultant in doctrinal disputes, in Arabia, Greece, and Asia Minor. On one occasion he was invited to Antioch by Julia Mammaea, the mother of Emperor Alexander Severus, who sent a military escort to conduct him from Egypt to Syria. In his manner of living he was as austere as many a monk, sleeping on the floor, and at one time existing daily on the equivalent of a few cents earned as a copyist of manuscripts. In his over-eagerness to comply literally with a certain injunction in the Gospels (Matt. 19:12), he performed an act on his own body which was severely condemned by many, despite the good intention that prompted it. He was never canonized by the Church, although there is none among the early Fathers who better deserved the title "Saint."

His writings numbered around 6000, too many, Jerome said, for anyone to read in a lifetime. At one period, with the financial help of Ambrose, he had a staff of nearly twenty, among whom were seven amanuenses, or secretaries, who wrote from his dictation. These relieved one another at stated times. The

Hexapla was in fifty volumes, and *Against Celsus* is of considerable length. The usual classification of his works is as follows:

> Exegetical Works: These contain short notes on the Bible; Commentaries on such books as Matthew, John, and Romans; 200 Homilies on the principal Scripture writings.
>
> Critical Works: *The Hexapla*
> Each page had six columns, and as many as nine in some sections, with the Old Testament in Hebrew in the first column, the same in Greek letters in the second, and in the fifth, the Septuagint or the standard Greek version of the day. The other columns had different Greek versions of the original Hebrew. In the fifth column Origen inserted critical notes of his own. Only this part as copied by Pamphilus and Eusebius is extant. The work itself is lost.
>
> Apologetic Works: *Against Celsus* in 8 books.
>
> Dogmatic Works: *Stromateis* in 10 books, only 3 fragments in Latin remain; *On the Resurrection,* of which only 4 fragments are extant; *De Principiis* in 4 books.
>
> Practical Works: *On Prayer,* which includes an exposition of the Lord's Prayer; *Exhortation to Martyrdom* (written while Ambrose and others were in prison); *Letters.*

Two of his works, *De Principiis* and *Against Celsus*, are of special interest. *De Principiis* was translated into Latin by an admirer called Rufinus of Aquileia (350-410). This interpreter of Greek theology took upon himself to change some of the original expressions, in an effort to make them appear more in keeping with Catholic beliefs. This important work, written during the author's early activities in Alexandria, is a presentation of the main doctrines of the Christian Faith. *Against Celsus* was written at the end of his life. It is in the form of an Apology against an attack on Christianity written in the reign of Marcus Aurelius, that is, about eighty years before his own time. The name of Celsus' treatise was *A True Discourse.*

This work was typical of paganism of the second century, which paid more attention to the way a man thought than the way he lived. The Christian Church knew nothing of this preference. Right thinking and right living went together, for what a man believed had to be expressed in a behavior worthy of it. What paganism regarded as valid thinking about the problems of existence passed as virtue. The intellectuals were considered in a class of their own, and ignorance was worse than moral depravity.

It is against this background that Origen's Apology is to be understood. Celsus was as brilliant an opponent as could be found in those days. He was well versed in the Scriptures and in Greek thought. He attacked not only the outposts of Christianity, but also its most sacred strongholds. He questioned and refuted the Christian's conception of God and man and everything that his Rule of Faith stood for, from the Virgin Birth to the Resurrection. When argument failed him, he tried to blast the Faith with mud. His gibes and slanders and childish accusations show how a keen intellect can degenerate.

Origen's defense follows in general the pattern set by the Apologists. He is genuinely sympathetic with the quest of an enlightened pagan to find the truth, and he recognizes with even greater understanding than any before him the role of philosophy as a tutor leading finally to Jesus Christ. He is full of enthusiasm as he describes the culture produced by the Gospel, as revolutionary in its moral power as in its intellectual grasp. Christianity is both a philosophy and a way of life. As such it has universal appeal. There is no discrimination. All have come short of the glory of God and all must be saved by grace. Christians, through the transforming impact of God's love, are the outstanding citizens of the Empire. They "decline public offices, . . . that they may reserve themselves for a diviner and more necessary service in the Church of God — for the salvation of men" (*Against Celsus*, Bk. VIII, lxxv, ANF, IV, 668):

> For "in secret" and in our hearts, there are prayers which ascend as from priests in behalf of our fellow-citizens. And Christians are benefactors of their country more than others. For they train up citizens, and inculcate piety to the Supreme Being; and they promote those whose lives in the smallest cities have been good and worthy, to a divine and heavenly city, to whom it may be said, "Thou hast been faithful in the smallest city, come into a great one" (Bk. VIII, lxxiv, p. 668).

(i)

In the Preface to *De Principiis*, a summary of the Apostles' teaching is presented. What we have in the Apostles' Creed and in Irenaeus' Rule of Faith is given in greater detail. Besides, other material is included. For instance, Origen adds the belief in the soul as having a substance with a life of its own and in man's moral duty. He also held to the belief that every rational soul has a free will which operates in a world of hostile forces

The Faith and Fusion

where man, none the less, is his own master, whose fate is in no wise controlled by the stars above, as many then believed. He further mentions the Church's view of the Bible as containing a double meaning, one being apparent to most, the other less obvious. All this seems to sum up the unequivocal teaching of the Church.

He points out that the Apostles were clear and positive about the essentials of the Faith, but in the case of other matters there is no guidance given as to the best way to interpret them. Nothing is said about the following:

1. Whether God has a body, or some form, and whether it is of a different form from ours.
2. Whether the soul comes into being with the body, or whether it has a prior existence.
3. Whether something existed before the present world, and whether another world will follow this.
4. When were God's angels created, and of what nature are they?
5. Whether the sun, moon, and stars have life on them or not.

With regard to God's nature, his answers, as given in *De Principiis*, were later accepted by the Church as valid and catholic, despite Jerome's contention that his view of the Trinity was misleading, and Augustine's unfavorable reaction to most of his work. The following is an abbreviation of his statement of the doctrine as given in the Preface:

> There is one God, the Creator . . . a just and good God, the Father of our Lord Jesus Christ . . . the God of the Old and the New Testaments.
> Jesus Christ was born of the Father before all creatures . . . the servant of the Father in the creation of all things . . . became man and was incarnate, although God, and while made man, remained the God which He was . . . assumed a body like our own, differing in this respect only in that He was born of a virgin and of the Holy Spirit. . . . He suffered and died . . . after His resurrection conversed with His disciples and was taken to heaven.
> The Holy Spirit is associated with the Father and the Son in honor and dignity as the Apostles taught. . . . It was He that inspired men under both dispensations.

In *De Principiis* (Bk. I, i, 3, 4, pp. 242ff.) he adds that the Spirit is in the "unity of the Trinity . . . along with the unchangeable Father and His Son." Salvation has been made possible through "the cooperation of the entire Trinity." We cannot become partakers of the Father and the Son, without the Holy Spirit. Both the Son and the Spirit are the ground of our knowledge of the Father. Both reveal the Father to whom they will. "All knowledge of the Father is obtained by revelation of the Son through the Holy Spirit."

As he proceeds, there is a certain amount of confusion in his thinking, to say the least. In Book I, ii, 2, p. 246, he stresses how both the Son and the Spirit share with the Father the goodness within the Godhead. There seems an inconsistency, however, as he seeks to explain how that goodness was put into operation. As regards certain forms of existences within the universe, the Spirit seems *quiescent*. It is by the almighty power of God, shared by both the Father and the Son, that rational and even inanimate forms came into being, the Spirit having no part in their creation:

> I am of opinion, then, that the working of the Father and of the Son takes place as well in saints as in sinners, in rational beings and in dumb animals . . . and in all things universally which exist; but that the operation of the Holy Spirit does not take place at all in those things which are without life . . . not even in those who are endued indeed with reason . . . the operation of the Holy Spirit takes place [(in those persons)], who are already turning to a better life . . . [(and in those)] who are engaged in the performance of good actions, and who abide in God (Bk. I, iii, 5, p. 253).

Compare with the above his contention that men derive their existence from God the Father; their rational nature from God the Son; and their holiness from God the Holy Spirit (*ibid.*, 8).

In his answers to the questions concerning nonessentials, what he offers are speculations. These were acceptable to some and severely condemned by others. Such problems as he mentions in the Preface were bound to arise, and the human mind has to find some kind of an explanation, though the result may be mere guesswork. It is when fanciful solutions are turned into dogmas to be believed in at all costs that man's ingenuity is to be deplored.

Among those who were inclined to accept his teaching unchallenged were Heraclas, who relieved him at times as head of the seminary and who later became Bishop of Alexandria (233-247); his successor in the see, Dionysius the Great (247-265); and Pierius, head of the school around 270. Athanasius (300-373), another Alexandrian bishop, agreed with the less speculative part of his teaching; Rufinus, Pamphilus (martyred in 310), and Eusebius (260-340) were among his defenders. Some of his daring innovations were denounced by Methodius, Bishop of Olympus and Padara (260-312), who wrote two books against him, *On the Resurrection* and *On Things Created*. Marcellus, Bishop of Ancyra (4th century), blamed him for "the mischievous mixture of philosophic speculation with Christian doctrine." Epiphanius, Bishop of Salamis in Cyprus (320-403), was also a bitter opponent. The Ecumenical Council of Constantinople (553) condemned his theory of pre-existence.

As a matter of fact, Origen assures us that he did not regard his strange conjectures about the universe dogmatically. He would have been the last to suggest that any of his speculations concerning nonessentials made the essentials of the Christian Gospel less imperative as the sole basis of man's salvation. Should we ever discover that some of the planets are inhabited, what difference would that make to human welfare? Copernicus and Galileo did not make the message of Peter and Paul obsolete. A trip to the moon is not likely to increase the speed of the pilgrim's progress, nor is the man in the moon likely to share his burdens. We are driven back to the Cross, however far we travel, and to an empty tomb, however full the universe seems to be of our distant relatives.

(ii)

Although most of his solutions to the problems listed in the Preface of his *De Principiis* are speculative and submitted "simply as opinions, treated in the style of investigation and discussion" (Bk. II, ix, 4, p. 290f.), they are nevertheless important, for they illustrate how firmly he thought of the universe as being spiritually made. Whether stars or souls, celestial dominions or devils, they all share in a common origin. The form of existence brought forth by the will of God is neither in fragments nor in conflict, as the Gnostics believed. Freedom of action is a hallmark of all existences which from their original spiritual state developed to be either angels or powers, principalities or planets, human souls or demons. The story of man's fall as given in Genesis is illustrative of a cosmic disorder. It is through the Word that all beings, whether angels or men, regain their lost Paradise.

In his interpretation of Colossians 1:16-18, he reaffirms Paul's claim that

> in Christ and through Christ were all things made and created, whether things visible, which are corporeal, or things

invisible, which I regard as none other than incorporeal and spiritual powers . . . . viz., thrones, dominions, principalities, powers, influences (Bk. I, vii, 1, p. 262).

By "logical inference" he concludes that the sun and moon and stars "are to be included among the principalities," whose purpose is to "illuminate day and night." These, too, along with all other beings, living and rational, have been clothed with bodies to perform their function within a "distinguished principality of labor." The angels, again, each with his particular office, are regarded as "rational creatures, capable of good and evil" (Bk. I, viii, 3, pp. 265f.).

Concerning the matter whether the soul comes into being with the body or has previously existed, he has this to say. The soul of man existed before he was born in a spiritual realm. It was in this pre-existent state that it first sinned. For transgressing against the divine purpose in its original abode it was transported to a physical body, to be kept captive as a prisoner. At the final restoration of all things the soul will return to its native air as pure as in the day it was originally brought forth. Even the devil and his assistants will be included in this restoration. All of the souls created by God fell except one. It was this perfect soul that the Word took to Himself before appearing in the flesh (Bk. II, vi, 5, pp. 283f.; ix, 1, 2, 6, pp. 297ff.).

As to what existed before the present world and what is to follow, his answer can be briefly summarized thus: There is an eternal process, originating in God's own volition, in which He brings into being an indefinite series of worlds and ages, in a regular procession, until He wills otherwise, when again He will be All in All (cf. I Cor. 15:24). Existences, with the exception of those on our world, are incorporeal and spiritual. To enter the world or age that follows ours we must be clothed upon with spiritual bodies:

> It is not to be supposed that several worlds existed at once but that after the end of the present world others will take their beginning . . . ages that are not seen are eternal (Bk. III, vi, 3-6, pp. 345ff.).

In dealing with the question of God's form he stresses throughout *De Principiis* God's spiritual nature. God cannot be seen because He is without body or form to make Him visible. The invisible God, none the less, can be known through certain manifestations of Himself.

(iii)

In addition to his many speculations, he has made an extensive and liberal use of the allegorical method, a feature of practically all schools of thought at Alexandria, as has been pointed out. To mention but one instance, he follows Paul in spiritualizing the rock that quenched the thirst of the Israelites in the wilderness and identifies it with Christ (Num. 20:8; I Cor. 10:4; *De Principiis*, Bk. IV, i, 13, pp. 361f.; *Against Celsus*, Bk. IV, xlix, p. 520).

Justin Martyr, Clement, and Origen were trained philosophers and thinkers. They spiritualized Scripture passages in order to give what they taught permanent significance. Otherwise, what is recorded would be of interest only to the historian or to the moralist, who draws from the past lessons for the guidance of the present. For example, the journey of the Israelites from Egypt to Canaan is an experience in the life of a particular people. The allegorists find in it the story of man's pilgrimage to the Land of Promise, so that we can sing in many a tongue, "Guide me, O Thou great Jehovah, pilgrim through this barren land...." The incidental, in this way, can have an eternal import, and an ordinary narrative can become Holy Scripture. It is by help of the imagination that the universal meaning in an allegory is unveiled. Once the intellect takes over and seeks to base a doctrine on what is arrived at by the imagination, then trouble begins. It is for this reason that the Apologists, including Origen, and the Gnostics, were often caught in a dilemma. A simple statement like the Apostles' Creed, based as it is on Christian truth, without any attempt to read anything into it, had a greater doctrinal value than all the allegories taken together. Any expansion of the primitive creed by subsequent Church councils was never a deviation from the essentials of the Christian Faith.

(iv)

Origen's imagination traveled uncharted theological regions, seeking to discover truths that had not interested the Apostles, or were left indefinite by them. Here again his originality and novel approach were questioned. One example is his view of the Resurrection. Since he has been accused of spiritualizing the whole process, it would be well to find out what he actually wrote.

Jerome (*Epistle to Avitus*) argued that it was contrary to Christian belief for Origen to say that when Christ delivers the

Kingdom to God the Father the need of bodies will cease (*De Principiis*, Bk. II, iii, 3, p. 272). This statement seems contradictory to Scripture, but if considered in the light of his teaching as a whole, it is seen the body that he has in mind here is that which is made up of material particles. He explains in the context that the soul on its return to God will enter a realm far more tangible than anything suggested by the teaching of Plato. He cannot think of Christ or the saints ever entering that kind of world:

> We, however, who believe in its resurrection, understand that a change only has been produced by death, but that its substance certainly remains; and that by the will of its Creator, and at the time appointed, it will be restored to life; and that a second time a change will take place in it, so that what at first was flesh (formed) out of earthly soil, and was afterwards dissolved by death, and again reduced to dust and ashes . . . will be again raised from the earth, and shall after this, according to the merits of the indwelling soul, advance to the glory of a spiritual body (Bk. III, vi, 5, p. 346). (Cf. I Cor. 15, II Cor. 5:1).

He went beyond the Apostles in maintaining that the Scriptures are subject to a threefold interpretation. "For as man is said to consist of body, and soul, and spirit, so also does sacred Scripture" (Bk. IV, i, 11, p. 359). There is, first of all, the literal or historical meaning, which corresponds to the body. Then, corresponding to the soul, there is the moral sense, which represents a higher stage in Scriptural truth. Finally, there is the highest sense of all, corresponding to a man's spiritual nature. It is only by allegorizing the Bible that we can enter into its Holy of Holies.

His view of the death of Christ involves certain ideas which were novel at the time. It was the common belief that Satan had a right to the soul of Christ as a ransom from God (cf. Irenaeus). Origen held that the devil was deceived in the transaction in the following way. As soon as the payment was made on Calvary, Satan found to his dismay that what he had expected to be a gain had turned out to be a loss. It would have been better for him if Christ had not died at all, for His death spelled the doom of his evil influence over the lives of men. He was deceived, so Origen explains, by his own conceit in thinking that he could have done what he liked with the Ransom (Commentaries: *On John*, 2:21; *On Matthew*, 13:9, 16:8; *On Romans*, 2:13).

There is in his writings, however, a more evangelical view. In his comments on John 12:24, where a grain of wheat, through a process of death, bears much fruit, he writes of Jesus producing an abundant spiritual harvest through His own suffering. He goes on to say how God the Father spared not His own Son, but delivered Him up as His Lamb for us all, so that the Lamb of God, by dying for all men, might take away the sin of the world (*Against Celsus*, Bk. IV, xliii, p. 517). Origen does not seem to be aware of any conflict between this conception of the death of Christ as a sacrifice and that of a ransom to Satan. He also thinks of His death as an incentive to deeds of righteousness on the part of the believer. This is known in theology as the moral theory of the Atonement. Compare with this Paul's reference to the "fellowship of his suffering" as a means to attain unto the resurrection of the dead (Phil. 3:11). As in Irenaeus, man's redemption is closely associated with the Incarnation:

> [(Christians)] saw also that the power which had descended into human nature, and into the midst of human miseries, and which had assumed a human soul and body, contributed through faith, along with its divine elements, to the salvation of believers, when they see that from Him there began the union of the divine with the human nature, in order that the human, by communion with the divine, might rise to be divine, not in Jesus alone, but in all those who not only believe, but enter upon the life which Jesus taught (*Against Celsus*, Bk. III, xxviii, p. 475).

(v)

As a theologian, he has a penetrating grasp of the essentials and a comprehensive point of view. The Gnostics failed to co-ordinate their theories of the universe. They left the mind to wander from sphere to sphere and from aeon to aeon, without ever finding a principle to embrace the variety of gradations and existences. Origen, on the other hand, was able to bring into one system of thought all aspects of truth as it is in Jesus. He constructed what he called "one body of doctrine," a synthesis combining all ideas harmoniously. From whatever angle we look at it, truth in its entirety, sooner or later, will come into view. The moment the Christian thinker discovers that Jesus is the answer to Pilate's question, "What is truth?" he is given the secret to unravel all the mystery of being.

He tells us in the Preface to *De Principiis* that this system, which he describes as a "connected series and body of truths," is based, first of all, on what has been handed down by the

Apostles, especially as contained in the Bible, which is written by the Spirit of God. This tradition, as he summarizes it, is fundamentally the same as that presented by Irenaeus and Clement in their Rule of Faith, although, in keeping with his common practice, he adds something new, on the basis of deduction from Scripture (Preface, 2, 8, 10).

A circle could very well serve as a symbol of Origen's conception of reality. At the center of the circle stands God in Christ, who through His Son brought all existence into being. He sustains all that exists within the circumference. In *Against Celsus*, the combination, "the Most High God and His only-begotten Son," appears time and again, as if it were a refrain in a hymn. The Son is the perfect manifestation of all that exists at the center. None knows the Father but the Son and anyone to whom the Son chooses to reveal Him. What belongs to the nature of Deity is common to the Father and the Son (*De Principiis*, Bk. I, i, 8, pp. 248f.). As the *interpretation* of God's mind, the Son is called Wisdom. As an *expression* of God's mind, He is called Word. As *image* of the invisible God, He is Truth (Bk. I, i, 2, p. 242). It is through the Son that the Father is Almighty, for it is through the Son everything was made (Bk. II, 1, pp. 249f.). Both share the same omnipotence. The Son has the same nature, power, and goodness as the Father. At times the Son is spoken of as being inferior or second to the Father, an idea taken up by the Arians later. The Son is only second, as regards His function. As One sent by the Father, He is inferior to the Father (cf. John 14:26, "The Father is greater than I"). As one begotten by the Father's will out of His very nature, the Father and the Son are one. There never was a time when God the Father and God the Son did not exist, sharing with the Holy Spirit the eternal source of life. He stresses with Irenaeus and Clement the function of the Word as Mediator between God and His creation, and as the One in whom and through whom all that was within the Godhead became explicit. It is through Him that the Father "communicates" Himself. He is both the Revealer of God and the Redeemer of man. Origen was the first to refer to Christ as the God-Man (*Theanthropos*). He is as positive as Athanasius later concerning the divine and the human natures in Christ.

There is much in his teaching that recalls Plato and the Neo-Platonists. It was an axiom with him that what is seen must have a body. Hence the inference, since God has no body or form, He cannot be seen. "God, therefore, is not to be thought of as being either a body or as existing in a body" (*De Principiis*, Bk. I, i, 6, p. 243). Because of this fact "He is incomprehensible. God's nature cannot be grasped or seen by the power of any human understanding, even the purest and brightest" (*ibid.*, 5).

The invisible God, nevertheless, can be known. As Creator, He can be known through His work. As Father, He can be known through the Son. His nature and purposes can be known through the Bible, especially when we are guided by the Holy Spirit in our understanding of it. It is by the intellect and the mind that man can know God the Invisible. Thus he parts company with John and Clement, whose stress was on the necessity of spiritual affinity. One of the Beatitudes is changed by him. His version of "Blessed are the pure in heart, for they shall see God" reads, "Blessed are those with intellectual power, for they shall know God." He argues that "mind" and "heart" have the same meaning in the Sermon on the Mount. Whatever meaning is given to the term "heart," Origen is still convinced that man, because of his spiritual nature, can know God. By the help of the intellect he can know Him as the Source and Sustainer of all being, and as Saviour (*ibid.*, 1-9). Though God cannot be "measured," He can be known by His mission of love. Though He is incomprehensible, He communicates His goodness. Though God is a Spirit, the truth brings the worshipper into contact with Him, whether in Jerusalem or Gerazim, Alexandria or Caesarea.

The Neo-Platonists held that the One at the center of reality is beyond definition; One that cannot be comprehended in any manner; One that is impersonal; One that knows not that He or It exists. If He or It could be defined, He or It would cease to be the ideal of those who are concerned with mere abstractions.

The God of Origen is a Spirit who is eternally active. There is nothing fragmentary or static about the universe, the creation of His will through the Word. The cosmic order follows a set pattern of repetition. Worlds, like the sun, rise and set, to be followed at each sunset by the dawn of a new experiment in creative activity. Begetting the Son is a process that belongs to the same framework. The Saviour is ever being begotten. The story of man's fall is not something that happened once and for all. Every man has his own Eden to lose or to keep. The work of sanctification goes on and on in heaven.

In his thinking, there is a close attachment between the One at the center of existence and the manifold life of the circumference, whether angels or men, things seen or unseen, things spiritual or material. It is of the nature of Deity to be manifesting His perfection and purpose without ceasing. It is of the nature of Him to be constantly revealing Himself through the many. It is of the nature of God the Father to disclose the secret of His heart in the One sent to save the world. Finally, because God, the center of all reality, is Good, everything in the end will unite in a glorious Doxology.

Origen's conception of God as containing within Himself unfathomable depths of wisdom and love is appropriately expressed by John G. Whittier in the well-known stanza:

Immortal love forever full,
Forever flowing free;
Forever shared, forever whole,
A never ebbing sea.

VI

The Faith and Fallacy

THE FAITH AND FALLACY

Celsus, against whom Origen wrote his comprehensive Apology, is typical of the attitude of the intellectuals to Christianity in the second and third centuries. It appeared to these thinkers that the believer paid allegiance and homage to two Gods. As an argument, this would have a certain validity at the time, for the Christian was supposed to believe in one God alone. Justin, Clement, and Origen, who were as conversant with Greek philosophy as with the Old Testament, were greatly impressed by the Hebrew conception of the unity of the Godhead. They even went so far as to claim that the loftiest ideas of Plato in this direction reflected the influence of the Scriptures upon him. Whether true or not, it shows that the leading Apologists and thinkers knew of no higher conception of the Supreme Being than that revealed to Moses as the I AM THAT I AM, and later to the Prophets as the sole Ruler of the universe.

The Christian Church, as direct heir to this tradition, continued to stress the fact that God is one. To the pagan thinker, this basic emphasis appeared inconsistent because Christ was also accepted and worshipped as God. To Celsus, Christianity offered the world two Gods. As a pagan he would have no ground for complaint. Many a Greek thinker at the time subscribed to Plato's belief in one ineffable Being, and yet worshipped inferior gods. As a thinker, however, his argument was logical enough for there was evidently a contradiction in the Christian presentation.

At the end of the second century there appeared within the Church the beginning of a movement to explain in terms of thought its faith in the unity of the Godhead, the deity of Jesus Christ, and the eternal existence of the Holy Spirit. As in the case of most doctrines, it was some time before a final interpretation was arrived at. Rome and not Alexandria became the initial setting for the theological conflict involved. One of the emphases was represented by the Monarchians, who seemed very concerned about the ancient doctrine. In an attempt to safeguard the unity of the Godhead, they made it rather doubtful whether God had any contact with man in the way implied by the Incarnation of Christ. They agreed with the apostolic belief in the Fatherhood of God.

They were called Monarchians because they were out to protect the *monarchia*, or sole rule, of the Father. This they tried to achieve in a variety of ways. Some regarded God the Father as the sole Power which used Jesus as His vehicle for the salvation of the world. Some thought of God the Father as the sole Saviour who appeared on this earth in the role of the Son for the same purpose. Others, again, who seemed nearer the Christian position, held that it was an aspect or mode of the Deity that became manifested in the man Christ Jesus. According to these views, Jesus was the Father's Man, the Father's Mean, or the Father's Mode. The first held that Jesus was the Father's Man, because by gaining His favor Jesus was endowed with His power at His baptism. The second asserted that He was the Father's Mean, for in order to save us the Father Himself became incarnate at His birth. The third maintained that He was the Father's Mode, assumed by Him for the purpose of our salvation.

The technical terms for these distinct theories are Dynamic or Rationalist, Patripassian, and Modalist. Monarchianism originated in Asia Minor, where other strange ideas were born from time to time (cf. Montanism), but Rome became its stronghold while Victor, Zephyrinus, and Callistus (189-222), were bishops, all of whom were accused by one Christian writer or another of being partial to certain aspects of it.

Before the main expressions of Monarchianism are dealt with, a summary of the Catholic position as expressed by Origen, for example, in contrast with what the Sabellians and the Patripassians held, may clarify what was really involved in the conflicting interpretations.

When Origen speaks of the essence or nature of God, it is something non-corporeal and absolutely spiritual. In itself it is incomprehensible, invisible, without body or form (*De Principiis*, Bk. I, i, 5, ANF, IV, 243). None the less, the human mind can conceive of this nature assuming forms or expressions which, like the essence itself, are spiritual and invisible. These are regarded as peculiar to the nature of Deity because of God's complex character. The term used by him for these forms or expressions is *hypostasis*, a Greek word translated *substantia* in Latin, and "subsistence" in English. The expression used by theologians is "person." This does not mean "individual." Person as applied to the Trinity means the "form" or "mode" of expression of the Godhead.

The following analogy may be of some help, although inadequate in all respects, like most comparisons. A man's nature or essence is human. Of himself and in himself, in contrast with the lower creation, he is a human being. Yet his existence as a man may assume certain forms or relationships. He is capable of being father, husband, son, or brother. These do not affect his manhood, but they do express what he is capable of being (Tertullian, *Against Praxeas*, x, ANF, III, 604f.). Whether father, son, brother, or husband, he still remains a man. These facts of being father, son, brother, or husband could be called "subsistences" or "persons" in the theological sense. This analogy is imperfect because the subsistences, or persons, as regards the Godhead are essential to His very being. There was no *becoming* anything in the nature of God, Origen maintained. There is nothing accidental or conditional about it. God is Father, Son, and Holy Spirit, because He is what He is.

One of the important words in the interpretation of the Trinity is "until." This word implies that there was a "before" and "after" in the experience of God. Those who say that God is potentially Three Persons imply that the Trinity is simply a potential "until" something happens, like bringing a universe or a way of redemption into being. When theologians introduced this "untilism" into their thinking, the most profound among the guardians of the apostolic position knew instinctively that there was something false in their approach although it took some time to find an adequate means to refute the fallacy.

The concept of potentiality cannot be applied to God. If it does seem to protect the unity of the Godhead, it positively denies His unchangeableness. He has to be at any given moment what He is at every moment. We cannot think of God *becoming* Father, Son, and Holy Spirit. If He seems to us to become Father, Son, and Holy Spirit, He must of necessity be such from everlasting to everlasting (*Against Praxeas*, xxvii, pp. 623 f.). When John said that God is Love, he did not mean to suggest that that love was dormant within the Godhead, like the potentiality of a musical instrument waiting for someone to avail himself of it. Nor is it to be conceived as being in a process of becoming, as an oak, for instance, within an acorn. Every definition of God has to be in the present tense of the verb, as "God is," or "God is a Spirit," for He has to be what He is, always.

Furthermore, for our knowledge of God, to know what He is, is more important than to know what He does. Since that kind of knowledge is beyond our reach, and since all we can possibly know on our own is by inference, God in the fullness of time disclosed the nature of His being in His Son who became one of us.

The I AM THAT I AM who spoke to Moses has this to say in Jesus: HERE I AM WHAT I AM. Arius and many like him, in their approach to a doctrine of the Trinity, especially that part of the theory concerning the relation of the Son to the Father, were more concerned with what God did than with what He was. They took the activity of God as the basis of their knowledge of Him. Hence they repeated the fallacy of the Gnostics of giving us everything but a direct comprehension of a First Principle or of God. The massive and complex display of the Gnostics did not reveal what He really is. Nor did the more subtle and intricate presentation of Arius. The latter had the face of Christ painted in beautiful colors and displayed on the most conspicuous part of his screen. If the Gospel was meant to present mankind with an art gallery, this likeness by the Master Himself, the greatest of all His works, would have been its most outstanding exhibit. Creation in all its forms, whether it includes the physical power of the atom or the spiritual magnetism of Jesus Christ as conceived by Arius and many of the Monarchians, is not God. God would have been God if He had not created anything at all.

Sabellius and his followers were perfectly orthodox in saying that the Father and the Son and the Holy Spirit were aspects or modes of the Deity. They were justified in asserting that the whole of God appeared in each of these modes. Where then was the fallacy, according to the Catholic view? It was in the fact that they did not agree that the whole of God was in each of these aspects simultaneously. The whole was there consecutively, but not concurrently. They could not have admitted anything else, for to them the Father and the Son and the Holy Spirit did not stand for distinctions within the Godhead. For the purpose of self-expression, God was Father when doing one thing, Son when doing something else, and Holy Spirit when doing something different again.

In the light of this view the Three Persons are truly "persons" or "masks" in the original sense of the word, that is, different aspects assumed by God to suit the occasion, after the manner of the Greek actors in a play. To the Sabellians He can only be one Person and can wear but one mask at a time. They did not say what He would look like if He did not wear any of these. It follows therefore that God, in order to be anything at all, must be continually appearing under the aspect of Father, Son, or Holy Spirit, for He cannot be all of these simultaneously. This theory makes God dependent upon His expressions, instead of the other way around. To the Trinitarians, God

The Faith and Fallacy

appears as Father because He is Father by nature. He does not cease to be Father when He appears as the Son or the Holy Spirit. He is a Trinity of Persons by the nature of His being. The Patripassians got over the difficulty by saying that God is one Person, and they identified Him with the Father. What of the Son? If we mean by that expression the One who walked this earth as man, then He, too, was the Father. Tertullian charged them with crucifying the Father, and nicknamed them, "Patripassians." *Patri* in Latin is "father" and *passian,* "suffering." If it is the Father that suffered, what difference does that make to our salvation? Nothing, apparently, for the Father is God. Both Praxeas and Tertullian, both Noetus and Hippolytus, agreed that our salvation is of God, whether He suffered as Father or Son to bring it about. Praxeas and Noetus were denounced as heretics by Tertullian and Hippolytus for saying that it was the Father that became man in Jesus. The reason for the denunciation is found in the New Testament and the teaching of the apostolic Church.

I

Leading Monarchians

Active in Rome while Victor (192-198), Zephyrinus (198-217), and Callistus (217-222) were bishops

Chief opponents: Tertullian (160-220) and Hippolytus (in Rome 200-235)

Dynamic or Rationalist
(1) Theodotus — a leather-seller from Byzantium, an admirer of Euclid, Galen, and Aristotle — Excommunicated by Victor
(2) Theodotus — a banker of Rome
(3) Artemon or Artemas — Excommunicated by Zephyrinus
(4) Paul of Samosata — Bishop of Antioch, belongs to a later period and was never in Rome

Patripassian
(1) Praxeas — from Asia Minor; also visited Carthage, N. Africa, where he met Tertullian — Not mentioned by Hippolytus
(2) Noetus — a native of Smyrna, Asia Minor — Not mentioned by Tertullian

Modalist
- (1) Epigonos — a disciple of Noetus and head of a theological school
- (2) Cleomenes — continued Epigonos' work along with
- (3) Sabellius — from Pantapolis in Lybia, N. Africa, whose teaching is referred to by Hippolytus, Athanasius, and others — Excommunicated by Callistus

In the East the Monarchians were generally known as Sabellians. Origen calls them Patripassiani. In the West they were known as Monarchians or Patripassians.

The Monarchians at Rome were laymen. The bishops of that city had jurisdiction over them. In the case of Paul of Samosata, about fifty years later, many bishops from Palestine and Asia Minor discussed his form of the heresy at three synods held at Antioch. Since he was a bishop, he could only be tried by a council of his fellow churchmen, including bishops, presbyters, and deacons. Eusebius says that his deposition was reported by his judges to "the Catholic Church under heaven" (*Church History*, Bk. VII, xxix, NPNF, 2nd ser., I, 313). By so doing they must have considered their action as affecting the whole Church, and not a particular section of it.

All the Monarchians accepted the Gospel as God's way of salvation, although some of them were more interested in Euclid than in the Bible. These treated the Bible's contents as if they were problems in geometry or mathematics. In general, however, there was agreement that God the Father was man's best Friend. It was in trying to decide to what *extent* He could be regarded as Saviour that they disagreed with one another and with the Church. The Dynamic Monarchians, whom we shall refer to from now on as Rationalists, held that it was only the power of God the Father that took possession of Jesus. The Patripassians taught that the Father Himself came all the way via Bethlehem to be born of a virgin and finally to die on Calvary. The Modalists found the secret in the divine mode or aspect that appeared in Jesus; therefore there was no real incarnation or real suffering, for what happened was merely a semblance.

The greatness of Jesus is recognized by most of them. To the Patripassians, He was the Father Himself. With a slight change in Charles Wesley's hymn they could have sung, "Veiled in flesh the Father see." To the Modalists, He was not the Father Himself, but an expression or mode of His being. Sabellius called

The Faith and Fallacy 119

Him the Son-Father (*Huiopator*). Even the Rationalists, on the whole, regarded Him as Man-Plus. There was a difference in their interpretation of the Plus. To some of them Jesus the man became Man-Plus through an endowment of divine power which, in a lesser degree, inspired Moses and the Prophets. By playing the man the way He did, He became greater than man. To some, He attained divinity at His resurrection, as a reward for a life of complete obedience to the Father's will. In respect of this status, He was worthy of all honor and glory.

What is known of the Rationalists is mainly based on Eusebius' *History of the Church*, in which he incorporates a work called the *Little Labyrinth*, assigned by some to Hippolytus. It is from this lost treatise that he quotes when describing the early Rationalists and their teaching (cf. Tertullian, *Against All Heresies*, viii, ANF, III, 654). What he tells us of Paul of Samosata is taken from other sources. In addition to what he writes of the Patripassians and the Modalists, there is the *Refutation of All Heresies* by Hippolytus, the leading and the most enlightened defender of the Faith in Rome at the time. Another important work by a contemporary is Tertullian's *Against Praxeas*, which contains his brilliant exposition of the Doctrine of the Trinity. Later writings in support of the catholic point of view are: *On the Trinity*, by Novatian (at Rome, 251); *Against the Sabellians*, by Dionysius, Bishop of Rome (259-269); *Against Heresies*, by Epiphanius (347-407); *Against Arius*, by Athanasius (300-373).

It is of interest to note that both Montanism and Monarchianism harassed the Church in Rome about the same time. Tertullian became the head of a Montanist group at Carthage in order to promote a sterner discipline among his followers. Hippolytus left the Church in Rome and founded a group of Anti-Monarchians of all types for the sake of the purity of doctrine. This undaunted scholar and theologian was as severe in his condemnation of the bishops and their biases as he was of the Rationalists and the Modalists. His arguments were so convincing that Callistus on becoming bishop was constrained to expel Sabellius, despite his own leanings toward certain aspects of Monarchianism. During his term, Zephyrinus had to depend on Callistus, one of his deacons, for his knowledge of Christian doctrine. Hippolytus calls him "an ignorant [man] . . . and . . . unskilled in ecclesiastical definitions" (*Refutation of All Heresies*, Bk. IX, vi, ANF, V, 128). Had he been trained for Christian leadership at that crucial time and less impressed by the subtle maneuvering of his lieutenant in an effort to please all, he would have sided with Hippolytus against Epigonos and Sabellius, and with Tertullian against Praxeas and Noetus. Callistus had a romantic career. In early manhood, while acting as a slave in charge of his master's finances, he was deported to the mines of Sardinia, where Hippolytus himself was sent later, in 235 with Bishop Pontianus. On his return to Rome, Zephyrinus made Callistus chief of his deacons, in control of his temporal affairs. Hippolytus accuses him of making Sabellius a Monarchian.

The Rationalists are of importance because some of their ideas were repeated later by Paul, Bishop of Antioch (260-270). At the early stage they were known as Artemonites and Theodotians. This latter group had their own bishop, named Natalius, whose monthly salary was 150 denarii, a little over $25. According to a number of this group, Christ became deified after His resurrection. Artemon and his followers were much more secular in their thinking and more strictly rationalistic in their approach. To some of them, Euclid was superior to Christ, and mathematics of greater interest than the Bible. Artemon held that the Church, down to the time of Victor, had always taught that Christ was a mere man. A change in the teaching occurred during the bishopric of Zephyrinus, under Emperors Septimius Severus and Caracalla. Eusebius refers to Justin and many others to refute the absurd contention (*Church History*, Bk. V, xxviii, pp. 246ff.).

Paul of Samosata was influenced by the theories of the Artemonites. He was a Syrian, and was appointed bishop of Antioch in 260. It is one of the ironies of history that the very city which inaugurated Christian evangelism among the Gentiles became the birthplace of a heresy that was to trouble the Church for many years. Besides being the head of an important see, Paul was also chancelor to Zenobia, Queen of Palmyra, a kingdom that was separate from the Empire. Judging from Eusebius' vivid portrait, this picturesque prelate preferred the pomp and regalia of a procurator to the ordinary duties of a servant of Christ. On his visits to the market place, his person was protected by a bodyguard. His church services resembled a concert hall where the worshippers were encouraged to applaud his oratorical feats. At Easter, psalms to the risen Christ were abandoned, in favor of others composed in his own honor (Eusibius, *Church History*, Bk. VII, xxix, p. 313). He had started out as a poor man, as a beggar in fact. By regarding "godliness as a means of gain," and bribery and corruption as his recompense for sainthood, he had accumulated a large fortune. He was so sure of his position and popularity, that he dared the synod (which finally de-

The Faith and Fallacy

posed him) to expel him from his episcopal residence. The bishops were forced to appeal to the civil power. Emperor Aurelian gave a decision against him. Some of his ideas were to live on to worry both the Church and the state.

Basically, his view of the Person of Jesus Christ was no different from that of Artemon. The Jesus of history was a human being and nothing else. The Logos, or Word, so he argued, could never claim a personal existence. It existed in God, as reason in man. As regards Jesus, the Logos dwelt in Him in the form of a quality. Through submission to the Father's will He became one with that will. Because of an identity of will and disposition, Jesus could be worshipped as God. An Incarnation was impossible, but not an Ascension. This part of his theory was like that of the Roman Catholics concerning Mary. There was no descent from God, but an ascent to God, with all the honors that go with such an ascension.

II

On the appearance of Monarchianism in Rome, Tertullian and Hippolytus played a leading role. The former, in particular, is a worthy exponent of the catholic and apostolic position. The latter falls into a number of errors in his interpretation.

(i)

As Calvin admitted centuries later, the early Church had no better or abler champion against Patripassianism than Tertullian (*Institutes*, I, 13). His practical method of handling theological problems and his legally trained mind enabled him to be both definite and clear in many of his expressions. Before his conversion, he had studied Plato and the Stoics. Eusebius refers to him as Tertullian the Roman (Bk. II, xxv, p. 129). His father was a centurion in the service of the emperor. The son was the creator of what is known as Church Latin, with its ecclesiastical terms and expressions. These were adopted later by Western theologians. His presentation of the doctrines of the Trinity and the Person of Christ is regarded as the first attempt to give a scientific definition of them. His genius for coining epigrammatic and poignant sayings reminds us of Carlyle and Churchill in our own day. The following are often quoted: "Christians are not born; they are made." "The soul of man is Christian by nature." "It is no part of religion to compel religion, which should be adopted freely, and not by force." "Praxeas did twofold service for the devil at Rome: he drove out prophecy and introduced heresy; he put to flight the Paraclete and crucified the Father." This last quotation refers to Praxeas' opposition to Montanism and its stress on prophecy, which Tertullian interpreted in a more orthodox sense than was the case with most Montanists.

In his Rule of Faith he writes as follows:

> We . . . believe . . . there is only one God, but under the following dispensation or *oikonomia*, as it is called, that this one only God has also a Son, His Word, who proceeded from Himself, by whom all things were made, and without whom nothing was made. . . . who sent also from heaven from the Father, according to His own promise, the Holy Ghost, the Paraclete, the sanctifier of the faith of those who believe in the Father and in the Son and in the Holy Ghost (*Against Praxeas*, ii, p. 598).

The term *oikonomia*, translated above, "economy," or "dispensation," is used by him in contrast with *monarchia*, rendered "monarchy" in English, which stands for the sole rule of God, as the Monarchians stressed. Tertullian argues that among men the sole ruler sometimes shares the work of governing with chosen ministers, with a son perhaps, in certain cases. When a monarchy is so administered, the name given to that principle of government is "economy" or "dispensation." To his way of thinking, "monarchy," or *monarchia*, represents rule by a single individual; and *oikonomia*, or "economy," stands for the order of its administration.

As applied to God, *monarchia*, or monarchy, means that He is the sole Ruler. Economy, or *oikonomia*, stands for the Trinity, for it is under this form or dispensation that the Godhead functions. This does not mean that the Monarchy is subject to a division because it operates as an Economy or *oikonomia*:

> Do you really suppose that Those, who are naturally members of the Father's own substance, pledges of His love, instruments of His might, nay, His power itself and the entire system of His monarchy, are the overthrow and destruction thereof? (*ibid.*, iii, p. 598).

He is very concerned about accurate thinking when contrasting the Three (his name for the Three Persons in the Trinity) and the One, or the Economy and the Monarchy. With regard to the Economy, or the way the Monarchy is administered, the Three are not three in condition, or status. They are three in relation, or degree. They are not three in substance. They are three in mode, or form, of existence. They are not three in power. They are three in special characteristics or aspects. That is, there is a difference in their relation, in their form of being, and in their various aspects. The Father is not the Son, and the Son is not the Holy Spirit. They differ as administrators of the Monarchy in their relation to one another, in their peculiar form of existence as Father, Son, and Holy Spirit, and in respect of the distinct aspects of their activity (*ibid.*, ii, pp. 598f.).

When the distinction between the Monarchy and the Economy is set aside, and the Three are regarded in relationship to the Godhead Himself, then the Three are one in substance, of one condition, and of one power, for they are not three Gods, but one God who is Father, Son, and Holy Spirit (*ibid.*).

In an effort to define the distinctions of the Economy more clearly, Tertullian refers to the Son as being a portion of the Father's substance, the Father Himself being regarded as the entire substance (*ibid.*, ix, pp. 603f.). He also alludes to the Son and the Holy Spirit as if they were administrators acting temporarily for the Father. He again writes of the Holy Spirit as being third from the Father and the Son, and the Son as if He were inferior to the Father. The Father, for instance, exists of Himself and is not born. The Son, on the other hand, is born of the Father, and the Holy Spirit proceeds from the Father through the Son.

It is difficult, however, to conceive of distinctions in the Godhead without implying, because of the inadequacy of human analogies, a difference in their degree and mode of existence. As regards the Deity, there is no suggestion that anyone of the three is either greater or lesser, higher or lower. They are all one in their eternity and glory. He uses this analogy:

> Now the Spirit indeed is third from God and the Son; just as the fruit of the tree is third from the root, or as the stream out of the river is third from the fountain, or as the apex of the ray is third from the sun. Nothing, however, is alien from that original source whence it derives its own properties. In like manner the Trinity, flowing down from the Father through intertwined and connected steps, does not at all disturb the *Monarchy*, whilst at the same time guards the state of the *Economy* (*ibid.*, viii, p. 603).

Strictly speaking, it is not correct to say that the Trinity flows from the Father. Nor is it correct to refer to the Spirit as being third from God and the Son. Novatian, in his *On the Trinity*, an "epitome of Tertullian's work" (Jerome), confuses the Monarchy and the Economy, because he also identifies God with the Father.

For the contrast between the two to stand, the sole Ruler must be God and not the Father. The Spirit is third in relation to the Father and the Son, and not to God and the Son. In relation to God, there is no first or second or third.

Tertullian does not stress the eternal activity of the Godhead after the manner of Origen. His conception, nevertheless, implies that the Monarchy always functioned as a Trinity. He is far from suggesting that the Economy was ever a potentiality. In his interpretation of John 1:1 he asserts:

> There is without doubt shown to be One who was from the beginning, and also One with whom He always was: one the Word of God, the other God (although the Word is also God . . . not as the Father); One through whom were all things, Another by whom were all things (*ibid.*, xxi, p. 615).

In his refutation of Praxeas' theory that the Father suffered, he uses the analogy of a fountain and the stream that proceeds from it. On its course the stream may become polluted, without the fountain being affected at all. He thinks of the Father as the Fountain of the Godhead and the Son as the stream proceeding from Him. The Father could not have suffered, any more than the fountain in the foregoing analogy could become polluted because the stream is polluted. He goes on to show that although God the Father could not suffer, God was capable of suffering in the Son, and He did suffer because the Son of God became the Son of Man (*ibid.*, xxiii, xxix, pp. 618f., 625f.).

(ii)

Hippolytus asserts that he bases his doctrine of the Trinity on the Bible. Many of the features in his exposition, however, recall Plato rather than Paul, and Philo rather than John. Tertullian's *Against Praxeas* is far more scientific and scriptural than Hippolytus' *Against the Heresy of Noetus*. There are obvious flaws in Hippolytus' reasoning. He has no patience with Noetus for saying that the Father was born of the Virgin. Yet his own view of what happened at Bethlehem strongly implies, as we shall see later, that it was then that the Father became really Father.

The following statement is scriptural and in agreement with Christian tradition:

> As far as regards the power . . . God is one. But as far as regards the economy there is a threefold manifestation. . . . For there is one God . . . unoriginated, impassible . . . doing

all things as He wills, in the way He wills, and when He wills (*Against the Heresy of Noetus*, 8, ANF, V, 226).

For the Father indeed is One, but there are two Persons, because there is also the Son; and then there is the third, the Holy Spirit. The Father decrees, the Word executes, and the Son is manifested, through whom the Father is believed on. The economy of harmony is led back to one God; for God is One. It is the Father who commands, and the Son who obeys, and the Holy Spirit who gives understanding: the Father who is *above all*, and the Son who is *through all*, and the Holy Spirit who is *in all*. And we cannot otherwise think of one God, but by believing in truth in Father and Son and Holy Spirit (*ibid*., 14, p. 228).

It is when he seeks to explain the *oikonomia*, or Economy, that discrepancies appear. The Word, so he holds, has a threefold existence. First, it was in the form of Idea, or Intelligence, or Mind, in God who existed by Himself. The Word was *in* God, but not *with* God as a distinct personality. In its second stage of existence, the impersonal Word became a separate person for the purpose of creation. He is so distinct at this stage as to be treated as another God. He is called the Author, the Fellow Counselor, and the Framer of things that are in formation. By being begotten as Light of lights, the Word that was visible to God alone, became visible to the world. This manifestation makes it possible for the world to be saved (*ibid*., 10, p. 227). Hippolytus is himself aware of the paradox and goes on to explain:

Thus there appeared another beside Himself. But when I say *another*, I do not mean that there are two Gods, but that it is only as light of light, or as water from a fountain, or as a ray from the sun. For there is but one power, which is from the All; and the Father is the All, from whom cometh this Power, the Word. And this is the mind which came forth into the world, and was manifested as the Son of God (*ibid*., 11, p. 227).

The final form of the Word's existence came about through the Incarnation. It is by being born of the Virgin that He became the Son of God and the Father indeed Father. The second stage in His development reminds us of Philo's idea of the Logos. Both Philo and Hippolytus think of the Word as God's partner in the work of creation. To the latter, the Word at that stage was a person as real as the Father, a conception that the Alexandrian did not subscribe to. It is at the stage when He became man that the Word became the *Son* of God: "For neither was the Word, prior to incarnation and when by Himself, yet perfect Son, although He was perfect Word, only begotten. . . . Thus then one perfect Son of God was manifested" (*ibid.*, 15, p. 229).

III

(i)

In the fourth century the Catholic thinkers had to defend the Church's position against Arius (318) and Macedonius (360). The former, a priest of Alexandria, had received his early training under Lucian of Antioch, the head of the theological school in that city when Paul of Samosata was bishop. He was martyred in 312. This scholar and saint differed from the bishop in some respects. He accepted a kind of Incarnation, although his Christ was no better than a semi-divine creature and a demigod. Macedonius was bishop of Constantinople until deposed by the Synod of Constantinople in 360. These two challenged the doctrine of the Trinity at what seemed to be its strongest and weakest assumptions, namely, the relation of the Son to the Father and the relation of the Holy Spirit to both.

To these rationalists, Sabellius' Trinity of Three Phases became a Trinity of Three Faces, belonging respectively to three individuals called Father, Son, and Holy Spirit: one, not created, the other two, created beings; hence the charge against Arius and his followers of being Polytheists, or worshippers of many gods. Macedonius turned the whole doctrine as held by the Church into an absurdity by arguing that the Son and the Holy Spirit were brothers, if both were begotten of the Father. If, again, the Holy Spirit was begotten of the Son alone, then God the Father had a grandson. In his less humorous mood he used to refer to the Holy Spirit as a minister, servant, and creature.

(ii)

Among the theologians that confirmed and somewhat strengthened the teaching of Tertullian and Origen, are Hilary, Bishop of Poitiers (290-368), a Roman town in west central Gaul, who wrote *On the Trinity* against the Arians, a work that influenced Athanasius, Bishop of Alexandria (300-373), whose best known work is *On the Incarnation*, written when he was a young man; Augustine, Bishop of Hippo Regis, N. Africa (354-430), a convert to Christianity, like Tertullian and Hilary, whose *On the Trinity* is the outstanding work on the doctrine; and the Cappadocian Fathers, Basil the Great, Bishop of Caesarea in Cappadocia (329-379);

his brother, Gregory of Nyssa (330-395); and Basil's friend, Gregory of Nazianzus (330-390).

All these were conscious of the difficulty in finding the best terms to define God in Himself and God in His various expressions. Tertullian had employed the terms *monarchia* and *oikonomia*. Origen had defined the expressions as *hypostasis* (Latin, *substantia*; English, "person"). Hilary, writing in Latin, used *substantia* (English, "substance") for God as He is in Himself. His term for each of His three expressions was *persona* (English, "person"). He defined *substantia* or "substance" as "that which exists," and *persona* or "person" as "one who acts." Father, Son, and Holy Spirit are one in substance, or divine nature. They are distinct as persons who act. In their eternal relation, the Holy Spirit is from the Father through the Son. Later the Church held that the Holy Spirit proceeded from the Father and the Son. Athanasius was at a loss to know what term to use for God's expressions, or modes, so when he seeks to explain the relations of the Three Persons, he can only say, "Another, and Another, and Another." The Father, so he held, is not the Son and the Son is not the Holy Spirit, and yet they are one in "substance." Augustine feels that he is bound to use the term "Person," not from choice but because he knows of no better:

> For, in truth, as the Father is not the Son, and the Son is not the Father, and the Holy Spirit who is also called the gift of God is neither the Father nor the Son, certainly they are three. And so it is said plurally, "I and the Father are one." For He has not said, "*is* one," as the Sabellians say; but, "*are* one." Yet, when the question is asked, What three? human language labors altogether under great poverty of speech. The answer, however, is given, three "persons," not that it might be [completely] spoken, but that it might not be left [wholly] unspoken (*On the Trinity*, Bk. V, 10, NPNF, 1st ser., III, 92).

He is as fortunate as Tertullian in his analogies and finds within himself instances of a trinity. For example, the mind is a trinity consisting of memory, intelligence, and will. As forms of mental activity, the three are distinct, but as part of the mind itself the three are one, equal, and inseparable.

In defining the unity of the Godhead, Augustine is at his best. As sharing in the one substance, each of the three Persons is in each and each in all, and each contains the other. To show how intimately connected they are, he uses a term like "interpenetration," or "coherence." They are so inseparable, and the interpenetration is so coherent, that one wonders whether the Administrators of Tertullian's Economy are as distinct and separate as he thought they were.

The Cappadocian Fathers are important, for they fixed the terminology for subsequent thinkers. In the chapter on "The Faith and Formula," the term *ousia* will appear time and again. It is a Greek word for "substance." This was used by the Cappadocians to define God as He is in Himself, irrespective of any distinctions within the Godhead. The word they used for Father, Son, and Holy Spirit, or God's way of expressing Himself in three Persons, was *hypostasis*, the term employed by Origen. From this time on the Church adopted the expressions, "one *ousia*," or "one substance," and "three *hypostases*," or "three persons."

(iii)

The following statement of the Trinity is from the *Quicunque Vult*, which was written in Latin in the first half of the fifth century. It is better known as the Athanasian Creed, although the Alexandrian bishop had nothing to do with its composition. In fact, it owes more to the influence of Augustine than of Athanasius:

> And the Catholic Faith is this: That we worship one God in Trinity; and Trinity in Unity; Neither confounding the Persons: nor dividing the Substance. For there is one Person of the Father, another of the Son: and another of the Holy Ghost. But the Godhead of the Father, of the Son, and of the Holy Ghost is all one: the Glory equal, the Majesty coeternal . . . . So the Father is God: the Son is God: the Holy Ghost is God. And yet they are not three Gods: but one God. . . . The Father is made of none: neither created, nor begotten. The Son is of the Father alone: not made, nor created, but begotten. The Holy Ghost is of the Father *and of the Son*: neither made, nor created, nor begotten, but proceeding. . . (ANF, VII, 366).

VII

The Faith and Fellowship

THE FAITH AND FELLOWSHIP

Enough has been written in the preceding pages to justify to some degree the assertion that Christianity in the early centuries was transformed into a "metaphysics of wonderland." This criticism has in mind theology's effort to express what is essential to the Gospel in terms of thought. Laymen as well as Church leaders defended the Faith against pagan thinkers of those days as if it were a mere theory. They were constrained to present what they knew as a *way* of life, far superior to anything offered by either the Stoics or the Neo-Platonists, as a *philosophy* of life too. Although this fact gets the headlines, yet the Gospel had not been by-passed, nor its spiritual and moral power abandoned. While thinkers were busy with doctrinal disputes, Christians were still worshipping. Some were dying for the Faith; others were denying it; and some were preferring the soothing solitudes to the exciting thrills of secular society.

At no time during the early period in the Graeco-Roman world, from the far East to the far West, did the Church cease to be a new-life movement, an experiment in Christian evangelism, and a base, wherever the local group happened to be, of missionary expansion. If we could form a church which combined all the best that the denominations and sects boast of at the present time, the early Christian fellowship would have been equal to it in doctrine and discipline, in worship and service. There was loyalty to tradition and love for God and man. Divine and human interests were well balanced. Had the Day of Judgment come to pass in those days, the majority of believers would have been placed on the King's right hand. The sick and the poor were cared for, and work was found for the unemployed. Strangers were entertained as brothers in Christ. Those who had lost all rather than to deny their faith, were given shelter and support. Our annual sunrise service was a daily concern, for every day brought its Easter message. One's private life belonged to a community of saints and was fashioned by its decrees and sustained by its resources. The home was also claimed as a spiritual reservoir to nurture the family in the love and fear of the Lord. They were citizens of the Kingdom of God and the greatest benefactors of the State.

A well-organized church like that of Rome, for example, strong in numbers and in many other ways, must have carried a tremendous influence in the imperial city. Eusebius quotes from a letter sent by Cornelius, Bishop of Rome (251-253), to Fabius, Bishop of Antioch, with the following facts in it. In the Church of Rome at the time, there were, besides the bishop, 46 presbyters, 7 deacons (the accepted number in many sees [cf. Acts 6:1-6]), 7 sub-deacons, 42 acolytes or altar attendants, 25 exorcists or healers, many readers and doorkeepers, more than 1500 widows and persons in distress, and a large number of lay members (*Church History*, Bk. VI, xliii, NPNF, 2nd ser., pp. 286ff.).

As the years passed, the Church had to meet in regional and general councils to formulate its basic creeds. At no time was it called upon to plan together further conquests of men's souls. Such a commitment was accepted as a bounden duty of every Christian fellowship. From time to time there was an urgent pressure from within and without for a clearer understanding of the Faith. To save and transform the world, on the other hand, had become a matter of routine. Even the Arians were as keen and successful as the orthodox, by whom they were called heretics, in evangelism and missionary work. Other heretical groups have left records of similar endeavor and achievement. In spite of opposite theological views, the truth as it is in Jesus was still a passion for converting sinners into saints. There was unpardonable divergence in the thinking about Jesus, but in the experience and expression of Him there was hardly any difference. The Marcionites, for instance, were as notable for their moral behavior and as praiseworthy under persecution in His name as the Catholics. Those historians who write of the early Church as "a debating society" are obviously more interested in the headlines than in the heart throbs of the consecrated Christian cells scattered throughout the Empire.

Whether operating above- or under-ground, these cells, as Irenaeus tells us at the end of the second century, were one and holy. They were apostolic in doctrine and fellowship. The tradition which was their common heritage was guarded as a sacred trust both in spirit and letter. It was by reference to its form and content that some were called catholic, and any conflict with it a heresy. Whenever the meaning was uncertain or any of its expressions were to be changed, the Church as a whole acted as judiciary, or interpreter, under the guidance of the Holy Spirit.

Origen claimed the right to speculate concerning nonessentials on the ground that the Apostles had left so many questions un-

The Faith and Fellowship

answered. To those listed by him, which are in themselves of secondary importance in comparison with the essentials of the Gospel, the following could be added: What constitutes the authority of the Church? What guarantees its unity? Is it all here on earth, or has it its ideal counterpart? What about the Sacraments? Are they just symbols or something more? Has Baptism but one form?

In seeking an answer to these questions, and others like them, the Church did not act as one body. It was different in the case of the essentials. There were general councils to interpret how the Son is related to the Father, for example. At times, however, there were certain exceptions. The Ecumenical Council of Nicea had on its agenda such matters as the observance of Easter or the status of the Bishop of Alexandria. It is important to note that discipline, like doctrine, was a concern of councils and treated as among the essentials.

I

In dealing with the nature of the Church, two distinct ideas stand out, the Mystical and the Actual. These in fact are simply complementary aspects. The Christian Fellowship is both visible and invisible. Visibly, it is made of people. Invisibly, it is spiritual power produced by the presence of the unseen Christ. Its dual character is similar to the relation that exists between a man's body and his spirit. Many of the expressions denoting its spiritual structure are reminiscent of what is found here and there in the New Testament. To Ignatius it is another form of the truth expressed in the Incarnation, namely, the union of flesh and spirit. Irenaeus writes of it as a new birth and an "entrance to life." He refers to it as the "guarantor of immortality," and the "ladder by which we ascend to God." Clement of Alexandria alludes to it as the "'Virgin Mother," and as the "Bride and the mystical Body of Christ."

Clement was the first among the Fathers to stress the distinction between the visible and the invisible Church, between the mystical Body of Christ and the actual fellowship on earth. Cyril of Jerusalem (348-450) identifies the invisible with the visible, the unseen with the external society. He is most concerned, nevertheless, with its spiritual character. He says that the Holy, Catholic Church is the "Mother of all and the Bride of the Lord Jesus Christ," which to him corresponds to the heavenly Jerusalem.

In defining the actual, visible fellowship among men, the four epithets, One, Holy, Catholic, Apostolic, appear from an early period. It had become by the end of the second century the "Guardian of the Faith." Had there been no writings by the early followers of Jesus, the witness of the Church itself and its teaching would have been sufficient, so Irenaeus maintained. It was within the Church alone that communion with Christ was possible. Its very existence guaranteed the presence of God. It had been endowed with miraculous power to heal, to raise the dead, and to foresee the future. As opposed to the Montanists, whose ideal fellowship of saints was postponed until the final consummation, it was held that it had a definite divine purpose to fulfil here on earth. A realm of truth and righteousness was to be established through it. Lot's wife was a type of the Church, the salt of the earth (Irenaeus, *Against Heresies*, Bk. IV, xxxi, ANF, I, 505; Bk. III, iv, p. 416; cf. Lactantius, *Divine Institutes*, Bk. IV, xxx, ANF, VII, 133f.).

At one time Tertullian was in full agreement with Irenaeus. He, too, considered the Church as the sole repository of truth, the witness and keeper of the Holy Scriptures, the preserver of the apostolic tradition, divine in origin and authority. Later, his association with the Montanists led him to emphasize what they believed to be the "Israel within Israel," the righteous few who had received a special endowment of the Paraclete.

Augustine, Bishop of Hippo (354-430), recognized the importance of both its mystical and actual aspects. Its dual character is expressed by what he calls the *externa communio* and *the communio sanctorum*. The former stands for the Church as we know it, irrespective of any degree of holiness the members may possess. The latter is founded on the will of God, and not on any confession of faith. Everyone within the *communio sanctorum* has his name recorded in heaven, free of any quarterly statements from the financial secretary. Each was predestined to be saved before the ages. The Visible Society is made up of good and bad, of tares and wheat. The Invisible Society consists only of the elect. It follows therefore that "outside the Church there is no salvation." Origen held a similar belief. Cyprian regarded it as the medium of salvation. Augustine, however, confines the Church, outside of which there is no redemption, to the Invisible Spiritual Fellowship. It is possible to be within the earthly fellowship and out of its heavenly counterpart. Further, the Invisible Fellowship may have among its chosen ones some who never identified themselves with the *externa communio* (*The City of God*, Bk. XVIII, 47, NPNF, 1st. ser., II, 390).

He is free of the extreme theories of the Gnostics and the

Montanists, whose *gnosis* and spirituality were the respective signs of superiority within the visible society. To him the Church on earth is a reservoir of spiritual and moral power within the reach of all. What consists of good and bad is also the home of the Holy Spirit. This source of all blessings is there whether its members are among the elect or not. The soil within which both the wheat and the tares grow is of a divine constitution. The Visible Fellowship has a universal appeal. As a means of grace its portals are open to all who are baptized in the name of the Holy Trinity. All are welcome, for only God knows who the elect are.

II

Cyprian, Bishop of Carthage (248-257), is important in this connection because, first of all, the Church, the central theme of his teaching, was considered by him to be the medium of salvation. His constructive thinking about its organization and the statesmanlike manner in which he handled the problem of discipline made him an outstanding figure in his day. He was converted in middle age while residing in Carthage with a presbyter called Cecilius. His wealth and training in law and in the classics were put to good use when he was made the "bishop of the parish at Carthage." In less than three years after his baptism he was raised to the bishopric. His period in office was conspicuous for persecutions which made martyrs of some and apostates of others. In 250 he retired to a place of security until Decius had done his worst, whence he wrote a number of letters, many of which are still extant, to encourage and exhort the faithful. A year later he was back with his work, and more epistles were written to sustain the sufferers under Gallus (250-253). In 257 he was banished by Valerian and continued his letter writing till the eve of his martyrdom, on September 14, 258. As he states in his correspondence, his actual ministry among his flock was not more than six years in all.

Considering the short span of his episcopate, he was a prolific writer. The *Epistles* now extant are eighty in number. Many of them consist of his correspondence with Cornelius, Bishop of Rome, who abandoned his see under Gallus. Others deal with the separatists, Novatian and Felicissimus, and the schisms connected with their names. Twelve *Treatises* are also among his works. The most important is *On the Unity of the Church*. One is an address to the Proconsul of Africa to defend Christians against the charge that they were responsible for the wars and famine and pestilence, which were harassing the Empire at that time, because of their refusal to sacrifice to the gods. Another is entitled, *On the Lapsi,* namely, those who had betrayed their faith in the persecution. Others include the *Three Books of Testimonies Against the Jews, Works and Alms, On the Dress of Virgins, On the Lord's Prayer.*

Cyprian is usually regarded as the spiritual son of Tertullian. This recalls the influence of Clement on Origen. Like his master, he shows an exceptional grasp of some of the basic principles, considering that his activity as a Christian did not exceed thirteen years. It should be remembered that the men who were converted late in life must have been well acquainted with the Bible. It would be superfluous to compare him as a theologian with the thinkers of the third century and earlier. He was not called upon to express himself on such questions as the Person of Christ or the Trinity. What ideas he had to expound had to do with what constituted the authority of the Church when faced with such a problem as discipline. Under the existing system, confessors had the power to recommend or refuse pardon. He could not but recognize the splendid work of many of these. They were men whose own experience in trial fitted them to perform a job that required both wisdom and sympathy. Nevertheless, he believed that this prerogative belonged to the bishop, who was God's representative in dealing with man's spiritual struggle. Novatian, whom we shall consider later, indirectly agreed with him that the final judgment in doubtful and extreme cases of discipline lay with the chief officer of the Church.

Greater than any cleverness in settling abstruse subtleties of doctrine, was his prophetic instinct. He discovered, for his day, that the way along which the Master was traveling down the ages is both narrow and wide. So narrow it is, indeed, that the severest discipline should be immediately administered to the unworthy. Yet it is wide enough to make ample room for all the toleration and sympathy needed to raise the fallen and bring them back once again into step with the righteous claims of His will. That, in fact, was the greatest contribution of this Christian statesman to the Church of his time.

In his thinking about the Church, the Episcopate, and the Sacraments, there is at least a paradox, if not a contradiction, in some instances. He is emphatic about the bishop's authority, which he assumed to have been directly derived from Christ. He also recognizes the power of the laity, which functions in accordance with a similar divine arrangement. His arguments imply that the Roman bishop was unique among his brethren in the ministry as a successor of Peter. Yet he admits that it is the decision of all the bishops as a body that is final. As we shall see later, whatever personal views he had about Novatian and Felicissimus, it was the bishops meeting at Carthage and Rome that had the authority to determine their fate. Any action by the Roman bishop which did not represent the opinion of all the bishops was passed by. Again, his emphasis on the Eucharist as a sacrifice might lead one to think that there was a repetition of the offering by the celebrant.

Cyprian the statesman, in his approach to the problem of discipline, found the "way" to be both narrow and wide. His teaching in general reflects both a narrow and a wide outlook. What he says of the Bishop of Rome might be embarrassing to a Presbyterian. This idea of priority among peers might lead in time to the dogma of papal supremacy and infallibility. On the other hand, his conception of the laity might warm the heart of a Congregationalist, for there is in it that which could become the doctrine of the priesthood of all believers as conceived by the Reformers. This combination, which presents Cyprian as both a high and low churchman, is not so difficult to accept, if we think of him as being an idealist as well as a statesman.

Take, for example, his view of the Episcopate. As a statesman he has much in common with Ignatius, who also did his letter writing under persecution. These few quotations from his *Epistles* to the Churches will recall his teaching: "Look to the bishop as to the Lord Himself"; "Do nothing without the bishop"; "Be subject to the bishop." To Cyprian the "Church is founded upon the bishops, and every act of the Church is controlled by these same rulers" (*Epistle* XXVI, 1, ANF, V, 305). "The Church is established in the bishops and the clergy." Referring to the decision that has to be made in the case of schism, he says that the priest for the time is the judge instead of Christ, and the whole fraternity should obey him (*Epistle* LIV, 5, p. 340). Granting forgiveness of sins is the prerogative of the bishops, the successors of the Apostles (cf. John 20:11), he adds,

> Whence you ought to know that the bishop is in the Church, and the Church in the bishop: and if any one be not with the bishop, that he is not in the Church. . . . The Church, which is Catholic and one, is not cut nor divided, but is indeed connected and bound together by the cement of priests who cohere with one another. . . .Christ by His pres-

ence, both rules prelates themselves, and rules the Church by prelates (*Epistle* LXVIII, 8, 9, pp. 374, 375).

Thus speaks the statesman. The priests are the cement binding all together. The bishop is the visible symbol of unity. Such leaders are necessary to expedite the organized fellowship of saints as it functions. The Church as one body must also recognize the importance of all the members. So he tells us that the *lapsi* must be dealt with by an assembly for counsel consisting of bishop, presbyters, deacons, and confessors, as well as the laity who stand fast (*Epistle* LI, 5, p. 328).

Cyprian the idealist is convinced that God Himself is involved when His priests are disobeyed:

> No one, after the divine judgment, after the suffrage of the people, after the consent of the co-bishops, would make himself a judge, not now of the bishop, but of God. No one would rend the Church by a division of the unity of Christ (*Epistle* XLIV, 5, p. 322).

Further, the appointment and authority of the bishops is of God:

> The Lord who condescends to elect and appoint for Himself priests in His Church, may protect them also when elected and appointed by His good-will and help, inspiring them to govern, and supplying both vigor for restraining the contumacy of the wicked, and gentleness for cherishing the penitence of the lapsed (*ibid.*, 4, p. 322).

His conception of the nature of the Church and its unity reflects a similar idealistic point of view. The two or three gathered together in His name can make the Church as real as when large numbers are included. He writes of the "cement of concord." He refers to all being one in faith, in mind, in spirit, and in love: "all standing firm with the Gospel and the law of Christ." Peace and harmony are requisites to its unity, so he maintains. The Church stands for spiritual security. As with Noah's ark, the saved are within, the lost without. "He can no longer have God for his Father, who has not the Church for his Mother." The Church resembles a "robe, undivided, united, connected; it shows the coherent concord of our people who put on Christ." The Church, the Body of Christ, is a universal brotherhood. As the "episcopate is one, each part of which is held by each one for the whole," so is the Church one. There are many rays of the sun, but one light; many branches, but one root; many streams, but one source. None can be a martyr outside of the Church (Treatise I, *On the Unity of the Church*, 5, 6, 8, 12, pp. 422ff.).

III

In their view of the Sacraments, the early Fathers, on the whole, thought of Baptism and the Lord's Supper as means of grace. Only a few accepted the latter as a mere symbol, or simply a memorial. Many could have partaken of the present-day Mass without any scruples, provided no particular theory was involved. It was at the Council of the Lateran in 1215 that the Western Church first formulated the idea known as the Doctrine of Transubstantiation. The Council of Trent later reaffirmed it in 1555. This doctrine holds that the God-Man is truly, really, and substantially present under the forms of things sensible. By the act of consecration the substance of the bread becomes the body of Christ. A similar change affects the wine.

Baptism, generally speaking, was something more than a ceremony of initiation, or an outward sign of admission to the Church. It was more than a symbol. It stood for the means whereby the new life in Christ is bestowed upon the believer. Some of the metaphors for the rite were Bath, Illumination, Seal, and New Birth. An actual cleansing from all previous contamination, leading to a state of perfection, was believed in. Faith and repentance are its conditions. Only those that were fully aware of the spiritual meaning of the sacrament were encouraged to be baptized. Tertullian went so far as to maintain that none could obtain salvation without it. The water, so he held, was hallowed by the Holy Spirit, and the gift of eternal life was conferred by it (*On Baptism*, vii, xii, ANF, III, 672, 675f.). It is of interest to note that he taught laymen could perform the rite in the absence of a bishop, priest, or deacon, on the ground that what "is equally received can be equally given." But he has this to add: "Emulation of the episcopal office is the mother of schisms" (*ibid.*, xvii, p. 677). He was against infant baptism. Cyprian, his disciple, was in favor of it. Both Irenaeus and Origen refer to the baptism of children as part of the apostolic tradition. In certain cases, according to Cyril of Jerusalem, immersion was repeated three times. Occasionally, the naked body was anointed with oil. Ambrose, Bishop of Milan (340-397), held that Baptism was effective in cleansing a man of impurity produced by sins actually committed by him. The rite of washing the feet had to be added to purify him of original sin.

The Sacrament of the Lord's Supper was also regarded as a

symbol-plus. A symbol, to most of them, resembled a bridge connecting what is visible with what is invisible. The symbol, in some mysterious way, was supposed to become what it stood for. To us, a symbol, like the Stars and Stripes, for example, *represents* something, and nothing more. Something seen represents what is not seen. To the early Fathers, the elements in the Eucharist were believed to become what they signified, through the operation of the Holy Spirit.

The Sacrament of the Lord's Supper was regarded by Ignatius, Justin, Irenaeus, Clement, and Cyprian, as a sacrifice. What was offered was the body and blood of Christ under the symbols of bread and wine. They speak of a bloodless sacrifice. Cyril of Jerusalem also believed that the very body and blood of the Lord was received in the Supper as a spiritual sustenance. Tertullian rejected the idea of the elements as symbols. To him the bread and the wine were the body and blood of his Saviour: "The flesh feeds on the body and blood of Christ, that the soul may be made full of God" (*On the Resurrection of the Flesh,* viii, p. 551). Both Gregory of Nyssa (330-395) and Ambrose found the Sacrament to be a continuation of the Incarnation. The latter explains that the Christ presented in the Sacrament is Spirit, for the elements do not change from being what they are (*On the Mysteries,* VIII, NPNF, 2nd ser., X, 323).

Cyprian's view of the Sacrament as a sacrifice needs some clarification, since he refers to the priest as playing the part of Christ. His statement is as follows:

> For if Jesus Christ, our Lord and God, is Himself the chief priest of God the Father, . . .and has commanded this to be done in commemoration of Himself, certainly that priest truly discharges the office of Christ, who imitates that which Christ did; and he then offers a true and full sacrifice in the Church to God the Father, when he proceeds to offer it according to what he sees Christ Himself to have offered (*Epistle* LXII, 14, p. 362).

What he has in mind in the above quotation is imitation, not repetition. The priest is simply an imitator of the High Priest, "who first offered Himself as a sacrifice to the Father." Both the passion and the sacrifice are Christ's alone. It is in following the way that Christ Himself offered it that the celebrant plays the part of Christ. It cannot be a repetition. The cup of the Lord used by the priest in the time of Cyprian contained a mixture of water and wine. To him both the people, or the Church, and the Lord Himself were represented by the contents of that cup. The water stood for the people; the wine symbolized the blood of the Lord. Futhermore, the mixed cup stood for the union of both the communicant and Christ (*ibid.*, 13, p. 362). Clement of Alexandria, Origen, and Augustine accepted the allegorical and symbolic meaning. To Clement, Christ Himself was received through a "spiritual potency" at work in the institution. Bread and wine were "hallowed food." Origen also looked upon the elements as symbols. Augustine was in agreement with the Alexandrians. Both the bread and the wine remained what they were, and were not of themselves what they were supposed to signify. The flesh and blood of the Lord which they represent become spirit and life, a sustaining support to those who exist by faith. He also regarded the Sacrament as a memorial of the death of Christ.

IV

A leading hymnodist once asked

> *Tell me, Lord, is there forgiveness*
> *For repeating the same sin?*
> *Tell me, Lord, shalt Thou e'er enter*
> *Into hearts too hard to win?*
> *What do weigh the greatest failures*
> *Thou forgivest? Of what count?*
> *Which is heavier, my transgression*
> *Or the groans of Calvary's mount?*
>
> (Pantycelyn, 1716-1791)

The Church, in an effort to produce Christian character within a hostile and critical world, felt that a line had to be drawn somewhere. There had to be a limit to the transgressions it could absolve. When and how to discipline became a crucial problem in the third century and later. The extreme Puritans had their redeeming feature. They bore witness to the high standards of conduct which had made the Church so entirely distinct from anything the best culture of the day produced. Pliny in his well-known letter to the Emperor Trajan (c.112) testified to the purity of the Christian life. The superior quality of Christian morality was one of the basic arguments in the Apologists' defense of the Faith and for toleration within the Empire. Minucius Felix measured a man's religion by his righteousness. Polycarp, some years earlier, enjoined the faithful "to walk in the precept of the law, none avaricious, but temperate in all things, tender-hearted." One of the chief virtues of the early Church was chastity.

The Fathers, from the beginning, had accepted certain criteria concerning belief and behavior. It is worth mentioning that moral laxity, as well as some forms of doctrinal fallacy, are condemned by many of the leaders. The Montanist movement, at its best, was a reaction against both the rationalism of the Gnostics and the materialism condoned by many Catholics. Tertullian and Hippolytus are individual instances of a similar attitude. Zephyrinus, the Roman bishop, whom Tertullian denounces so severely for his Patripassianism, is called to order for being too lenient in his treatment of sinners. Callistus, his successor, with whom Hippolytus crossed swords because of his Monarchian leanings, is accused by him of being ineffective as the moral conscience of his flock. Novatian, again, was not only critical of Cyprian's policy concerning the *lapsi*, but he also prematurely called the "exile and martyr of Curubis" a coward.

By and large, it was far easier to gain admission to the Church than to re-enter it, once its ideals had in any way been renounced by its adherents. The initiated, through baptism, were given a clean sheet. Whatever evil had previously stained a man's life, it was forgiven and forgotten, as a new adventure in Christ began. It was when the Church had to deal with those who had soiled the sheet after their admission, that difficulties arose. Light offenses were met by different forms of censure, such as temporary exclusion from Holy Communion or varying degrees of penance. In dealing with the mortal sins of idolatry, murder, and adultery, not to mention apostasy, Church leaders differed concerning the form of punishment. Tertullian and the Montanists demanded final expulsion from the Church. Accordings to Eusebius, Dionysius, Bishop of Corinth (169), favored readmission (*Church History*, Bk. IV, xxiii, NPNF, 2nd ser., I, 150ff.). Origen, years later, believed in absolution for mortal sins committed after baptism.

Penitential discipline as imposed by the Fathers was severe and exacting. It was as punitive as any penal system in our day. Whatever freedom the penitent enjoyed, his feeling of guilt and remorse in many a case was worse than confinement within prison walls. In the fourth century penance would extend from ten to twenty years, long enough to prove whether a man was sincere or not. Readmission was impossible unless he brought forth "fruit meet for repentance."

Both the rigorists and the more lenient could have referred to the mandate given by the Master to His followers: "If you forgive the sins of any, they are forgiven; and if you retain the sins of any, they are retained" (John 20:23). The Puritans stressed the letter of the Law and not its spirit. Their opponents stood for the principles of toleration and love, as advocated by Cyprian and Augustine. The Bishop of Hippo had learned the hard way to be temperate in his judgment, as his *Confessions* so graphically show.

(i)

In the case of the *lapsi*, that is, those who had fallen from grace during the persecution of Decius (249-251), the Church was forced to intervene. It had to decide whether the lapsed were to be treated as heretics or as sinners beyond redemption. Novatus or Novatian, the presbyter who had written a treatise, *On the Trinity*, against the Monarchians, represented the Puritans in Rome. He formed a sect known as *Cathari*, or Pure Ones, who held that no clemency should be extended to the apostates. Felicissimus, his deacon, headed a similar group at Carthage with Fortunatus, chosen as rival bishop to Cyprian. The incumbent favored a more lenient treatment, but was against readmitting all kinds of penitents. Among the latter were many of those who were recommended by the Confessors. Both the Churches of Rome and Carthage agreed on accepting even these, provided the officers appointed by a council of bishops approved their readmission. Cyprian and Carthage had no pity on any clergy who had lapsed, such as Basilides and Martialis, two Spanish bishops, who had been deprived of their sees. Stephen of Rome disagreed with their deposition and reinstated them.

The first Church body to condemn Novatian was held at Carthage early in 251 and was attended by a large number of bishops. A similar action was taken later in the same year in Rome by a synod consisting of sixty bishops, and more presbyters and deacons, with Cornelius the bishop in charge (Eusebius, *Church History*, Bk. VI, xliii, pp. 286ff.; Cyprian, *Epistle* LI, 6, p. 328). Others outside of these churches joined in the controversy. Dionysius, Bishop of Alexandria (248-265), wrote a number of letters to Rome concerning those who had betrayed the Faith in Egypt. One was sent to Novatian, whom he greets as "brother," arguing that to become a martyr to prevent division of the Church was even nobler than to suffer to avoid sacrificing to idols (*Church History*, Bk. VI, xlv, pp. 290f.). Fabius, Bishop of Antioch, was inclined to side with Novatian. Eusebius says that Cyprian pleaded with him, in a letter now lost.

The persecution which tested so grievously the loyalty of Christians started in 249, when Decius was made emperor, following a fairly long period of noninterference by the State. During most of the two years he was in power, he was fighting the Goths. His decrees against the Church were piously and cruelly carried out on a vast scale. To his way of thinking, protecting the State against an alien system like Christianity was as imperative as to defend its frontiers against barbarians. His policy, like that of the prophet-statesmen of Israel in the eighth century B.C., was to bring the people back to the ancient altars. He seemed to hold with them that the threat from the outside was a judgment on something that was happening inside. Everywhere the people were abandoning the old gods and their temples. New allegiances were on the increase on the religious front. Decius, nevertheless, differed from the Hebrew prophets. Isaiah, for example, emphasized faith, not force; voluntary commitment, not compulsion. Dionysius of Alexandria, in a letter to Fabius of Antioch, poignantly declared that the only kind of piety in the emperor's religious reformation was an unholy thirst for the blood of Christians, or cruelties such as piercing the eyes of an old man with reeds till he became blind, or dragging a saintly woman over rough pavements and then stoning both to death (*Church History*, Bk. VI, xli, pp. 283f.). Inhuman methods of this nature succeeded in forcing many to renounce their faith.

Throughout practically the whole ministry of Cyprian at Carthage (248-257), persecution continued. Gallus (251-254) blamed the Christians for the plague from which the Empire suffered at the time. To him it was a divine vengeance on infidelity and adoption of a foreign cult. Under Valerian, his successor (254-260), there was severe suffering. Among the victims of the period was Fabian, Bishop of Rome, martyred in 250. In the same year Cyprian retired to a place of safety but returned in 251. Cornelius, Bishop of Rome, fled in 253 to Civita Vecchia, where he died. Babylus, Bishop of Antioch, and Alexander, Bishop of Jerusalem, suffered martyrdom in 250. Origen died in 253 as a result of torture under Decius. Valerian, who demanded of the senate the lives of all bishops, presbyters, and deacons, executed Xystus, Bishop of Rome; Laurentius, with four other deacons; and Cyprian. Lucius, Bishop of Rome (253-254), was exiled by Gallus, but freed later.

In 257, the year Cyprian was banished to Curubis, Dionysius of Alexandria fled to Kephro in the Mareotis. His own description of the flight, as given by Eusebius (Bk. VI, V, pp. 281f.), reads like a modern Western with all the thrills. On his way from the city he was taken captive by Valerian's men. While lying one night in a house, a rescuing party came suddenly on the scene, and the military guard took immediately to their heels. The bishop was placed on the bare back of an ass, with but a linen garment covering his body. He was rushed to safety under the cover of darkness, where he stayed until Gallienus proclaimed toleration three years later.

On the accession of Stephen to the Roman see, the problem of the lapsed assumed a new form, which brought Rome and Carthage into conflict. They disagreed on whether the fallen should be rebaptized on entering the Church. A council of seventy-one bishops at Carthage adopted the principle of rebaptism. The Roman bishop, following the custom in that city for years, readmitted the apostates to communion without a repetition of the baptismal rite. He maintained that laying on of hands was sufficient. Cyprian was supported by the bishops of Africa and Asia Minor. Dionysius of Alexandria wrote a number of letters bearing on the matter to Stephen, to Xystus, his successor, to Philemon and Dionysius, two presbyters, and to the Church at Rome (*Church History*, Bk. VII, v, vi, vii, ix, pp. 294ff.).

Stephen's reaction to the principle adopted by Carthage is of significance. He excommunicated the church there and the churches of Asia Minor in agreement with Carthage. Cyprian, whom the Roman bishop called a "false Christ" and a "worker of deceit," defied the whole procedure. Part of his answer, as recorded in the minutes of the seventh Council of Carthage, reads as follows:

> For neither does anyone of us set himself up as bishop of bishops, nor by tyrannical terror does any compel his colleague to the necessity of obedience; since every bishop, according to the allowance of his liberty and power, has his own proper right of judgment, and can no more be judged by another than he himself can judge another (end of first paragraph, ANF, V, 565).

Firmilian, Bishop of Caesarea in Cappadocia, in a letter to Cyprian, has this to say: "They who are at Rome do not observe those things in all cases which are handed down from the beginning, and vainly pretend the authority of the apostles" (*Epistle* LXXIV, 6, p. 391).

This mass expulsion had no detrimental effect on the churches. Firmilian, one of the victims, maintained that Stephen, by usurping a position and power not rightly his, had excommunicated himself. Up to that time, Catholicism had produced no ecclesiastical autocrats in Rome or anywhere else. Papal supremacy in any shape or form was unknown to the early Fathers.

With regard to the question of rebaptism, the Council of Arles, in 314, attended by a large number of Western bishops, including those of York, Lincoln, and London, in Britain, agreed with Rome against Carthage.

Modern Roman Catholic writers, especially, refer to Stephen and all other bishops of Rome belonging to the early period as "Popes." This kind of anachronism is as absurd as if we were to call present-day Americans "Red Indians." It is just as incongruous for church historians to put the cart before the horse as it is for other writers to do so. But in whatever position the cart is placed, the dogma of papal infallibility cannot be put in it during the first centuries of the Christian era. If the doctrine were pressed, it would be more consistent to use such a vehicle for the bishops of Alexandria, Carthage, Hippo Regis, and Milan, than of Rome. The only Roman bishop of any outstanding merit belonged to the middle of the fifth century. All the rest were very mediocre, compared even with laymen such as Clement, Origen, Justin, and Tertullian. Many of the Fathers, however, did recognize the bishops of Rome as the successors of Peter. Yet it is as difficult to prove that the Church of Rome was built on this Rock as if someone tried to verify a claim that our Constitution was founded by Columbus on Plymouth Rock. As regards origins, there does not seem to be any closer relation between Rome and Peter than between our democracy and the Pilgrim Fathers. There is no doubt that the latter landed in America, and Peter in Rome. Nevertheless, it is a precarious undertaking to base any important theories or doctrines on such happenings.

Eusebius the historian was unaware that the Roman bishops were any different from the rest. If anyone had the priority, Dionysius the Great of Alexandria would probably have been in the lead. It is interesting to note that he was the first to apply the Greek word *papa* (pope) to a bishop. In one of his letters on baptism he alludes to Heraclas, a former bishop of the city, as "our blessed father (*papa*)" (Eusebius, *Church History*, Bk. VII, vii, p. 296). It was Gregory VII, in 1057, who limited the term to the Roman bishops alone.

(ii)

The Meletian Schism, formed at the beginning of the fourth century, was confined mainly to Egypt, with lapsed Christians its chief cause. Peter, Bishop of Alexandria (300-312), is praised by Eusebius for his saintly character and illustrious control of the churches. He had presided in peace until Diocletian issued his edict for the demolition of the churches in 303. In the ninth year of the persecution, he was beheaded by Maximin (*Church History*, Bk. VII, xxxii, pp. 317f.). At the outbreak of the imperial attack, he had retired to a place of safety, as Dionysius had done in the time of Valerian. As in the case of Cyprian, the Puritans condemned his action. One of these was Meletius, Bishop of Lycopolis in the Thebaid, who took upon himself to apply stern measures against the lapsed in parishes beyond his own. On his return to Alexandria, Peter suspended him. The Council of Nicea (325) failed to end the schism that followed. The Meletians turned out to be bitter enemies of Athanasius and sided with the Arians. They lasted for about a hundred years when they finally ceased to exist as a distinct body.

(iii)

Following the Diocletian persecution, a new term was coined, namely, *traditores*. It stood for those who had surrendered sacred writings to their pagan tormentors in exchange for their lives. In all probability, heretical works such as those of the Gnostics must have suffered destruction along with Bible manuscripts. This may account for the fact that the earliest of the New Testament Codices belong to the fourth century, that is, when the State was at peace with the Church. In the case of the *lapsi*, it was only on rare occasions that any of the leaders gave in. The two Spanish bishops, mentioned previously, were exceptions. It is reasonable to infer that more of the bishops would be included among the *traditores*, the logical guardians of sacred writings.

The impetus for the survival of the Novatians seems to have come from among the people themselves. They lingered on till the sixth century. The struggle concerning the *traditores* was of shorter duration, but more intense and bitter. It was more ecclesiastical, and the State intervened. Church leaders on both sides were numbered by the hundreds. The final disappearance of the Donatists synchronized with the entrance of the Arian Vandals into North Africa in 428. The ruthless tactics of these converted barbarians destroyed the churches of that influential sector of Christendom.

The first test case affecting a bishop happened at Carthage. The rigorists, who like the Novatians before them showed no mercy, had as many as seventy bishops in Numidia alone. They were led by Bishop Secundus. Mensurius, Bishop of Carthage, like

Cyprian years earlier, stood for a more lenient policy. At his passing in 311, Caecilian, an archdeacon, succeeded to the bishopric. Bishop Felix of Aptunga, who ordained him, was suspected of having been a *traditor*. The Numidian bishops therefore questioned the validity of his election. As a countermove, they made Majorinus the Catholic appointee. On his death in 315 Donatus, called "the Great," was appointed bishop, and the new Puritans took their name from him.

Eusebius gives the two letters sent by Emperor Constantine to Miltiades, Bishop of Rome, and Chertus, Bishop of Syracuse, when requested by Anulinus, his proconsul in North Africa, to intervene in the dispute. In answer to the first of these, a synod met in Rome in 313, attended by Caecilian, with ten of his supporters. The Donatists had a similar number. The point at issue was the validity of Caecilian's appointment. There were other complaints against him. The synod or council convened by Chertus met at Arles in the south of France in 314. At both of these gatherings the Donatists lost their case. Caecilian and his followers were recognized as the true representatives of the Catholic position. Unsatisfied with the verdict, the rigorists appealed to the emperor himself. Constantine not only approved the decision of the councils, but also threatened them with banishment and confiscation of their Church property if they continued to resist. In a letter, accompanied by a sum of money, to Caecilian he instructed the bishop to bring, "without hesitation," any opposition on the part of his opponents to the notice of his judges, in order to turn them from their error. The emperor, according to his letters, was most concerned about keeping the "lawful and holy Catholic Church" from being divided by any schism (*Church History*, Bk. X, v, pp. 378ff.).

The next important step in the conflict between the two parties is connected with the name of Augustine. In 411 another council was assembled, with Marcellinus, representing the emperor, presiding. Two hundred and eighty-six Catholic and 279 Donatist bishops were present. Extreme measures were approved by the majority. Three years later it was considered a crime against the State, punishable by death, for the Donatists to hold any meetings.

In his *Anti-Donatist Writings* Augustine appears as a strong and convincing opponent. This brilliant thinker had to admit, however, that the Donatists, like the Church as a whole, had consecrated bishops, presbyters, and deacons. They followed the same Rule of Faith as the Catholics. The Sacraments were administered by them

The Faith and Fellowship

in the traditional manner. What they did not possess, according to him, was *caritas*, or love. Without love, so he argued, the unity of the Church was bereft of its most essential cohesive power. Without love, the episcopate was no guarantee of the Church being really one and apostolic. Even the Sacraments were meaningless without love. Yet strangely enough, he found no inconsistency in adopting a policy of retaliation in the case of recalcitrant Puritans.

The Novatians and the Donatists were worthy of the highest praise for their stress on what seemed to them essential to Christian conduct. The Catholics could not but be one with them in that respect. Yet they believed that leniency, toleration, and love were also in God's will.

VIII

The Faith and Freedom

THE FAITH AND FREEDOM

Up to the time of Augustine, the Church was principally concerned with a statement of its faith and the application of some principles. To the Apologists, a doctrinal presentation was deemed necessary to defend Christianity against calumny and slander. In the struggle with Gnosticism, the Gospel as interpreted by Clement, for example, was the true knowledge, the goal of the saint, and the scholar's quest throughout the ages. In refuting the Monarchians, such leaders as Tertullian and Hippolytus formulated a doctrine of the Trinity that would safeguard belief in the unity of God. Later, the catholic position was put to the test at the council of Nicea, as we shall see in the last chapter.

In the conflict with Novatianism and Donatism, a new stress was noticeable. With the exception of Cyprian's and Augustine's specific efforts to arrive at a doctrine of the Church, the Catholics were mainly engaged in the application of such principles as toleration and love.

Broadly speaking, the Fathers up to now were concerned with doctrinal questions and practical issues, such as discipline. This dual interest reminds us of the sequence so typical of some of Paul's epistles. Take, for instance, the Epistle to the Romans. The first part shows how God's righteousness is essential to man's salvation (1:17-11:36). The second deals with Christian duty and concord (chaps. 12-16). In the Epistle to the Ephesians, his classic on the Church, the second section emphasizes Christian behavior.

Augustine (354-430), as compared with the Greek Fathers, had a Pauline approach in his apprehension of the Christian Faith. His *Confessions* should be carefully studied if we want to follow his teaching on many subjects. His well-known saying, "Thou hast made us for Thyself, and our hearts are restless until they find their rest in Thee," has in it something which belongs to the atmosphere of the Upper Room in John's Gospel. There, all the bliss of following the Master is enjoyed by just resting in His presence and listening to His eloquent whispers. His teaching is that of one who had found in Christ the answer to the longing of his soul. It is in the light of this personal discovery that most of his teaching is to be understood. Knowing the inner struggle so well, it is no wonder that his approach is more subjective than that of his predecessors. He had found through his own experience that a sinful state affects both the will and the emotion, and not merely the mind, as the philosophers taught.

With the help of self-analysis, he had discovered that he himself was an "I," functioning in a trinity of modes: "I exist and I am conscious that I exist, and I love the existence and the consciousness, and all this independently of any external influence." By reflecting upon this psychological fact, he was able to go beyond the Eastern Fathers. In their conception of the Trinity, the stress was on the eternal distinction of the Three Persons. Augustine emphasized the eternal relation existing between them through love: "The communion or unity or holiness which links each to the other is properly called love, for it is written, 'God is love.' And herein may be seen how the Persons in the Deity are three, and not more than three: One who loves Him who is from Himself, and One who loves Him from whom He is, and love itself."

The term "person," as we have seen, was found to be inadequate and confusing when applied to the Father, the Son, and the Holy Spirit. There is no ambiguity as he thinks of God as a person. He conceives of Him as holy and loving. His will and power are absolute. His sovereignty and supremacy are ultimate facts. As he recognizes the ideals of both Greek and Hebrew, he is conscious of no conflict, for the secret to unravel the mystery of His being is personality. He is one with Origen in regarding the universe as being spiritual and a realm where hearts are in unison. In the light of the Greek ideal, he is aware of an absolute distinction between God and man. God is God and man is man. In the light of the Hebrew ideal, man, through grace and the redemptive power of love, is capable of being brought into fellowship with God, in whom he finds eternal rest. He would have found no difficulty in singing with us today,

> *O Love that wilt not let me go,*
> *I rest my weary soul in Thee;*
> *I give Thee back the life I owe,*
> *That in Thine ocean depths its flow*
> *May richer, fuller, be.*
> George Matheson

A stanza from Oliver Wendell Holmes' well-known hymn combines the Greek and the Hebrew ideals:

> *Lord of all being, throned afar,*
> *Thy glory flames from sun and star;*
> *Center and soul of every sphere,*
> *Yet to each loving heart how near!*

The Faith and Freedom

In his controversy with Pelagius, the British monk, Augustine is more concerned with the *facts* of experience than with any *theory* of them: first of all, on the lower level of his own natural make-up; then, on the higher plane, where all is of God through grace. The "freedom" that enters into the argument is to him as much of a fact as the Exodus to the Israelites. Any theory concerning it is simply an explanation. He is not looking at the wonders of God's merciful intervention as an observer. He is himself a living witness of its effect. He had sought many ways of deliverance, but sin had a strangling hold on him, until the break came through the miraculous power of grace.

Augustine was born in 354, at Tagasta in Numidia (Tunisia), in North Africa. As in the case of Moses, a mother's heart entered into the conflict to emancipate the slave from the tyrant's grip. Monica was a devout Christian. She brought into the struggle the most potent forces of the soul: prayer, persuasion, and example. Nothing seemed to affect her brilliant son. He abandoned himself without restraint to a life of dissipation in the city of Carthage, where he spent his student days. His escapades, however, did not blur or blunt his exceptional intellect. From twenty on, he earned his living as a teacher of rhetoric, or the art of effective expression in speaking and writing, first at Carthage, then Rome, and finally Milan. Throughout this period he was also a student. Like Justin, he was continually changing his masters in his eagerness to find the truth that makes men free. His father planned to make a lawyer of him, but philosophy had a greater appeal than law. The Manichaeans interested him first. He attended their meetings for nine years till he was twenty-seven. Their crude efforts to solve the problem of evil and their quaint reasoning left the facts of his own life unexplained. Neo-Platonism, his second attraction, raised him to a higher plane, and his intellectual acumen was further quickened as he was led to think of God as an eternal Spirit, without form or change, the very soul of the universe. All this satisfied the intellect only. This kind of philosophy identified sin with ignorance. Such an identification means that actual facts of experience are not realistically met. Conscience, emotion, and will are by-passed and divorced from man's moral struggle.

At Milan, under the preaching of Ambrose, the erudite bishop who had himself been a teacher of rhetoric, he soon discovered that the Gospel had something to say to him as a man, with his passion and conscience, with his emotion and will. Here was a message that forced him to see himself not as a thinker but as a moral being. He could not get away from its challenge to readjust his life in the light of his new discovery. It was while the heart and the mind, the intuition and the intellect, were struggling for the upper hand, that he heard the voice of a little child saying to him, "Take up and read." The response needed but the slightest prompting, for, unawares, he was on the way to a great decision. As he read Romans 13:14: "But put on the Lord Jesus Christ, and make not provision for the flesh to gratify its desires," there was saved for the Church an intellect that has influenced its thinking more than any other of the early Fathers. Luther and Calvin were among his debtors. His views of the Church and the Sacraments, the Trinity, man's redemption and freedom, predestination, justification by faith, and the mystical ideal, are of importance even today.

His conversion took place in 386, when he was thirty-two. At Easter, the following year, he was baptized by Ambrose and, like Saul of Tarsus, he, too, retired to the solitudes after becoming a Christian (Gal. 1:17). The churches of North Africa did not take long to appoint some of the ablest converts to the highest offices. As in the case of Cyprian of Carthage, he was made Bishop of Hippo Regis a few years after his baptism, much against his will. This section of North Africa gave to the Church Tertullian, Cyprian, and Augustine.

Among his most important works are: *The Confessions; The City of God; On the Trinity; On the Spirit and the Letter; On Nature and Grace; On the Predestination of the Saints; On Grace and Free Will; Anti-Manichaean, Anti-Donatist,* and *Anti-Pelagian Writings;* also commentaries and expositions and sermons.

As compared with Origen, the greatest of the Greek Fathers, he is less theoretical and more practical. Origen had a Christian upbringing. Augustine was in his thirties when he was converted. Origen knew of no conflict within himself. Augustine was conscious of a struggle between the heart and the mind. Both men tried to reconcile faith and thought. Origen followed the process from faith to thought: Augustine, the process from thought to faith. Augustine knew but little Greek, and was less versed in Greek philosophy than Origen. Theology had its beginning with the Alexandrian. Like Origen, Augustine went beyond the ideas of his own age. Both were innovators and creators of new conceptions. Origen belonged to a period of persecution. He died from the effects of suffering for the Faith. Augustine was born in an era of peace, and died a natural death. In the first period, Catholics and heretics struggled against one another within the Church. In the second, the state took sides with those who had the greater influence on the emperor at the time, and heretics were persecuted by the state.

In his speculative thinking, Augustine is less adventurous than the Alexandrian, yet some of his emphases, like those of many of the Easterners, led to strange paradoxes. His conception of the Church, for instance, seems to vary.

As regards the Church, strictly speaking, there is no common denominator to the *communio externa* and the *communio sanctorum*. Taking the two together, all that can be said is that both are fellowships, one on earth, the other in heaven. The contrast between them simply brings out their inherent difference. There is no guarantee that those who are within the visible Church are also within the invisible. It is possible for many who are not members of the earthly fellowship to reach the heavenly. The function of the visible Church, so far as the elect are concerned, is utilitarian. God's chosen can grow spiritually within it by means of the Sacraments. As regards world redemption, the unity of the earthly Church is not of the Pentecost type, where individuals are made one by a common prayer, a common expectancy, and a common desire — the original requisites for a Church born of the Holy Spirit. Again, the *communio sanctorum* is not in any way an *ecclesia* which has been called out of anything. It is concerned with a state of being which is shared by the elect. The Church of the New Testament has been called out of the world for active duty. It is therefore an *ecclesia*. The *communio sanctorum* is also distinct from the Kingdom of God. The former is not only a state of being, but also one that is sufficient of itself, detached and transcendent. The Kingdom can come. The Church of the New Testament prays, "Thy Kingdom come." The *communio sanctorum* has not come out of anything like the apostolic Church, nor can it come out of anything like the Kingdom of God.

Whenever he reflects the influence of Neo-Platonism, to which he was once attracted, it is the timeless and the spiritual that are real. He is less of an idealist in his conception of the City of God. This he contrasts with the *civitas terrena*, which stands for the secular and civic society of his day. The *civitas Dei* has elements in its structure which have affinity, to that extent, with the Kingdom of God and the visible Church, or the *communio externa*. One could pray, "Thy City come, that its spirit and principles be realized on earth through the Church."

Many of his paradoxes are due in part to readjustments, as the philosopher is superseded by the theologian. Another reason for this is the lack of logical unity in his system of thought. In the early stages, he thinks of the human will as being free of all restrictions. As a theologian, in later years, he abandoned this position. In his theory of predestination, God alone is free. Man finds his freedom through fulfillment, on his part, of the divine will. As in the case of Origen, Augustine had his champions and opponents. In its sixth-century form, his theory was condemned by the Council of Orange, which held that "none were predestined to evil by the Divine Power." His stress on the Church, again, with its authority and sacraments and creed, can be contrasted with the more evangelical aspects of his teaching. Faith, in the light of the latter emphasis, is not a mere affirmation of what should be believed, but a means of contact with the soul's spiritual resources. Protestants agree with him in the power of God's grace working in and through the individual, whereas Roman Catholicism reaffirms his ecclesiasticism.

I

During his bishopric, he was faced with two issues that tested his genius as a Christian theologian. The first had to do with Donatism, already discussed; the second, with Pelagius, a man of great piety who had come to Rome in 405 to call people to repentance. The British monk was one with the Montanists of years past, especially Tertullian, in their condemnation of the worldliness that threatens the Christian life in every generation. As compared with the Novatians and the Donatists, there was a positive side to his missionary fervor. His stress on action calls to mind the Epistle of James, which Luther under the influence of Augustine's teaching called an "epistle of straw." Since man's efforts count for something, he brought into the forefront of his message the claim that if Christians took themselves and their Master seriously, they could, by their own power, lead a life worthy of Him. The fault was not so much in man's nature but in his will. If he wanted to be good, he could. This Neo-Paganism, in its extreme form, was a denial of what is basic to Christianity. All that is needed is Christ's help in man's attempt to attain perfection. With a little encouragement, the goal can be reached. To him, grace is but an assistance and a reward (*On the Grace of Christ*, 34, NPNF, 1st. ser., V, 229f.).

It was Coelestius, whom Pelagius had converted in Rome and who had settled at Carthage, who brought into the open the theological theories that were implied in the reformer's stress on man being the master of his fate. The implications embraced such matters as the nature of man and the power of the human will. As he was being examined for ordination, he greatly surprised the brethren by asserting that man's sin affected none but himself, that every man was born as perfect as Adam in his creation, that little children who died in infancy stood in no need of baptism, which was believed to be a means of purification. On being excommunicated at Carthage, he moved to Ephesus, where he was ordained (Augustine, *On Original Sin*, Bk. II, ii, iii; *On the Proceedings of Pelagius*, 62, NPNF, 1st. ser., V, 210, 237f.).

Pressure was brought to bear on Pelagius himself while he was vacationing in Palestine. Jerome was near at hand, and Augustine was not too far away to bring a strong case against him. To the former, he stood for the heresy of Pythagoras and Zeno in a new guise (*Preface to Jeremiah*, Bk. iv). Two meetings were held in 415, one in Jerusalem, the other at Lydda, presided over by John, Bishop of Jerusalem. At the trials, the Eastern judges knew only Greek; the Western accusers, only Latin. The accused knew both. Pelagius was too clever to commit himself. No maneuvering on the part of the Westerners could induce him to admit that he condoned unreservedly his disciple's teaching. On the strength of his defense, the ecclesiastical court failed to indict him. Carthage and Rome in 418 condemned both, with Zosimus, the Roman bishop, at last in agreement. Pelagius and his followers were banished from Rome by an imperial decree. At the General Council of Ephesus in 431, he was branded as a heretic and excommunicated. It is believed that he died in Palestine around 440, ten years or so after Augustine. (*On Original Sin*, 2, 3, 12, NPNF, 1st. ser., V, 237ff.; *On the Proceedings of Pelagius, ibid.*, pp. 183ff.).

(i)

Augustine accepted Paul's contention, in I Corinthians 15, that "in Adam all died and in Christ all shall be made alive." Pelagius' version would have read as follows: "In Adam we do not die and in Christ we are all made better." To Pelagius Adam's fall was his own concern, and had no effect on his descendants, who stand or fall on their own merit, without any previous pressure to determine their actions, whether good or bad. Pelagius broke absolutely with the past, maintaining that with every birth there is a new beginning. Man's nature, whether in Adam or his children, is morally neutral. The soul as it is brought forth is neither good nor bad. It becomes moral through an action of the will. It is through his actual choices that man becomes a moral being. From his first creation, he was meant to stand at a crossroad, with nothing in himself to tell him which of the roads to follow. He stands there, with his will poised between good and evil. If he takes the wrong turning, he is morally doomed. It is by his choices that he is saved or lost. There is no such thing as original sin. At the crossroads, man has two means of assistance. He has Christ's example. There is no doubt which of the roads He would have taken. Not only has man His divine example, but he is also sure of His grace. There is nothing in His grace, however, to force him to make the right decision, but once made it can be availed of. Sin is the result of misusing one's responsibility, due to the influence of education and bad example (*On the Proceedings of Pelagius* and other works).

His stress on personal responsibility has obviously a positive value. It re-emphasizes what Ezekiel among the Hebrew prophets had to tell his contemporaries in Babylon when they were inclined to blame their ancestors for their misfortune. Everyone was held responsible, for God's judgment is an exceedingly personal affair. Theoretically, Pelagius was justified in making a similar emphasis. Many of the Fathers recognized that there is a difference between original sin and man's own evil doing. Ambrose, to mention but one, taught that personal sins could be cleansed by baptism, but that washing of feet was necessary to purify the effects of original sin. The belief in original sin, however, does not make any man less responsible for his own actual performances.

(ii)

Many of the early Fathers had taught that the will is free. Justin in his *First Apology*, XLIII, ANF, I, 177, argues that

> Since if . . . all things happen by fate, neither is anything at all in our power. For if it be fated that this man, e.g., be good, and this other evil, neither is the former meritorious nor the latter to be blamed. And again, unless the human race have the power of avoiding evil and choosing good by free choice, they are not accountable for their actions, of whatever kind they be.

Irenaeus, in his exposition of Matthew 23:37, "How often would I have gathered thy children together . . . and ye would not," points out that here is "set forth the ancient law of human liberty, because God made man a free [agent] from the beginning pos-

The Faith and Freedom

sessing his own power, even as he does his own soul, to obey the behests . . . of God voluntarily, and not by compulsion of God" (*Against Heresies*, Bk. III, xxxvii, 1, ANF, I, 518).

Both Clement and Origen accepted a similar point of view. The former maintained that "he who is saved is not saved against his will, for he is not inanimate; but he will above all voluntarily and of free choice speed to salvation" (Origen, *Stromata*, Bk. VII, vii, ANF, II, 532ff.). The latter, a strong believer in man's freedom, tells Celsus that if the spontaneity of virtue is taken away, its essence is destroyed (*Against Celsus*, Bk. IV, iii, ANF, IV, 498). The Church teaches, according to him, that "every rational soul is possessed of free-will and volition . . ." and that "we are not to be subject to necessity, so as to be compelled by all means, even against our will, to do either good or evil" (Preface to *De Principiis*, 5, *ibid.*, p. 240).

He explains that this freedom does not mean that the mere exercise of the will, will produce virtue: "The human will of itself is weak to accomplish any good, for it is by divine help that it is brought to perfection in anything" (*ibid.*, Bk. III, ii, 2, p. 330).

Tertullian, in *Against Marcion* (Bk. II, vi, ANF, III, 301f.), held that since man was created in the image and likeness of God, it was only proper that he should be formed with a free will and a mastery of himself: "so that this very thing — namely, freedom of will and self-command — might be reckoned as the image and likeness of God in him." This gracious and large gift to man came of God's own goodness: "Both the goodness and purpose of God are discovered in the gift to man of freedom in his will." Gregory of Nazianzen believed with Tertullian that the will is free, although he agreed with Augustine that man was completely corrupted through the Fall.

In the West, before Pelagius appeared on the scene, Augustine is one with the other Church leaders in affirming the freedom of the will. Practically all held that man was fallen because of Adam and has lost a state of perfection with him; nevertheless, they asserted that man's will has still a certain amount of freedom. Hilary would have it that he still has the initiative. Ambrose, although his emphasis on human freedom is less explicit, also allows for man's ability regarding his moral recovery, provided enough grace is given to assist him.

II

Augustine holds, against Pelagius, that there is a spiritual condition in man to be accounted for, something that is beyond his choices, and which is characterized by pride and selfishness. Augustine's reply to Pelagius is given in the following works: *Merits and Remission of Sins, Nature and Grace, The Grace of Christ and Original Sin, Man's Perfection in Righteousness, The Soul and Its Origin, Grace and Free Will,* and *Predestination of the Saints.*

In his analysis of man's spiritual state he says that to hold that a man's soul, as made at the beginning, was neutral, conflicts with the teaching of Genesis, where we are clearly told that man was created in the image of God. Whatever else that image stood for, it is reasonable to infer, so Augustine argues, that it contained a will with a holy inclination, which through the Fall became perverted. He is in agreement with Paul in saying that as a result, sin, as far as the descendants of Adam are concerned, has become a natural condition and disposition, passed on from generation to generation. The Apostle was conscious of something besides morality, with its choices and subsequent actions, when he uttered those heart-rending words in Romans 7:22-25:

> For I delight in the law of God after the inward man: But I see another law in my members, warring against the law of my mind, and bringing me into captivity to the law of sin which is in my members. O wretched man that I am! who shall deliver me from the body of this death? I thank God through Jesus Christ our Lord. So then with the mind I myself serve the law of God; but with the flesh the law of sin.

When we consider further the account of man's creation as given in the Bible, such questions as these arise: Was man in the beginning immortal? Pelagius claimed that he had a mortal body and that he would have died whatever happened. If Adam was made in the image of God, why did he sin? If the first man was originally free, what of his descendants? In what way does the sin in Eden and its results affect succeeding generations?

With regard to the first two questions, Augustine introduces into the dispute the conception of capability. Adam, so he asserts, was created with the ability not to sin, but since he preferred to sin, his descendants cannot but sin. It could have been otherwise in the case of Adam, but not in ours. Again, Adam could have been immortal, but all his descendants live under a sentence of death and are doomed to die sooner or later. With regard to the freedom of the will, man's original power to do as he pleases is gone forever. All that is salvaged from the Fall is a kind of natural freedom which may lead to some acts of moral worth. Spiritual freedom is God's own work, and enjoyed by the elect alone. Hence, grace is absolutely and not relatively necessary, as Pelagius held. It is also irresistible. Under its impact and pressure, man is certain to act in accordance with God's will, without the least suspicion that what he is doing is not being done of his own free will. In his description of the elects' perfect state he writes as follows:

> Neither are we to suppose that because sin shall have no power to delight them, free will must be withdrawn. It will, on the contrary, be all the more truly free, because set free from delight in sinning to take unfailing delight in not sinning. For the first freedom of will which man received when he was created upright consisted in an ability not to sin, but also in an ability to sin; whereas this last freedom of will shall be superior, inasmuch as it shall not be able to sin. . . . For as the first immorality which Adam lost by sinning consisted in his being able not to die, while the last shall consist in his not being able to die; so the first free will consisted in his being able not to sin, his last in his not being able to sin (*The City of God*, Bk. XXII, 30, NPNF, 1st. ser., II, 510).

If by freedom is meant absolute independence, then man is not free under grace. The fact is, he is bound to be under *something* whenever he is called to exercise his freedom of choice. At the crossroads of decision, no one is independent of some kind of pressure. It is what has directed him thus far that will decide in most cases which of the roads a man will take. Philosophers are apt to call this pressure character, habit, and disposition. Psychologists speak of impulses and desires, which spring from the unconscious to play the role of tyrants, and the strongest wills alone can resist their power. Unless the tyrant is turned into a slave by the power of the will, its tyranny will be expressed in action. These experts of the mind claim that if they could but discern what pressures there are within, a man's action at the crossroad could be foretold. That is, what a man *is* will determine what he *does*, unless something like conversion intervenes and a new character is formed. No choice is a leap in the dark. Consciously or unconsciously there is a determining factor which is not of the will alone. It is the nature of the pressure, as Augustine holds, that decides whether the will is really free or not. Certain pressures make man a captive, despite his apparent freedom of choice. No man is free if he is constrained to choose the lower instead of the higher. Such a freedom is capricious and arbitrary. It is when the choice is made in accordance with the will of God that true freedom is realized. Whatever pressure is needed to bring this about, it is only then that man is really free. George Matheson has expressed this truth thus:

> *My will is not my own*
> *Till Thou hast made it Thine;*
> *If it would reach a monarch's throne,*
> *It must its crown resign;*
> *It only stands unbent*
> *Amid the clashing strife,*
> *When on Thy bosom it has leant*
> *And found in Thee its life.*

(i)

If we were to examine this pressure in terms of what is usually called Original Sin, then we would have to decide whether it affects the soul alone, or the body alone, or both.

We have seen how Origen believed that the soul sinned in a preexistent state. Only the soul which the Word united to Himself was pure. All the others are transported to this world to serve a life sentence within the human body until their final release, when they shall return whence they came. The human body is mortal, but not moral. The idea that the body is either good or bad is not itself part of the problem of evil, as Origen conceived it. Every soul is created on its own. What happens to one, does not affect the others. Each fell on its own. Each is saved on its own. Although he abandoned this theory before the end of his life, a Church Council at Constantinople in 553 condemned him for it.

The majority of the Eastern Fathers, with whom Jerome and Hilary of Poitiers from the West agreed, maintained that the pressure from the past came through the body. Each soul is a new creation, free of any contamination. The name given to this theory is Creationism. The theory accepted in the West was called Traducianism. Gregory of Nyssa and a few other Easterners subscribed to it. According to this view, both the body and the soul are derived from the parents, who are the immediate transmitters of the evil that has come down from Adam. In him all his descendants became corrupt in both body and soul, and none is born free of a bias and an inclination to sin.

Augustine believed in the solidarity of the race as thoroughly as Paul and Irenaeus before him. Sin to him is a family concern, with every member of it a part of a "sinful mass." The sin of the first man is our sin. So closely are we related, that we are held responsible with him for it. His guilt is our guilt, an assumption that Tertullian repudiated. Augustine recognized the

The Faith and Freedom 165

rightful claim of the devil, conceived as a personal power, to every child of Adam. The release came through the death of Jesus whose blood set the captives free. There is no idea of deception, as in Origen or Gregory of Nyssa. The Cappadocian regarded Satan as a ravenous fish caught by his own bait. Augustine held that he had a right to sinful man, but had no claim on Christ, the pure and holy. Since it was innocent blood that was poured on Calvary, it was therefore just to free those who are His. By the death of the Innocent, justice was at last satisfied. Satan had no reason to complain if what was rightfully his became the possession of Another, through a transaction that was fair and just. Augustine disagreed with Ambrose's assertion that God stood in need of being reconciled. He was the sinner's Friend, who of His infinite mercy gave His own Son to emancipate him.

(ii)

In contrast with Origen, Pelagius found the origin of evil in the experience of the individual here and now. Both he and the Alexandrian left Adam out of the picture, as far as the origin of sin was concerned. Every soul in a pre-existent state was his own Adam, according to Origen. To Pelagius, every soul is his own Adam in this present state. Augustine thought of sin first of all as a fact affecting all, whether they liked it or not. His approach, therefore, is not that of a theorist. He is out to furnish the most rational interpretation of what he accepts as true. This fact of human experience he does not consider by itself. He considers also the grace of God, which counterbalances any evil effect sin has on the race. The fact of sin as involving all mankind is an undeniable reality. It is not an idea. The fact is there and must be accepted, whether we can account for its origin or not. The most reasonable thing in such a situation is to find another fact which will diminish its influence or do away with it altogether. This other fact is the grace of God, for as Paul says, "Where sin abounded, grace did much more abound" (Rom. 5:20).

(iii)

It is for this reason that Augustine introduces his theory of predestination. To him it is the divine guarantee that grace must triumph over sin. If he were to agree with Origen that all are to be saved in the end, that in itself would neither weaken nor strengthen his position. What he seeks to explain is that God saves and that His grace is mightier than the power of evil. A general may not win all his battles, but if he finally carries the day, he has proved himself the victor. God, by electing to eternal salvation those whom He wills, proves that the ultimate triumph is His. Evil is helpless to keep His own captive. Not all of the Israelites were saved, but a remnant was protected against all odds. Christianity finally appeared, to guarantee that the original plan of redemption will not fail. Pharaoh and Antiochus Epiphanes had their day, but the books of Exodus and Daniel are ours because it was not all their day. Predestination, as conceived by Augustine, is our proof that God is sovereign Lord and that He has the final veto. The theory that some are predestined to perdition is a corollary which, in this case, is not necessary to prove the other. His followers, by missing his own emphasis on the power of abounding grace, led some of the councils to condemn the idea that people were ever elected to be doomed (cf. Synods of Orange and Valens in 529). It is important to note that he is far from suggesting in any of his works that God was responsible for the existence of evil (*On the Predestination of the Saints*).

We have mentioned before how the Gnostics used a massive canvas to portray the vastnesses as they thought of them, and how Irenaeus conceived of Christ in like manner. Augustine's mind is not only captivated by the irresistible power of grace, but also by its immense scope. The universe itself is a mission of grace. All that exists is an expression of a will that is benevolent and good. Everything witnesses to and is governed by the mercy of God. Whether redemption is limited or unlimited, whether all are to be saved or only a certain number, it is in harmony with the divine will that man will find his destiny. Whether the Fall happened in a pre-existent state or in Eden, both Origen and Augustine agree that man's recovery of his original status is due to God's will and grace.

III

What could be called a compromise between the views of Augustine and Pelagius is represented by two men, John Cassian, a pupil of Chrysostom, and Faustus of Rhegium (Riez). Both belonged to the fifth century and had some connection with Monasticism in Southern France. The former gave to posterity handbooks on the life of the cloister. The latter was abbot of the monastery of Lerins before he became Bishop of Rhegium. Their semi-Pelagianism conflicted with the extreme views of both sides, and they sought to combine what was of value in both. Augustine referred to certain Massilians, who had Marseilles as their chief center. He praises them for renouncing the error of Pelagius in some of its forms. Their views of predestination are contrary to his (*On the Predestination of the Saints*, ii, NPNF, 1st ser., V, 498).

The semi-Pelagians in general held that man was created immortal, with nothing to worry him in the way of pain and suffering. He was without sin, but free to determine his own destiny. Through the Fall he became mortal and morally corrupt, with the freedom of his will weakened, but not wholly lost. As against Pelagius, they stressed the need for grace, because sin has produced moral impotency. Since man is a free agent, he is capable of co-operating with God. As regards the question which comes first, man's volition or the grace of God, they held that in some instances man's will power takes the initiative and in others, divine grace. They disagreed with Augustine that man is entirely corrupt, for they believed there is some goodness in everyone. John Cassian rejected predestination as impiety because it seems to put a limit to God's power to save. He did, none the less, admit that God knew beforehand who would be saved. Faustus and his supporters even doubted this much.

The Council of Orange agreed with Augustine with the exception of one aspect of predestination already referred to. It condemned the semi-Pelagians for teaching that man may take the first step in his own salvation. They were denounced for not perceiving that grace is a gift of God, given of His own good pleasure even before man shows any willingness to receive it. The council felt that Augustine's treatment was more in harmony with what Paul had in mind when he told the Philippians, "Work out your own salvation, for it is God that worketh in you both to will and to do of his good pleasure" (2:12-13).

IV

Augustine was justified in teaching that the center of salvation was God, from whom emanates all grace, as healing rays from the sun. Man can never be the center. That was Pelagius' mistake, despite his insistence, at times, that man needs God to make anything of his life. To maintain that man is absolutely helpless and completely corrupt is of secondary importance. It is just as reasonable to argue that God's image in man is seldom entirely erased, but to hold that man can be made perfect through his own volition is a pernicious heresy.

In order to appreciate what is fundamental in his approach, we must not take his negative attitude to free will too seriously.

Pelagius' view has in it elements of truth, for if morality has any meaning at all, the will must be free. Salvation, however, is not an ethical matter. It is simply a question of accepting what is being offered. God gives and man accepts. Neither does the acceptance or the refusal to accept make man any more or less moral. The fact that I accept or refuse what is offered me in a business transaction has nothing to do with morality, or even with what is called freedom, as when we talk about human freedom and human worth, the big things in the case of a free people. Freedom in the latter sense is a principle which governs a certain way of life. When God offers man the salvation that is in Christ, what man is there who thinks at that moment of his right to accept or refuse? Nor does the idea of duty ever enter. If a man accepts the grace of God because he ought to, or from a sense of duty, then he is guilty of the heresy known as Pelagianism. When a man exercises his freedom to accept God's grace, it cannot be put to his credit; otherwise he is not saved by grace, and we are back with the legalists of every age. He needs no more will power than when he reaches out his hand to accept what is offered him from the other side of a counter in a store. Otherwise his acceptance has a moral, not a religious, significance. As Augustine maintained, it is by faith that we are justified. That is to say, the act of reaching out to accept God's mercy itself has no merit.

The higher freedom of which he writes is something different still, and should be taken in all seriousness. This is not the power to accept or reject, but the ability of the will to abide in perfect freedom under God. This kind of freedom resembles the principle which is peculiar to a democracy, and without which its way of life would cease to exist. Man, through grace, becomes a citizen of a realm where freedom is essential to its very being. His freedom is the birthright of his citizenship. This can only be enjoyed to the full when his will is in perfect harmony with the divine will, without ever feeling the least degree of pressure or constraint. He is not able to act otherwise, for of such is the City of God.

IX

The Faith and Fetters

THE FAITH AND FETTERS

The Church up to the time of Constantine was on the defensive, and its way of life was branded as something hostile to the best interests of the State. Marcus Aurelius, the Stoic idealist, had no scruples when called upon to decide the fate of certain Christians. What their Master seemed to stand for was a threat to the security of the Empire. The power which He had over His disciples had to be destroyed at all costs. The following table will suggest at a glance what opposition the Church had to endure at the hands of the State from the beginning of the second century until toleration was granted in 313:

Emperor	Attitude to the Church
HADRIAN (117-138)	Tolerant, on the whole, yet Christians attacked by the people.
ANTONIUS PIUS (138-161)	Disapproved illegal procedure. Polycarp martyred at Rome.
MARCUS AURELIUS (161-180)	Policy of intolerance. Justin martyred.
COMMODUS (180-192)	Both friendly and hostile. Apollonius, a Roman senator, martyred.
SEPTIMUS SEVERUS (193-211)	Attacked Seminary at Alexandria. Leonidas and others martyred. Issued an edict against Jews and Christians. Areas affected: Africa, Syria, Cappadocia.
BASSANIUS ANTONIUS nicknamed Caracalla (211-217)	A tyrant who murdered his brother Geta. Continued persecution.
HELIOGABULUS or El-Gabel (218-222)	In his youth a priest of the sun god at Emesa in Syria. Tolerant?

ALEXANDER SEVERUS Pupil of Origen (222-235)	Stood for toleration. His chapel contained statue of Christ, figures of Orpheus, Hercules. His private Pantheon had in it statues of Abraham, Achilles, Virgil. Origen visited his mother, Julia Mammaea, who was very devout.
MAXIMIN the Thracian (235-238)	Intolerance and persecution. Banished Hippolytus and Pontianus, Bishop of Rome, to the mines of Sardinia.
GORDIAN (238-244)	Tolerant.
PHILIP an Arabian (244-249)	Tolerant. Called First Christian Emperor.

Except for the reign of Maximin (235-238), 218 to 249 was a period of peace. During the subsequent period, the northeast border of the Empire was threatened by the Goths who crossed the Danube. There were obvious signs of disruption also from within. A new obligation to the ancient gods became compulsory. Opposition to Christianity on a wide scale was intensified. Many denied their Master.

DECIUS or TRAJAN (249-251) GALLUS (251-253)	Both represent a systematic attempt to destroy the Church, bishops being special targets. Decius' Edict of 249 demanded sacrifice to the gods. Many renounced the Faith. Schisms followed. Many martyrs.
VALERIAN (253-260)	Out to destroy the Church. His edict (257) commanded Christian leaders to sacrifice to the gods. Many martyred.
GALLIENUS (260-268)	Tolerant.
CLAUDIUS II (268-270)	Tolerant.
AURELIAN (270-275)	Assisted Church against Paul of Samosata. Later planned persecution, but was assassinated before it was put into effect.

From 260 to 303 the Church enjoyed peace. Within the Empire itself, from 278 to 284 was a period of anarchy.

TACITUS
(6 months)

PROBUS (276-282)	Tolerant.
CARUS and his sons CARINUS and NUMERIANUS (282-284)	Tolerant.
DIOCLETIAN (284-305)	During first 20 years the Church was unmolested. In 303 and 304 edicts were issued to destroy churches and burn sacred writings. Christians were deprived of civil rights. Many suffered death, and property was confiscated.

At this time the Empire was divided into two parts, East and West, under four rulers, two called Augusti; and two, Caesars. At the beginning of his reign, Diocletian was emperor and sole ruler, but now he became Augustus of the East, with Nicomedia, in Bithynia, as his capital, and Galerius, his son-in-law, as Caesar, to protect the Empire against the Persians. In the West, with Milan as capital instead of Rome, Maximian ruled as Augustus and Constantius Chlorus as Caesar, entrusted with the defense of Gaul and Britain.

Under the new arrangement the Augusti were to retire after twenty years in office and the Caesars to take their place.

Both officers in the East acted as despots in their attitude to the Church. The Western rulers were more tolerant. It was at this time that Neo-Platonism, with Alexandria as its center of influence, rose to challenge Christianity. The State's hostility to Christianity was aggravated by this. In 311 Galerius, from his deathbed, issued an edict of toleration, beseeching the Church with his dying breath to pray for the State and its rulers. Maximin II continued to harass the Church, but in 313 he was driven from power by Licinius, the brother-in-law of Constantine who was the son of Constantius. In 312 Constantine overcame Maxentius, a tyrant and the Roman Senate's nominee for the title of Augustus in the West, at Milvian Bridge, near Rome. The following year at Milan he issued an edict of toleration to all forms of religion, and the Church was given back the property taken by the State. Licinius followed a similar course in the East. In 319, however, this Augustus revived the old methods of persecution. In 323 he was defeated by Constantine, who became sole emperor. This epochmaking victory weakened the forces of Paganism, and before the end of the century Christianity was accepted as the official religion of the Empire.

While the Empire was undergoing a radical change with regard to its leadership, the Church was seeking to secure its own unity through a better understanding of certain doctrines concerning the Person of Jesus Christ. Arius questioned the orthodox claim that the Son was equal to the Father in all respects. Such a challenge had to be met. A large assembly of Churchmen from all over the Empire and beyond came to Nicea, not far from Constantinople, in 325, and there, in obedience to the Emperor's request, they arrived at a decision. A majority condemned Arius and his supporters, and their own belief was expressed in what is known as the Nicene Creed. This victory was only apparent. The struggle, the different aspects of which will be explained in the next chapter, continued for a number of years.

It is important to note how the emperors reacted to this doctrinal conflict within the Church. Constantine himself, during the fourteen years he was sole emperor, knew that the Nicene Creed was not acceptable to all. He wrote a number of letters to Arius and his followers, Eusebius of Nicomedia, and Theognis, Bishop of Nicea, whom he had banished a few years after the Council of Nicea. Arius appeared in person before the emperor at Constantinople, the new capital. It was during this visit that the heretic died from a severe attack of dysentery. Athanasius, the Catholic champion at Nicea, was banished to Gaul for reasons partly economic and partly doctrinal. He had been falsely accused of interfering with a shipment of corn to be sent from Alexandria, the granary of the East, to Constantinople. He was also held responsible for keeping the opposing factions within the Church at loggerheads. Constantine was genuinely concerned. He played the role of arbitrator in the Donatist controversy, as we have seen, and he sought to reconcile the Novatians by inviting Acesius, their bishop, to a synod. The Meletians were out of favor, and he banished John, their leader (Socrates, *Eccles. History*, Bk. I, x, xxxvii, NPNF, 2nd ser., II, 17f, 34). On the death of Constantine, in 337, the Empire was divided among his three sons, Constantine II, Constantius II, and Constans, whom he had made Caesars years earlier.

The Faith and Fetters

The following data are based mainly on the *Church Histories* of Socrates and Sozomen, both of the fourth century.

Emperor	Attitude to the Church
CONSTANTINE II (West) (337-340)	Favored orthodoxy. Recalled Athanasius, whom he had banished after being accused by the Arians of usurping episcopal authority.
CONSTANS (West) (337-340: Caesar) (340-350: Augustus)	Favored Athanasius, who returned to his see at Alexandria. The bishop again left. Restored by Council of Sardica, an appointment which Constantius confirmed rather than fight Constans his defender. Protected the pagan temples.
CONSTANTIUS II (East) (337-350: Augustus) (350-361: Sole Ruler of East and West)	Bitter enemy of orthodoxy. Persecuted opponents of Arianism. Made Eusebius of Nicomedia bishop of Constantinople instead of Paul. Convoked a synod of bishops in Rome. Wrote a letter to the Synod of Ariminum in support of Arianism. Ordered pagan temples to be closed and prohibited idolatry. Yet patronized Paganism.
JULIAN (East and West) (361-363) Nephew of Constantine	Renounced Christianity. Ordered pagan temples to be reopened. Favored heathen institutions and permitted persecution of Christians. Secularized education and forbade Christians to attend State schools.
JOVIAN (East and West) (363-364)	Accepted the Nicene Creed. Closed pagan temples. Proclaimed general tolerance.
VALENTINIAN (West) (364-375)	Stood for Nicene orthodoxy and was tolerant to all sects. The temples left open and Paganism unopposed.
VALENS (East) (364-378) Brother	Supported the Arians and persecuted the moderates and other Christians.

GRATIAN (West) (375-383) Son of Valentinian	Influenced by Ambrose, Bishop of Milan. Issued an edict of toleration. Excluded Eunomians and Manichaeans from the churches. Renounced title, "Supreme Pontiff." Inaugurated a religious reformation in a manner reminiscent of some of the kings of Judah. Confiscated the property of pagan temples and prohibited the priests to officiate.
THEODOSIUS I (East) (379-383: Augustus) (383-395: Sole Ruler of East and West)	Championed orthodoxy. Called the Second Ecumenical Council held at Constantinople, in 381, which secured a victory for the Nicene Creed in the East. Granted the Novatians freedom of worship. Confiscated churches of Arians, Apollinarians, and Macedonians. Destroyed pagan temples. His policy spelled the doom of Paganism. Christianity became official religion, but pagans were not forced to become Christians.

By comparing the tables of emperors before and after Constantine, we arrive at the following conclusion: The first period culminates with the Edict of Milan, when the State ceased to persecute. The second reaches another climax, with Theodosius I. What was legitimized by Constantine as another religion in the Empire and patronized without his forbidding Paganism, became the official religion of the Empire under Theodosius, with Paganism out of favor and renounced. Constantine accepted the pagans' recognition of him as their Supreme Pontiff (*Pontifex Maximus*), and temples were built by them in his honor. His immediate successors in office assumed the same title. It is not certain when he became a Christian. Sozomen favors the tradition that he was converted while serving in Britain prior to his conflict with Maxentius. He disagrees with the view that he was baptized in Rome in order to purify his soul after murdering his wife, Fausta, and his son, Crispus, for as the historian points out, his son was alive many years later (*Eccl. History*, Bk. I, v, NPNF, 2nd ser., II, 242f.). Socrates states that he received Christian baptism on his deathbed in 337, with Eusebius, the Arian bishop, officiating (*Eccl. History*, Bk. I, xxxix, pp. 267f.). Both historians tell of his vision the day before the Battle of Milvian Bridge. He saw a

The Faith and Fetters

pillar of light in the heavens, in the form of a cross, with the words, BY THIS SIGN CONQUER, inscribed on it. The following night Christ appeared to him in a dream and directed him to face his foes with the sign of the Cross upon his standard. According to Sozomen, he immediately consulted Christian leaders about the meaning of what he had seen and heard (Bk. I, iii, pp. 241f.).

His was an age of superstition. His own mother, Helena, is also supposed to have been divinely guided in a dream. The tomb where the body of Jesus once laid was found by her beneath a temple of Venus. In the sepulcher were found His cross and the nails. A church called the New Jerusalem was built to commemorate her discovery. Part of the cross was enclosed in a silver casket and placed in the sacred edifice. The remainder of it was concealed by the emperor in a statue of himself at Constantinople. Out of the nails he made bridle-bits and a helmet which he used on the field of battle. No stretch of the imagination could make us believe that Christ ever sanctioned this kind of caricature of His holy sacrifice (Socrates, *Eccl. History*, Bk. I, xvii, p. 21). Such sacrilege should save us from regarding the road to the Battle of Milvian Bridge as another road to Damascus.

The Edict of Milan did not make Christianity the state religion. What stands out in the edict of Constantine as given by Eusebius (*Church History*, Bk. X, v, NPNF, 2nd ser., 379f.), is its spirit of toleration. Freedom of worship was not to be denied to anyone, pagan or Christian. As regards Christians, not only were they free to worship their Deity in accordance with their own ritual, but their property was to be restored, without compensation to those who had seized it. Henceforth, the religious liberty enjoyed by pagans during the centuries of persecution is to be extended also to Christians. During his reign the emperor did something besides tolerate the newly legalized religion; he patronized it in a variety of ways.

If we compare the second table of emperors with the Old Testament kings, Constantine I stands out like Solomon as the temple builder, who did not completely abandon his interest in pagan deities. Constans reminds us of Ahab, with Athanasius as his Elijah, but still a protector of idol worshippers. Constantius II plays the part of Jezebel and plots the destruction of the servants of God. Julian is obviously the Manasseh, before his conversion, of the royal line. Gratian and Theodosius I represent the reformers, the latter, especially Josiah. The religious changes, in neither case, prevented the State from falling a victim to enemies from without. The Babylonians finally took Jerusalem. The barbarians sacked Rome under Alaric in 410, and Genseric, the vandal, in 455.

I

In considering the question whether the new alliance deprived the Church of its freedom and gave the State a power of control over it, certain basic principles and historical facts call for recognition. It is maintained that at this juncture in the life of the Church a new Christianity came into being, with the emperor its chief patron, along with many in his court who were out to gain royal favor, irrespective of the claims of Christ upon their hearts and minds. It is further stressed that the acceptance of Christianity as the religion of the State involved what is known as Erastianism, the doctrine which holds that the State is supreme in ecclesiastical matters.

The Church at no time, whether before or after Constantine, compromised in its teaching or action with the principles laid down in the New Testament. In the test case recorded by Matthew (22:15-22), Jesus settled a dilemma by recognizing the rights of both God and Caesar. To Him there was no contradiction: "Render therefore to Caesar the things that are Caesar's, and to God the things that are God's." Paul is in harmony with the principle laid down by his Master:

> Let every person be subject to the governing authorities. For there is no authority except from God, and those that exist have been instituted of God. . . . For the same reason you also pay taxes, for the authorities are ministers of God. . . . Pay all of them their dues . . . (Romans 13:1, 6, 7).

The Apologists of the second century made it crystal clear that the Church was free of any hostile attitude toward the State. Persecution was rampant for a long time because the emperors had no such principle to guide their action. The Caesars claimed all or nothing. The Church, on the other hand, under normal conditions kept an even balance between its duties, except in a crisis, when the claims of Christ had to come first. Suffering unto death was the usual procedure whenever the State interfered in matters of conscience. Such was the dominating principle before and after Constantine.

The State never succeeded in destroying freedom of thought despite its many edicts and persecutions of heretics. The Arians who were ousted at Nicea continued to worry the orthodox. In its various forms, Arianism had a popular appeal, and some of the emperors accepted it. As a missionary influence, it did as much as orthodoxy to safeguard the security of the Empire. In the West it was the Arians that led the Teutonic barbarians into the fold. They turned the attackers of the imperial power into defenders of the Faith, and thus saved the areas conquered by them from reverting to Paganism.

In the years following Nicea, Athanasius, often referred to as the Pope of Alexandria in his day, plays an important part. He is an instance of the fact that under the new alliance the State was helpless to destroy freedom of thought. At Nicea he was a deacon and was then around twenty-five years old. Three years later he was made Bishop of Alexandria, where he used his keen intellect and spiritual influence to stabilize the victory won at Nicea. During his forty-six years in office he was banished five times, but he never gave in. As it has been said, it was a case of one man standing against a hostile world. Eight emperors were involved directly or indirectly with his fight for freedom of thought. Two of them nearly took up arms against each other to decide whether he should be allowed to continue his struggle. Constantius finally agreed with his brother Constans that he had a right to his belief. His defense of the Nicene Creed was vindicated by the Council of Constantinople in 381, eight years after his death. This Council decided against the Arians. A victory was gained for the orthodox position in the East.

Under the new order the Church retained its pristine right to formulate its own doctrines. There is no such thing as the Creed of Constantine or the Creed of Theodosius. The Creed of Nicea is named after a city in Bithynia, in Asia Minor. At the Council held there, although the emperor had called it together and attended its opening session, the Church Fathers did not discuss or consider what to do with the policy of toleration just granted, a fact of epoch-making import. Their main concern was the Person of Jesus Christ. The new policy and the change in the attitude of the state were mere incidents compared with the question whether the Son is God or only the highest and the most sublime of all creatures. Empires come and go. States change in their attitude to the Church from age to age. Nicea became in truth a City of Victory, because at a Council there the early Fathers reaffirmed their faith in Jesus of Nazareth as God of very God, one in substance with the Father. Nicea was a victory for humanity as claimed and saved by God. The great victory of those days, as far as the Church was concerned, was the one won at Nicea and not at Milvian Bridge. In the well-known Apostles' Creed there is no reference to the Holy Roman Empire. The only form of fellowship that is considered holy is the Church and not the State, whether united to it or not. Nicea has made it clear that men do not think of Caesar, whether friendly or otherwise, when dealing with their own souls.

The Fathers under toleration continued to explore and advance in their conception of Christian doctrine and Church government. The period after Nicea produced leaders of exceptional distinction:

Augustine (354-430), the greatest of all.

Hilary of Poitiers (290-368), called the Athanasius of the West; also known as the first Church hymnodist.

Epiphanius (320-403), the bitter opponent of Origen and all whom he called heretics.

The Cappadocian Fathers: Basil (329-379); Gregory of Nyssa (330-395); Gregory of Nazianzen (330-390), the great Church orator.

Ambrose, Bishop of Milan (340-397), who influenced and baptized Augustine; also a hymn-writer.

Jerome (340-403), the eminent scholar whose translation of the Bible known as the Vulgate is still in use.

John Chrysostom (347-407), Patriarch of Constantinople, a famous preacher and commentator of the Bible.

Rufinus of Aquileia (350-410), who translated into Latin Origen's *De Principiis* and Eusebius' *Church History*.

Cyril of Alexandria (367-444) and *Leo of Rome* (390?-461), both noted churchmen.

Among the Church Historians: Eusebius of Caesarea (260-340), Theodoret (393-458), Socrates (379-444), Sozomen (380?-443).

At no time following Nicea could the imperial power dare to oppose what the majority of Church leaders believed in. When the orthodox were the stronger, as was the case for the most part in the West, the emperor supported them. His policy was determined by what the Church believed in at the time, unless he took an entirely hostile attitude to Christianity itself, as in the case of Julian. Valens also seems an exception, for he reverted to the policy of earlier persecuting emperors in forcing his preferences upon all, whether the Arians were in the majority or not.

The emperor was of service in convening Church synods and

The Faith and Fetters

councils. His military forces were effective in penalizing those whom the councils declared heretics. Occasionally, for the sake of concord within the realm, he would summon the leaders together to settle their doctrinal disputes. The actual formulation of the creeds was outside his jurisdiction. Piety was beyond his plenary powers. The State intervened in matters of discipline. The leaders of unpopular groups were expelled from their churches and often exiled. Constantine is again an exception. According to Eusebius, it was he that suggested to the Fathers at Nicea the term *homoousios*, which was satisfactory to the majority assembled there. By the time of Theodosius I, the emperor's attitude to Paganism reflected the strength of Christian influence and sentiment. His edicts against pagans were not the result of his own convictions. The time was ripe for recognizing Christianity as the state religion and for officially renouncing anything in conflict with it. Ambrose, Bishop of Milan, deplored the emperor's unchristian and inhuman actions. As Theodosius was approaching the door of the cathedral, the bishop held him by his purple robe and said in the presence of a large crowd that had come to worship, "Stand back! a man defiled by sin, and with hands imbrued in blood unjustly shed, is not worthy, without repentance, to enter within these sacred precincts, or partake of the holy mysteries" (Sozomen, *Eccl. History*, Bk. VII, xxv, p. 394).

Furthermore, the new alliance made the emperors Christian-conscious. The Edict of Milan determined their own fate. In giving the Church freedom of worship they lost their own freedom of action, and their success as rulers depended on their attitude to the Church. The Church has often been an exacting and costly partner. If the Church and State had been separate in England, Edward, Duke of Windsor, in all likelihood would be king today. Julian, the Apostate, tried to break away from this form of partnership, but it was too late. He had everything in his favor, a brilliant brain, a profound knowledge of pagan philosophy, youth, enthusiasm, and a powerful army to put his measures into effect. His policy was pathetic and recalls the attempt of Canute centuries later to roll back the waves of the incoming tide. Opening old pagan temples and prohibiting Christians from entering State schools were like hurling sand banks against the rush of a mighty torrent. The new order he inaugurated, apart from externals, had much in common with what the Church stood for. No reformer or reactionary could have revived Paganism as Nero or Marcus Aurelius knew it. The Roman Empire had undergone a radical spiritual change from within. Julian injected his resurrected Paganism with as much Christianity as possible. His priests were supposed to act and look like its clergymen. He dressed his Paganism in a Christian apparel. He stressed the kind of charity that reached out to suffering humanity in the form of hospitals and other beneficial institutions. During his short reign of two years he was in the service of the Galilean whose followers he despised. It is not surprising to hear him say with his dying breath on a Persian battlefield, "Thou hast won, O Galilean." Julian was another Saul of Tarsus, kicking against the pricks, and had he lived it is not improbable that he would have carried the sign of the Cross on his banners like his uncle, with the power of the Cross within his own heart.

The alliance also brought the emperors under the influence of the high moral standards of the Church. One of the remarkable facts about Constantine himself was his flexibility, combined with a certain amount of stability. As a statesman he soon saw that harmony within the Church meant greater security for the State. Hence his effort to settle doctrinal differences at Nicea, and his attempt to win the Novatians. His correspondence concerning the Donatian dispute is another instance of his interest in Church unity. As a reformer he showed readiness to apply Christian principles to social conditions. Crucifixion as a form of punishment and the combats of gladiators were abolished, as was also the law against celibacy. Divination and black art were done away with. White-slave traffic came under his ban, and the status of womanhood was raised. The home was recognized as a center of influence, and restored. Hostels and hospitals were built to protect and heal. Such reforms as these did not come because of his family's interest in the sun-god, but were all due to the impact of the Son of God through His Church upon the impressionable nature of the emperor (*Eccl. History*, Bk. I, xviii, p. 22; Bk. I, ix, pp. 245f.).

One evil effect of the association of Church and State was the imperial policy of making orthodoxy or its opposite the test of allegiance to the emperor. Under Valentinian in the West, acceptance of the Nicene Creed was the test of loyalty to the throne. In the East, under his brother Valens, the Arians alone were deemed loyal. The Catholics and the moderates were persecuted in the name of the law. Later, Theodosius I published edicts against all who did not subscribe to the Creed, and also against all pagans. In his case, loyalty meant accepting Christianity and its creed in the Nicene form. The old practice of paying allegiance to the emperor through worship, acknowledging thereby that his position as head of the State made him divine, appeared in a new guise. Under his patronage of the Church, any recognition of him as divine would have been regarded as sheer idolatry. None the less, allegiance to him henceforth was tantamount to a religious duty, for he looked upon himself as the official judge of belief in the East. Although citizenship did not involve paying divine homage to him, it did mean accepting the form of belief subscribed to by him at the time.

Many years after the experiment of uniting Church and State had been in operation, Ambrose and Augustine tried to rationalize the alliance. In practice, according to the latter, it was an early instance of co-existence. The hot war between the two had been finally turned into a cold war. There was, however, no change in the temperature on the spiritual front represented by the Church. On that front there could never have been an armistice or cessation of hostilities in the struggle against idolatry, unchastity, and worldliness. In Augustine's *City of God* stress is laid on the inevitable contrast between the Church and the State when considered from an ideal point of view. The structure and the governing principles of the Church are of God. The State is of the earth and is man's creation. Ideally, they are diametrically opposed. They have nothing in common in this respect. In practical experience, nevertheless, the *Civitas Dei* and the *Civitas Terrena* are interdependent. They need the support of each other. The State relies on the Church for its conscience and moral standards; the Church needs the State for protection. As an idealist, Augustine conceived of the Church's influence gaining so conspicuously in the process of time that the State would become less distinct and less of a partner. Ultimately, the *Civitas Dei* would turn out to be a theocracy, where the State is the servant of the Church, as in the days of Samuel and the Hebrew kings.

Christianity had been in the ascendancy long before the Edict of Milan. When the inevitable happened, the Church was under no constraint to enter into any agreement with the State. It was the State that surrendered, not the Church. There was never anything like a concordat. No political matter was discussed at Nicea. The emperor was a mere guest at the Council. He stood until he was told to sit. It was the State, not the Church, that came to recognize a new Master. Before the end of the fourth century Jesus of Nazareth, a crucified alien, had become the spiritual Head of the Empire. Hence the Church of those days never compromised with the State or gave up any of its peculiar prerogatives. There were leading churchmen and certain groups too apt to forget their allegiance to the King of kings, whose claims know no change. Under our two-party system daring experiments may be indulged in at times, but our democratic way of life remains basically the same. Despite its many factions, the Church continued its witness to the apostolic tradition. Imperial patronage did not affect or alter that witness. The tendency toward worldliness after the union was not entirely due to the new relationship between Church and State. Such a tendency is possible, whether the Church and State are separate or not, especially in a time of peace. Church and State, for example, are apart in the U.S.A., but not in England. That does not mean that the Church is less worldly here than there. The fact is, the early Church did not become more or less of what it was capable of becoming because of Constantine's policy. The rapid growth of Monasticism was due to something far more profound than a mere reaction to the worldliness which is supposed to have resulted from the union. Among sections of the Church there had been reactions against overindulgence in the things of this world many years earlier. The Montanists left the Church in the second century as a protest against its supposed secularism. Anthony, the founder of Monasticism, had been active for some time before the Edict of Milan.

It was a statesmanlike gesture on the part of Constantine to face the situation realistically. No special manifestation of divine guidance or even conversion was required to bring this about. The victory had already been won, and he was wise to admit it. The legend of the vision of the Cross, however, is less difficult to believe in than the supposition that he could have overcome the Church even if he had adopted the methods of Diocletian and Galerius. Sterner measures would have made the faithful more resolute to persist. Whenever they were driven underground, in the early stages, there was always a resurgence. The resurrection of Jesus, upon which the Church is founded, represents a process that is as sure of success as that which makes the death of a grain of wheat produce an abundant harvest. The fact that the Church triumphed over hostile forces is not so remarkable after all. The truth becomes more challenging the more vehemently its standards are questioned and opposed.

II

During the first three centuries the antagonism of the State had been ineffective. In the period that followed the edict of toleration, the Church was still as faithful to its mission as it had been under persecution. There is nothing to show that the new imperial policy produced within the Church complacency, inertia, or spiritual stagnation. Christian leaders were capable of performing yeoman service and were prepared to die for the Faith if need be. To take but one instance, Basil the Great (329-379) offered to give his life for his belief that the Saviour was very God of very God, as the Creed of Nicea asserted, rather than give in to the prefect sent by Valens for the sole purpose of making an Arian of him (Sozomen, *Eccl. History*, Bk. VI, xvii, p. 356).

It was a creative period, with experiments in ecumenicity and asceticism. Both Athanasius and Anthony are typical of a movement toward unity of the Faith through a better knowledge of the Son of God and toward deepening the spiritual life through ascetic living. It is obvious that Athanasius, the champion of the first General Council, did not regard Anthony as a reactionary, for it was he that gave the world the first biography of the founder of Monasticism. Other leading theologians and thinkers were sympathetic to the movement and tried experiments of their own. Basil, Bishop of Caesarea in Cappadocia, organized the interest in the movement within his see. Hospitals, schools, and homes for charity were built. He formulated a Rule to regulate the lives of the adherents of the new order. Jerome and a number of ladies from Rome visited Egypt to see for themselves what the monks had accomplished there.

It is only partially true that "monastic piety sprang up as an antidote to the increasing worldliness of the Church." To account for the success of this movement, an analysis of the mood and the temperament that made it possible is very necessary. Predispositions and biases are much more difficult to overcome than ideas. Christian thinkers, from the time of the Apologists, were equal to the task of overcoming the peculiar theories associated with the Gnostics, the Manichaeans, and the Neo-Platonists. But the asceticism of these systems continued in its appeal to certain people. The rank and file among early Christians lacked the special training of the philosophers and theologians. While the victory was being brilliantly won by Church leaders on the intellectual front, the people were still lured by the spiritual appeal these systems made to them. An interesting example of how certain types of people were attracted by asceticism is the case of Augustine. He was acquainted with both Manichaeism and Neo-Platonism. Immediately after his conversion, he sought solitude in order to reflect on a way of life that seemed to him in harmony with his change of outlook as a Christian. After a short time in Rome, he retired to the outskirts of Tagaste, in Numidia, where he was born. There he founded a religious community with his friends. It was with reluctance that he gave up his seclusion to become Bishop of Hippo.

Monasticism to a large extent was religion in the rough, with refinements reduced to a minimum. To claim it was anticlerical or anti-something-else, such as ritualist or formalist, is to forget that its environment had as much to do with its roughness as any conviction or prejudice. A man in the service of his country will undergo many hardships away from home, will survive on very small rations, not because he dislikes anything better, but because he is forced to do so by the conditions under which he is living. The monks were men who endured a similar kind of existence for the sake of their Master. Missionaries throughout the ages have given up much. It would be misleading to suggest that they do all this as a protest against a more civilized way of existence, although their form of service means abandoning their families and friends. Nevertheless, it is only fair to assume that many a monk led a life of simplicity in solitude in order to get away from something. As a group of religious enthusiasts, monks could be divided into those who were running away from a certain way of life and those who were forsaking familiar pursuits in search of a better way. In the case of the former, they disliked something either in the State or Church. The others were more concerned with spiritual adventure, free of the shackles of the social order.

The monasteries of this lay movement at Scetis and Nitria, west of the Delta of the Nile, a very fertile region capable of supporting a large population, gained prominence. It was in this vicinity that the first experiment in asceticism was made. It involved many thousands. Anthony (251-356), usually referred to as the founder, was an Egyptian. He sold all he had and lived in austerity. He struggled daily with demons. It was the belief of those days that Satan and his agents dwelt in the desert. St. Anthony's Monastery has been in use for nearly sixteen centuries, and it is the oldest in the world (Sozomen, *Eccl. History*, Bk. III, xiii, p. 291).

At the beginning there were no strict rules to control or restrain.

All did their daily exercises in freedom. They had left the market, the workshop, the army, and the professions, in order to develop their inner life on their own, by means of introspection, soul analysis, and discipline. There were two classes. The general term *monachi*, or monks, which means "men living on their own," covered both of these. The first group were called Erminites (cf. hermits). As the name suggests, they lived on their own, away from all normal social contacts. The second group were known as Caenobites. They mixed with others. They were less austere and ascetic than the first. Famous among the latter was a Copt called Pachomius, who blended piety with manual labor, a forerunner of the Moravians. In the Monastery of Nitria about five thousand followed different modes of life, and the monks were allowed to live alone or with others. On Saturdays and Sundays they came together for worship in a common sanctuary. There were many priests, but only the senior officer took charge of the services. The chosen leaders were called *Abbas* (abbot), a Syrian word for father (*ibid.*, xiv, pp. 292f.).

Monasticism had its critics from the outset. Among its defenders were Christian statesmen, scholars, and intellectuals, such as Athanasius, Basil, Jerome, and Chrysostom. Its ideal fitted the Beatitude which promises satisfaction to "those who hunger and thirst after righteousness." Whatever the means employed, the hunger and the thirst were there and the blessedness too. This way of life was regarded as the conversion of truth into practice. Socrates calls it "the philosophy of deeds" and "the apostolic life." As the Apologists sought to harmonize apostolic doctrine with Greek philosophy, the monks tried to combine apostolic life with the philosophy which finds its highest expression in the renunciation of the material for the sake of the spiritual, in making the soul less of a partner with the body and more of a master. In their enthusiasm to achieve this mastery the body too often ceased to be a slave. It became a hindrance and finally a thing to be shunned altogether. On the positive side, in the attempt to develop and perfect the inner man, the usual exercises were prayers at set times, a healing ministry, and the expulsion of devils from human abodes. The four cardinal virtues, Prudence, Fortitude, Temperance, and Justice, interpreted in a manner suitable to a life in isolation rather than in a city, were accepted by them (Socrates, *Eccl. History*, Bk. IV, xxiii, pp. 106ff.). On the negative side, their asceticism was carried to an extreme. Marcurius, the Egyptian monk, is quoted by Socrates as saying,

For twenty years I have neither eaten, drunk, nor slept to satiety; my bread has always been weighed, my water measured, and what little sleep I have had has been stolen by reclining myself against a wall (*ibid.*).

The historian tells of a young couple who the night they were to come together as man and wife decided on a life of chastity, the man arguing that virginity was God's ideal. Ammoun, the husband, considered it a sin to look on his own naked body, on the ground that "it became not a monk to see even his own person exposed" (*ibid.*). To this kind of thinking marriage was for sinners and not for saints. In its extreme form, Monasticism was more concerned with those who had a mind to renounce society than with those who tried to transform it from within. They thought that a desert was more advantageous to soul culture than a Christian home. In this respect their ideal was John the Baptist, and not Jesus of Nazareth.

The stress on asceticism had more in common with the Greek and the Oriental temper than with apostolic Christianity. The first Apostles had been called out of the world in order to evangelize it through daily intercourse. The Church is by nature a form of apostleship commissioned to save the world. It can never become part of the world, although it must of necessity function within it. The metaphors of salt and leaven, applied to the Church in the Gospels, imply that it cannot thrive in isolation. Its very mission calls for attachment, not detachment. It lives through losing itself. It dies if it loses others.

As regards its doctrinal bias, Monasticism was pro-Nicea. The monks of Egypt were severely punished by the Arians for siding with Athanasius and the Nicene Creed. Socrates gives a heartrending picture of the ransacking of their monasteries under Valens. They were forced out of their chapels, where they had gathered for prayer, by his soldiers. Lucius, the commander-in-chief, finally drove the abbots into exile on an island occupied by pagans who worshipped their priest as a god. What followed recalls an incident at Philippi, when Paul first visited the city (Acts 16:16-18); the priest's daughter, who was possessed by a demon, was cured. The father and all his votaries were saved on seeing a truly divine power at work (*ibid.*, xxiv, pp. 109ff.).

It was when Monasticism became interested in communal life that its novelty began to have a meaning. Its stress on spiritual growth and service attracted both saints and scholars alike. It came to be regarded not as a thing apart but as an adventure in

Christian behavior and industry, independent of the direct control of either Church or State. By combining the sanctuary and the workshop within its conception of the fuller Christian life, religion produced the right environment, and labor became sacred. It was a revolutionary idea and experiment because at the time work was thought to be for slaves alone and not for free men.

X

The Faith and Formula

THE FAITH AND FORMULA

"Formula" is here taken to mean a statement in a set form of words. In mathematics or chemistry it is usually expressed by the help of symbols and figures. If we were to formulate a particular statement of the early Church in figures and not in words, 3 in 1 or 1 in 3 is as valid to the trinitarian as 3 and 1 make 4 to the mathematician. Both have a similar axiomatic value. To the mathematician, his axioms are basic to his system. So are the formulas of the Creeds of the Church to the theologian. If the early Fathers had stated their Christological conclusions in accordance with a mathematical pattern, the formula $1 + 1 = 1$ would have explained how God and man are united in Christ. To Nestorius the formula was $1 + 1 = 2$. Apollinaris and Eutyches preferred $1 + 0 = 1$. The Arian expression was $0 + 1 = 1$. The '0' in the last formula stands for the divinity of Christ, which to the Arians was not equal to that of God the Father. His humanity was accepted as perfect. The '0' in the formulas of Apollinaris and Eutyches represents the human nature which, according to both, was not as perfect as His Deity. Nestorius, in seeking to explain the relation of God to Jesus Christ, arrived at the conclusion that He was a combination of two Persons and not of two natures.

If we were to express the faith of the early Church in words, the formula $1 + 1 = 1$ means that the Father and the Son are one in all that God is or stands for, and never apart in their essential being; one in their eternity and co-existence, one in their creative and redemptive power. There is no distinction, only in the form or mode of existence. To use again one of Tertullian's illustrations, the source and the stream are one with regard to content, but distinct in function; that is, what is spring in one case appears as flow of water in the other. The term used in the Nicene Formula for what the Father and the Son have in common is "substance" or "essence" (Greek: *ousia*).

In the controversies that harassed the Church following the statement presented in the form of the Nicene Creed in 325, the Catholic formula remained as it was originally accepted. The Arian formula underwent a number of changes. In its first form it was a denial that the Father and the Son were one in substance (*ousia*). An improved formula granted that there is a likeness or resemblance between the Father and the Son. Though Christ is not God in the apostolic sense, yet He is God as the Logos or the Word was to the Greek thinker. The Logos to the Greek was God in expression, and the most perfect of its kind, although it differed only in degree from other manifestations of the divine will. He was not really one with God, but He was one with us, who in our less finite way are also divine. The Arian idea was very much like that of the Gnostics, who regarded the *Pleroma* with all that existed within it, from the highest to the lowest, as a reflection of the Infinite.

In an effort to arrive at formulas concerning the Person of Him who is the Saviour of mankind, the Church met at a number of important councils, which for lack of a better name could be called Ecumenical, or General, Councils, all of which were held in the East with the bishops of that section of the Empire in the majority. These are the Council of Nicea (325), the Council of Constantinople (381), the Council of Ephesus (431), and the Council of Chalcedon (451). All these gatherings were summoned by the emperor in power at the time.

I

The Emperor Constantine was a wise statesman who recognized the strength and influence of the Church within his Empire. Its phenomenal growth, if properly nourished, could mean stability and security. Any disruption within it might therefore in all probability weaken the State at a time when the barbarians on its borders were becoming a greater menace as the years passed by. Under such conditions, peace within the Church seemed at the moment to be vital to the best interests of the State itself. As a shrewd statesman, it was his policy to favor the strongest party in the Church. As a theologian he had but the crudest idea about what the Arians were after or what the orthodox thinkers had in mind in resisting their theories. Despite the eulogies of Eusebius the historian, he seems to have known more about the corn of Alexandria than the creed of its bishop.

The idea of holding an ecumenical council appealed to the emperor and he adopted it. The majority of those who responded to his summons to attend were from the East; only a few of the Western sees were represented. At that time the West was free of the influence of the Arians of Alexandria and Antioch. There were at least 250 bishops present, accompanied by some laymen.

The Faith and Formula

This gathering is traditionally known as the Council of the Three Hundred and Eighteen. Sylvester, Bishop of Rome, was not there but was represented by a number of delegates. Among the Western bishops were Caecilian, Bishop of Carthage, and Hosius, Bishop of Cordova in Spain, who presided. Strangely enough, there were at the meeting bishops from beyond the "iron curtain" of those days, from among the Gothic and Persian enemies of the Empire. One of those present is better known to the world today than he was then. He was the original Santa Claus, namely Nicholas, Bishop of Myra in Asia Minor (*Eccl. History*, Theodoret, Bk. I, vi, NPNF, 2nd ser., III, 43; Socrates, Bk. I, viii, NPNF, 2nd ser., II, 12, 13; Sozomen, Bk. I, xvii, pp. 253f.).

Constantine, who was of lofty stature, entered the council last, with a few of his attendants. He did not take a seat until he was granted permission by the presiding bishop. He sat on a low stool in the center, where heretics or those tried by the councils usually sat. He was surrounded by what appeared, according to Theodoret, like an army of martyrs. Some were without eyes; others, without arms or the use of their hands, such as Paul, Bishop of Neo-Caesarea. They had come there on mules, asses, and horses, supplied by the State. The emperor's heart went out to this assembly of suffering saints, and he urged them to discard their differences for the sake of the concord and the unity of faith (Theodoret, Bk. I, vi, pp. 43f.).

The welcoming speech to the emperor was delivered by Eusebius, Bishop of Caesarea. The response was given in Latin and translated into Greek, the language of the council. The meetings continued from May 20 to August 25 of the year 325. Many matters were discussed, such as the Meletian Schism in Egypt and the time of keeping Easter. It was decided to set aside for Easter the first Sunday following each full moon after the 21st of March, an arrangement still in vogue. The bishops were impressed by the uniqueness of the Holy Land, and special privileges were granted to the Christian Church at Jerusalem. The Council recognized that the authority wielded by the Bishop of Alexandria over the churches of Egypt, Lybia, and Pentapolis, was equal to that of the Bishop of Rome in his see.

The main purpose of Nicea, however, was to settle the Arian dispute, which had created many factions within the Eastern Church. The leading representatives of the opposing points of view about the Person of Jesus Christ up to that time had been Alexander, Bishop of Alexandria, and Arius, a presbyter of the same city, who had derived his chief ideas from Lucian of Antioch, martyred in 312, and who is considered to be the real founder of Arianism. To arrive at a formula favorable to all was extremely difficult. The majority were strongly against incorporating any terms in their statement which were not in the New Testament. They were also unfavorable to toning down any expressions to appease Arius and his friends. Eusebius, Bishop of Caesarea, the Church historian, a man distinguished for his piety and fairness, and who was partial at the time to the Arian position, offered the creed in use in his own church.

In the opinion of Athanasius, a young deacon from Alexandria, who spoke for the minority, this statement did not go far enough. Moreover, its expressions, so it was maintained, could be interpreted in such a way as to allow the teaching of Arius, who regarded the Son as a sort of demigod and not as One coequal with the Father in respect of His very being. A new term was suggested, namely, *ousia*, a Greek word, translated *substantia* in Latin, and "substance" or "essence" in English, neither of which conveys the exact meaning of the original. Others had used the word before. Tertullian used the phrase, "of the substance of the Father" (*Against Praxeas*, 4). The Synod of Antioch in 269 condemned Paul of Samosata for the use he made of it. The bishop had in mind the belief that the Father and the Son were one in the Sabellian sense.

The following comparison shows how the creed subscribed to by the council differed from what was submitted by the Bishop of Caesarea:

The Creed of Eusebius	*The Creed of Nicea*
We believe in one God, the Father Almighty, the Maker of all things, visible and invisible; and in one Lord Jesus Christ, the Word of God, God of God, Light of Light, Life of Life, Only-begotten Son, First-born of every creature, begotten of the Father before all worlds by Whom all things were made; Who for our salvation was incarnate, and lived among men. He suffered and rose again the third day, and ascended to the Father; and He will come again in glory to judge the quick and	We believe in one God, Father Almighty, Maker of all things visible and invisible. And in one Lord Jesus Christ, the Son of God, begotten of the Father; only-begotten, that is, of the substance of the Father, God of God, Light of Light, Very God of very God, begotten not made, being of one substance with the Father: by Whom all things were made both in heaven and on earth: Who for us men, and for our salvation, came down from heaven, and was incarnate, and was made man; He

the dead. We also believe in One Holy Ghost. . . . suffered, and rose again the third day; He ascended into heaven, and is coming to judge both the quick and dead. And we believe in the Holy Ghost.

At the end of both creeds heretics are anathematized. The Creed of Nicea ends with these words:

> The holy Catholic and Apostolic Church anathematizes all who say that there was a time when the Son of God was not; that before He was begotten He was not; that He was made out of the non-existent; or that He is of a different essence and of a different substance from the Father; and that He is susceptible of variation or change (Theodoret, Bk. I, xi, pp. 49f.).

Any reporter at the council would have circulated the news that a formula had at last been found which was satisfactory to all except two. Theonas of Marmarica and Secundas of Ptolemais, both Egyptian bishops, could not agree and were exiled. Arian writings were burnt to celebrate the victory. Even Eusebius of Caesarea and Eusebius of Nicomedia, a supporter of Arius, accepted the Nicene Formula. To all appearances it was a complete triumph for those who adhered to the faith of the Apostles. Henceforth the orthodox position would be expressed by the newly adopted term *homoousios*, "of one substance." From now on this is to be the expression to test men's belief, whether it is apostolic or not; whether it is Nicene or something else.

II

At a second general council held at Constantinople in 381, where 150 bishops met at the summons of Theodosius I, the Nicene Formula was reaffirmed. At Nicea Constantine's interest was mainly political. Doctrine was left to theological experts. At Constantinople the Church had become such a power and its teaching so important in the sight of the State that the emperor was as concerned with theology as with politics. For the first time a creed was made legal by an imperial decree.

In the period between the councils of Nicea and Constantinople the Eastern section of the Empire was affected by a continuous struggle among Church members, some supporting the Nicene Formula and many more opposing it. Emperors and court officials became embroiled in the discussions. Athanasius, who stood for the original statement, was exiled time and again; so were others who agreed with him, whenever the emperor was Arian in his sympathies. Julian, who sought to counteract the influence of Christianity, freed the exiled bishops in the hope that a head-on collision between the two opposing forces would strengthen his own effort to re-establish Paganism within his realm. Ecclesiastics played into the hands of the emperors, and the emperors used doctrinal differences to further their own political ends. Eusebius, Bishop of Nicomedia, a past master in intrigue, used his sacred trust as a minister of the Gospel to scheme and overthrow all bishops in favor of the Nicene Creed.

It would be well to mention here that the people were keenly interested in what was going on, either as a means of diversion from the daily round or as something more serious. Arius, like Luther and Wesley later, adopted hymnody as a means of popularizing his teaching. The battle hymns of Arius used to disturb the peaceful slumber of the citizens as his choristers sang his compositions in the middle of the night. John, the Bishop of Constantinople, rather than be outdone, also organized nightly processional singing in favor of the Nicene Creed. Whenever any doubt arose which of the two teams of antiphonal chanters was the better, street fighting helped them to arrive at a decision. The Arian chief chorister on one occasion was Briso, one of Empress Eudoxia's eunuchs, and he stopped his warbling the moment the sound of the opposition reached his ears in the form of a mute stone. Before the hymn contest was over many on both sides had ceased their earthly chanting forever, all happy to die as martyrs for a worthy doctrinal cause (Socrates, Bk. VI, viii, p. 144).

The doctrinal conflict that followed Nicea can be more easily understood if we regard the council held there as being composed of two principal parties, which could be called Fundamentalists and Progressives. Arius and his sympathizers did not number more than twenty. Both of these groups were conservative and orthodox in their thinking about Jesus Christ. To them He was God and an object of worship. The first group are called Fundamentalists because they believed that in expressing the Deity of the Saviour nothing but Biblical terms should be used. Had they lived at the end of the first century they would have protested, in all probability, against the term Word or Logos in the Prologue to the Fourth Gospel. The Progressives, on the other hand, were innovators because they employed the Greek term *homoousios* to express their belief that the Son was of one substance with the Father. As Basil, Bishop of Caesarea, held later, the Scriptural

The Faith and Formula

reference so often quoted by the Arians, "My Father is greater than I" (John 14:28), really implies that the Son is of the same substance or essence as the Father; otherwise there is no point in the comparison (*Ep.* 8).

Although practically the whole council voted in support of the formula, the Progressives in the period that immediately followed, that is, from 326 to 336 (the year Arius died), were looked upon as dangerous liberals. Two of their leaders were singled out for attack: Athanasius, for his able defense of the Creed, and Eustathius, Bishop of Antioch, because he was suspected of Sabellianism.

In order to follow subsequent doctrinal development, the importance of the Conservatives or Fundamentalists to any final solution must be recognized. The majority of these, even in the East, were never really Arian. These, whatever happened, had to be won over, either by pressure or persuasion. Without their support the militant prelates on both sides would be helpless in any attempt to create harmony within the Church.

The Progressives never compromised as they sought to stabilize their position. They remained true to the Nicene Creed and came to be known as Homoousians. The Arians changed their formulas from time to time, and according to Sophronius, Bishop of Pompeiopolis, "they expressed a separate opinion from day to day." The semi-Arians altered the *homoousios* of the original orthodox formula to *homoiousios* (*homoi* in Greek means "like"), maintaining that the Son is *like* the Father in all things. The Anomoeans, another group of Arians, abandoned both *homoousios* and *homoiousios*. They denied that the Son is one in substance with the Father or even like the Father in all things.

The Arian dispute following Nicea can be explained with reference to distinct periods, starting with 325 and ending with the Council of Constantinople in 381, when final victory was won for the Nicene Creed. Between 344 and 353 there was a period of comparative peace throughout the Church.

Period One (326-337)

Arian Intrigue

(*Eccl. History*, Theodoret, Bk. I, xx, xxviii-ix, pp. 57ff.; Socrates, Bk. I, xxiv, xxviii, pp. 27ff.; Sozomen, Bk. II, xix-xxv, pp. 270ff.)

The first twelve years after Nicea was a period of plotting on the part of Eusebius, Bishop of Nicomedia, backed by the Emperor Constantine. Synods were held in the vicinity of Nicomedia to depose bishops such as Athanasius and Eustathius. Arius and his followers were readmitted into the Church on signing a formula in which Christ was accepted as the divine Logos, but not as the Only-begotten Son, not to mention His being one in substance with the Father, as the Nicene Creed claimed. During this period the Church in Rome exerted no influence.

Period Two (337-344; 350-361)
Imperial Arianism

(Theodoret, Bk. II, i, iii, vi, xii, xv, xxii, pp. 65ff., 76f., 79f., 86f.; Socrates, Bk. II, iii, x, xiv, xxv, pp. 37, 39ff., 53; Sozomen, Bk. III, ii, v, ix, xvii, xxii, pp. 283ff., 288, 297, 299f.)

Soon after assuming power in the East on the death of Constantine, Constantius his son made Eusebius Bishop of Constantinople, the new capital. Under the clever and subtle scheming of the bishop the court became saturated with Arian ideas and filled with sympathizers. Constantius, though unbaptized and not actually a Christian, was a militant Arian. He forced a favorite of his on the see of Alexandria to replace Athanasius, the rightful bishop. Constans his brother stood stubbornly against Arian infiltration within his dominion. On the death of Constans in 350 Constantius became sole ruler. The Bishop of Rome resisted every effort to Arianize the West.

During this period many important councils were held in the East and West. The Eastern councils were predominantly Arian; the Western, orthodox. In practically every one the Nicene Formula was considered directly or indirectly, as the following summary shows:

Council	Attitude to Nicene Creed	New Creed
Antioch (341) (90 bishops)	Non-committal	Reflects teaching of Lucian Sanctioned by emperor
Sardica (343) (100 bishops) from West	For Against	Reaffirmed Nicene Creed
Philippopolis (343) (70 bishops) from East		Reaffirmed Creed of Antioch (341)

The Faith and Formula

Sirmium (357) (East)	Against	Creed states Son is unlike the Father, hence not God. This is called, "The Blasphemy"; and its framers, "Anomoeans," from *anomoion*, Greek for "unlike."
Sirmium (359) (East)	Against	Creed adopts *homoiousios*, stating the Son *like* the Father in all things.*
Ariminum (359) (400 bishops from West: 80 were Arian)	For	A Creed not signed by majority held the Son to be God of God, like to the Father . . . according to the Scriptures.
Seleucia (359) (150 Eastern bishops, mostly Arian)	Against	Reaffirmed Creed of Antioch

As a result of the last two councils, at Ariminum and Seleucia, "the whole world," as Jerome tells us, "groaned and wondered to find itself Arian." Thus a victory was gained for Imperial Arianism.

Period Three (364-378)

Arian Persecution

(Socrates, Bk. IV, iii, vi, ix, xv, xvii, xxii, xxiv, pp. 97ff., 103ff.; Sozomen, Bk. VI, vii-x, xii, xiv, xviii, xx, pp. 350-352, 353f., 355ff.).

For a period of three years (361-363) the New Paganism of Julian challenged both the Arians and the Orthodox, whereas Jovian (363-364) championed the Nicene Formula. Valentinian, Emperor of the West (364-375), supported the Orthodox. Valens, Emperor of the East (364-378), condoned no compromises. Those that were not Arians through and through lost their sees. The monks were severely persecuted. Julian's political tactics were nothing compared with the intolerance and cruelty of Valens. His methods recall Diocletian, when massacre and pillage were the order of the day. A ship carrying eighty Conservatives and Progressives, who had protested against the nominee for the bishopric

---

*Liberius, Bishop of Rome, accepted this Creed for the purpose of refuting the Anomoeans.

of Constantinople, was destroyed by fire in the open sea by his orders.

There were forces, nevertheless, working for the resurgence of orthodoxy throughout the Empire. In 364 a council was held at Lampsacus, where the moderates renounced the minority Creed of Ariminum. They made their semi-Arianism look as much as possible like the Nicene Creed. Great influence was exerted in behalf of the Nicene formula by men of Ambrose's calibre in the West and by the Cappadocian Fathers in the East, Basil the Great, Gregory of Nyssa, and Gregory of Nazianzen, who was for a short while bishop of Constantinople at a time when the capital was mainly Arian. Gratian (375-383), a pupil of Ambrose, prepared the way for the final victory of the Nicene Formula in the West. The East, under Theodosius I (379-395), at last accepted the statement of the Fathers as presented at Nicea. At a council called by the emperor in Constantinople in 381, when 150 bishops met, the Nicene Creed was reaffirmed. Arians were prohibited by law from using churches or building new ones. The Macedonians, who held with their founder, Macedonius, Bishop of Constantinople (360), that the Holy Spirit was not God, but a minister of high order in His service, like the angels, suffered the same fate as other heretics.

III

At the Council of Nicea the problem concerning the question of the relationship of the Son to the Father had been settled to the satisfaction of the orthodox leaders by stating that the Son was of the same substance as the Father. At the Council of Ephesus they were confronted with what seems a more difficult problem, namely, the way both God and man are united in Christ. To the Apostles and Church Fathers up to then, both Godhead and manhood are brought together in Him through the unifying process of His Person.

The test word of the controversy that led to this council was another word in Greek, the language of the Eastern bishops. The term *Theotokos*, which means God-bearer, had been applied to Mary the mother of Jesus since the time of Origen. The common English translation, "Mother of God," is misleading, for the stress appears to be on "Mother," whereas the original has the emphasis where it should be, on the Godhead of Him who was born. It should be understood that any claim to divinity on the part of the mother was not the point at issue. That claim is a modern concern, without any apostolic basis. The dogma of the Immaculate Conception and the Ascension of Mary are recent inventions. What Christian leaders of the fourth century had in mind was the Deity of the Son. Neither Origen nor Nestorius nor Cyril had any intention of making the mother divine.

If the title *Theotokos* is analyzed, it is appropriate and befitting, provided, as Theodoret points out, we recognize that the term "Mother of man" is as applicable to Mary as "Mother of God," because the Lord Christ Himself is called both God and man in the Scriptures (*Letter* CLI, NPNF, 2nd ser., III, 325ff.). She is the mother of God in the sense that the One born of her is God. That does not mean that His Deity was derived from her. He that was born of her was conceived by the Holy Ghost, as the Scriptures state. The Master's humanity came by way of Mary, and it is not by accident that she is called "Mother of man," for as man He was born in accordance with the natural process that makes every child part of his mother's nature. It is because of that process that His manhood was complete and in possession of a soul with will and mind like any other human being.

Nestorius, Patriarch of Constantinople (428), protested publicly against the common use of the title, "Mother of God." First of all, he defended with great eloquence Anastasius, his presbyter, who had attacked the term *Theotokos* in a sermon preached at the Cathedral Church of the capital. Subsequently, the Patriarch defended his position in a correspondence with Cyril, Archbishop of Alexandria, who had declared in a synod held in that city that Nestorius was a heretic. The Archbishop was convinced that the Deity of Christ was being threatened by the Patriarch's denunciation of the term, "Mother of God." When Nestorius was pressed by an assembly of the brethren to clarify his teaching, he admitted, "I cannot term him God who was two and three months old," and he added, "I am, therefore, clear of your blood and shall in future come no more among you." Later, as he realized that his contention endangered the peace of the Church, he agreed that Mary was "Mother of God," declaring, "Let Mary be called *Theotokos*, if you will, and let all disputing cease" (Socrates, Bk. VII, xxxiv, p. 172).

At the Council held at Ephesus in 341, summoned by Emperor Theodosius II and attended by about 159 bishops, Nestorius was deposed. On the return of John the Bishop of Antioch to his see, he, along with a number of other bishops, deposed Cyril. Cyril on being deposed, appealed to the emperor, and he caused both

Nestorius and Cyril to be put in prison. He regarded the sentence passed on the former and the action of John of Antioch as legal. On their release Cyril returned to Alexandria to resume his duties as bishop, but Nestorius was never restored. His followers, years later, exerted great influence as monks and missionaries as far as China in the East.

On the orthodox side, the leaders in the dispute were Cyril, John, and Celestine, Bishop of Rome, under whose presidency a council of Western bishops held at Rome condemned Nestorius and threatened him with excommunication. Cyril issued twelve anathemas against the Patriarch, who in turn answered with counter-anathemas. At the request of John, who doubted the orthodoxy of Cyril, Theodoret, Bishop of Cyrrhus, or Cyrus, in Syria, an outstanding theologian and historian, issued twelve anathemas in answer to Cyril's.

From these verbal curses and other evidence concerning the controversy that resulted from Nestorius' attack on the term *Theotokos*, we find that the real question at issue was the relation of the Godhead and Manhood in Christ Jesus. Apollinaris, Bishop of Laodicea in Syria (362), had fallen into a heresy in his effort to define the union. This erudite scholar and writer had been a strong supporter of the Nicene Formula and was a friend of Athanasius and Basil the Great. In his controversy with the Arians he had stressed the sinlessness of Jesus. He absolutely disagreed with the Arians that the Logos in His incarnate state, that is, as man, could be tempted or be subject to sin. Since the rational soul or spirit is the seat of evil, the divine Word or Logos, according to him, occupied the place of the human soul in Jesus. God in all His perfection was in Him, but His human nature was not complete, because it was bereft of everything that is peculiar to the soul as possessed by other men. This approach emptied the Incarnation of all reality. Apollinaris' novel device of asserting that the archetype of true Manhood existed eternally in the Godhead did not appeal to the orthodox. He was excommunicated and his theories condemned by synods held at Antioch and Rome, and by the Council of Constantinople in 381. Later, they were refuted by the Definition of Chalcedon in 451. His supporters formed themselves into a distinct sect, with bishops and churches of their own.

Many of the heretics, as Theodoret reminds us, had their explanations of the person of Christ. Marcion denied that the Logos was truly man. His humanity was a mere semblance. Valentinus, among the Gnostics, asserted that the Son of God employed Mary as a conduit. Paul of Samosata held that Jesus was just a man. Arius believed that the human form in which the Logos appeared was capable of change and liable to sin (Theodoret, *Letter* CLI, pp. 325ff.).

Nestorius was obviously under the influence of the teaching of his master, Theodore, Bishop of Mopsuestia in Cilicia Secunda (392). Theodore, as his commentaries on the Bible show, was a great scholar and thinker. His theory of the relationship of God and man in Christ, however, is open to question. To him the union resembles that of the marriage bond. Husband and wife are made spiritually one in holy wedlock, yet they are still two persons with their peculiar traits and characteristics. In the union of the Logos and man, Jesus the man, who was the human partner and associate of the divine Word, could have sinned like all men. Theodore was anathematized by a council held at Constantinople in 553 for teaching that the Incarnate Son of God was subject to temptation as any other ordinary mortal. Nestorius was as confused as his master when attempting to account for the existence of two natures in Christ. Both seem to regard "nature" and "person" as one and the same.

Theodoret, who was also a pupil of Theodore, had a better grasp of the union of the two natures in Christ than either his master or his fellow student Nestorius. He suggests, for example, that every man has two natures. As regards his body he has a physical nature, in common with the lower creation. As regards his mind and will, he is in possession of a spiritual nature. Despite this duality he is still one person, and is held responsible whenever his hand steals or whenever his body does any other criminal action or even whenever evil thoughts enter his mind, as the Sermon on the Mount teaches. By failing to see that Christ, while in possession of two natures, was still one person, Nestorius arrived at the strange conclusion that in His incarnate state He was functioning as two Persons, one divine, the other, human.

Theodoret (393-458) expresses the orthodox position as follows:

> We confess that our Lord Jesus Christ, perfect God and perfect man, of a reasonable soul and body, was begotten of the Father before the ages, as touching the Godhead; and in the last days for us men and our salvation (was born) of the Virgin Mary; that the same Lord is one substance with the Father as touching the Godhead, and of one substance with us as touching the manhood. For there was an union of two natures. Wherefore we acknowledge one Christ, one Son, one Lord (*ibid.*, p. 326).

It seems from the controversy that the Incarnation was in the forefront of consideration. The Atonement, or what the death of Christ means to us men and our salvation, seems of a secondary consideration. Such a conclusion, however, is not supported by the facts. The orthodox party at Ephesus felt that Nestorius, like Theodore before him, regarded the suffering and the sacrifice of Christ as being the sole responsibility of the earthly partner in the union of God and man. In the opinion of those who had fully realized the implication of the victory gained at Nicea, God and God alone could atone and redeem. There was something far more important at stake than a doctrinal explanation of the union of God and man in Christ. The question at the heart of the problem was, Who is man's real and only Saviour? The Council of Ephesus, in denouncing and anathematizing Nestorius, reaffirmed its faith in the one Lord Jesus Christ, the only-begotten Son of God, who for us men and our salvation came down from heaven to be conceived of the Holy Ghost and to be born of the virgin Mary, the "Mother of God."

IV

An aftermath refers to a second mowing or crop of grass from land in the same season. In the period following the Council of Ephesus there arose a need for a second mowing by another council, and this was done by the Council of Chalcedon in 451. Well over five hundred bishops came together. There was a deep concern about Nestorianism. Many felt that it had not been completely destroyed. Theodoret, the Bishop of Cyrrhus, and a friend of Nestorius, was held in suspicion.

The opening session of the Council was a pandemonium, with the atmosphere of the sacred assembly rent with catcalls. The Alexandrians, who remembered too well Theodoret's anathemas against their beloved Cyril, whose passing had occurred in 344, shouted in unison, "Do not call him a bishop! He is not a bishop! Cast out the fighter against God! Cast out the Jew!" The whole scene followed the pattern at the Pretorium in the time of Pilate with its cry, "Away with him! Crucify him!" Their loyalty to Cyril made it impossible for them to endure Theodoret, so he had to be expelled. As his opponents were shouting, "He is a heretic! He is a Nestorian! Away with the heretic!" he met their slander with these words: "Anathema to Nestorius and to whoever denies that the Holy Virgin Mary is the Parent of

God, and who divides the only begotten Son into two Sons. . ." (Theodoret, *Prolegomena*, V, NPNF, 2nd ser., III, 10, 11).

Besides Theodoret another of the leaders was suspected of heresy. Since the Council of Ephesus, Eutyches, the Principal of a Monastery near Constantinople, had circulated theories about the Person of Jesus Christ, not very different from those of Apollinaris. He was a convincing opponent of Nestorianism. His contention that in Christ there was but one nature, namely, the divine, was condemned by some of the leading bishops. At a synod in Constantinople called by Theodosius II in 448, with 30 bishops present and presided over by Flavian, the bishop of that city, he was excommunicated. A year later, what is known as the *Latrocinium*, or Robbers Council, was held in Ephesus on August 8, with Dioscorus, Bishop of Alexandria, taking the leading part. At this Council Eutyches was acquitted and restored. Flavian was condemned and died later as the result of ill-treatment at the hands of the monks. Theodoret and other leaders suspected of Nestorian leanings were deposed. In the same year Leo, Bishop of Rome (440-461), whom Theodoret had consulted, wrote his very fine epistle, the *Tome*, in which the ideas of Eutyches are answered and severely denounced. As the following quotation shows, Leo was greatly astonished that Eutyches had ever been supported and restored to office:

> But when during your cross-examination Eutyches replied and said, "I confess that our Lord had two natures before the union: but after the union I confess but one," I am surprised that so absurd and mistaken a statement of his should not have been criticized and rebuked by his judges. (See NPNF, 2nd ser., XII, 43).

In his eagerness to protect the Faith against Nestorianism Eutyches was driven to another extreme. Nestorius had taught that in Christ were two Persons, for he had taken each of the natures in Him as a distinct personality, with the divine nature functioning as God and the human nature as man. Although both God and man were represented in the union, we are left, nevertheless, with a form of dualism that keeps the divine and the human forever apart. Eutyches felt that they had to be brought together in some way in the man Christ Jesus. The chasm had to be bridged. The Greek mind found no difficulty in believing that the gods appeared on earth in the form of men. In Acts 14:11-13, for instance, the people of Lystra, convinced that the gods had come down to them in the likeness of men, called Barnabas,

Jupiter, and Paul, Mercurius, and were prepared to worship them both as gods. To Eutyches God appeared in the man Jesus. It was not a case of God and man becoming united in one Person. In Jesus there was but one nature, and that was completely divine. His humanity resembled the burning bush Moses once saw, but the divine blaze in the case of Jesus was so strong and overpowering that the bush ceased to exist the moment the divine flame set it afire. The bush was very necessary as a means of displaying the Godhead among men, but Christ's humanity had but an apparent reality. His human nature was merely a symbol, the divine nature alone had substance.

At the Council of Chalcedon summoned by Pulcheria and Marcian, the newly appointed rulers of the Empire, the Nicene Creed and the creed attributed for the first time to the Council of Constantinople of 381, a creed that is very similar to the Nicene, were enthusiastically received. "The Tome" was read; Eutyches was condemned as a heretic, and Dioscorus, the Bishop of Alexandria, his chief supporter, was deposed. The following passages from Leo's work will give an idea of what the Council subscribed to:

> Without detriment therefore to the properties of either nature and substance which then came together in one person, majesty took on humility, strength weakness, eternity mortality: and for the paying off of the debt belonging to our condition inviolable nature was united with passible nature, so that, as suited the needs of our case, one and the same Mediator between God and men, the Man Christ Jesus, could both die with the one and not die with the other. Thus in the whole and perfect nature of true man was true God born, complete in what was His own, complete in what was ours. . . . For He who is true God is also true man: and in this union there is no lie, since the humility of manhood and the loftiness of the Godhead both meet there. For as God is not changed by the showing of pity, so man is not swallowed up by the dignity. (*Letter* XXVIII ["The Tome"], iii, iv, NPNF, 2nd ser., XII, 40).

Besides reaffirming the Creeds and approving "The Tome," the Council of Chalcedon produced its own Definition, which is the ecumenical answer of the Church of those days to the heresies known as Arianism, Apollinarianism, Nestorianism, and Eutychianism. Four of its expressions have by now become famous: "Without confusion"; "without change"; "without division"; "without separation."

The Church in its opposition to Nestorius and Eutyches discovered that the Gospel to the former was the story of man's struggle without God. To the latter it was an account of a divine accomplishment without man. The orthodox position, by claiming that both God and man were united in Christ, guarantees humanity's ascent through the descent of the divine. The individualism implied by the theory of Eutyches conflicts with the universalism of the Gospel message. The man Jesus to him was a mere symbol in whom actually our manhood is lost. Nestorius is positive concerning the dual representation that is in Christ, but the necessary unity is not there. The guardians of the apostolic teaching knew a bridge had been constructed. Time and eternity, earth and heaven, man and God, at last, had a point of contact in the Incarnation and had become one in Christ. The Cross gave the redeemed an access to the heart of the Eternal. The Holy Spirit found a new way to the hearts of men. Unless God in the fullness of His love is in Jesus, then our deepest need will never be met. Calvary is an absolute necessity. Human nature of itself can never change from being the seat of evil and decay.

BIBLIOGRAPHY

General

Angus, S., *The Environment of Early Christianity.* London: Duckworth, 1914.
An Outline of Christianity, Vol. II. London: The Waverley Book Co., n.d.
Bardenhewer, O. von, *Patrology.* Herder, 1908.
Bardy, G., *The Greek Literature of the Early Christian Church.* London, 1930.
———, *The Christian Latin Literature of the First Six Centuries.* London, 1930.
Bartlett, J. V., *Early Church History.* London: The Religious Tract Society, 1894.
Bate, H. N., *History of the Church to 325.* Rivingtons, 1912.
Bethune-Baker, J. F., *An Introduction to the Early History of Christian Doctrine.* London: Methuen, 1903.
Biggs, C., *The Church's Task in the Roman Empire.* London: Oxford, 1905.
———, *The Christian Platonists of Alexandria.* London: Oxford, 1913.
Bright, W., *The Age of the Fathers.* London: Longmans, 1903.
Bryce, J., *The Holy Roman Empire.* London: Macmillan, 1880.
Burn, A. E., *The Apostles' Creed.* Rivingtons, 1914.
———, *The Nicene Creed.* Rivingtons, 1913.
———, *The Athanasian Creed.* Rivingtons, 1918.

Cadoux, C. J., *The Early Church in the World.* Edinburgh: T. & T. Clark, 1925.
Caird, E., *The Evolution of Theology in the Greek Philosophers.* Maclehose, 1904.
Case, S. J., *The Evolution of Early Christianity.* Chicago, 1914.
Chadwick, H., and Oulton, J. E. L., (ed.), *Alexandrian Christianity.* Philadelphia: Westminster Press, 1954.
Chapot, V., *The Roman World.* New York, 1928.
Coulton, G. G., *Five Centuries of Religion.* Cambridge, 1923.
Cullmann, O., *Studies in Early Church History and Theology.* Trans. A. J. B. Higgins. Philadelphia: Westminster Press, 1956.

Dill, S., *Roman Society from Nero to Marcus Aurelius.* London: Macmillan, 1904.

Dorner, J. A., *Doctrine of the Person of Christ.* Edinburgh: T. & T. Clark, 1872-1884.

Duchesne, L., *The Early History of the Church.* London: Murray, 1912.

Eusebius, *Church History,* NPNF, 2nd ser., I.

Fliche, A., and Martin, V., (ed.), *L'Englise primitive.* Trans. E. C. Messenger. Burns, Oates, 1942-7.

Gibbon, E., *The Decline and Fall of the Roman Empire.* London: Methuen, 1923.

Glover, T. R., *The Conflicts of Religions in the Early Roman Empire.* London: Methuen, 1909.

Greenslade, S. L., (ed.), *Early Latin Theology.* Philadelphia: Westminster Press, 1956.

Gwatkin, H. M., *Early Church History to* A.D. *313.* London: Macmillan, 1909.

——, *Selections from Early Christian Writers.* London: Macmillan, 1893.

Hagenbach, K. R., *History of Christian Doctrine.* Edinburgh: T. & T. Clark, 1883.

Hardy, E. R., *Christology of the Later Fathers.* Philadelphia: Westminster Press, 1955.

Harnack, A. von, *The Mission and Expansion of Christianity in the First Three Centuries.* London: Williams & Norgate, 1908.

——, *The History of Dogma.* London: Williams & Norgate, 1899.

Hughes, P., *A History of the Church,* Vol. I. New York: Sheed & Ward, 1952.

Kidd, B. J., *A History of the Church to* A.D. *461.* London: Oxford, 1922.

——, *Documents Illustrative of the History of the Church.* London: S. P. C. K., 1920.

Knox, J., *The Early Church and the Coming Great Church.* New York: Abingdon Press, 1955.

Latourette, S. K., *A History of the Expansion of Christianity,* Vol. I. New York: Harper, 1937-1945.

Merrill, E. T., *Essays in Early Christian History.* London: Macmillan, 1924.

McGiffert, A. G., *The God of the Early Christians.* New York: Scribner's, 1924.

Pullan, L., *Early Christian Doctrine.* Rivingtons, 1899.

——, *The Church of the Fathers.* Rivingtons, 1903.

Ramsay, W. M., *The Church in the Roman Empire.* London: Hodder & Stoughton, 1893.

Richardson, C. C., (ed.), *Early Christian Fathers*. Philadelphia: Westminster Press, 1955.
Roberts, A., and Donaldson, J., *The Ante-Nicene Christian Library*. Trans. of the Writings of the Fathers to A.D. 325. London: T. & T. Clark, 1867-1872. American Editions: Buffalo, N. Y.: Christian Literature Publishing Co., 1885-1887; New York: Scribner's, 1885-1887; Grand Rapids, Michigan: Eerdmans.
Schaff, P. and Wace, H., *Nicene and Post-Nicene Fathers*. Buffalo, N. Y.: Christian Literature Pub. Co., 1886-1894; New York: Scribner's, 1890-1900; Grand Rapids: Wm. B. Eerdmans Pub. Co.
Schaff, P., and D., *History of the Christian Church*. New York: Scribner's, 1882-1910.
Socrates, *Church History*. NPNF, 2nd ser., II.
Sozomen, *Church History*. NPNF, 2nd ser., II.
Theodoret, *Church History*. NPNF, 2nd ser., III.
Tixeront, J., *Handbook on Patrology*. Chicago: Herder, 1947.
———, *History of Dogma*. Chicago: Herder, 1923.
Torrance, T. F., *The Doctrine of Grace in the Apostolic Fathers*. Edinburgh: Oliver and Boyd, 1948; Grand Rapids: Wm. B. Eerdmans Pub. Co., 1958.
Torrey, C. C., *Documents of the Primitive Church*. New York: Harpers, 1941.

Weiss, J., *The History of the Primitive Church*. New York: Macmillan, 1937.
Wright, F. A., *Fathers of the Church*. New York: Dutton, 1929.
Whale, J. S., *Christian Doctrine*. New York: Macmillan, 1941.

CHAPTERS

I

Barnabas, *Epistle*. ANF, I.

Clement of Rome, *Epistle to the Corinthians*. ANF, I.

Didache or *Teaching of the Twelve Apostles*. ANF, VII.

Hegesippus, *Fragments*. ANF, VIII.
Hermas, *The Shepherd*. ANF, II.

Ignatius, *Epistles*. ANF, I.

Lake, K., *The Apostolic Fathers*. London: Heinemann, 1914.
Lightfoot, J. B., *The Apostolic Fathers*. London: Macmillan, 1891.

Papias, *Fragments*. ANF, I.
Polycarp, *Epistle to the Philippians*. ANF, I.
Pseudo-Clementine Literature. ANF, VIII.

II

Arnobius, *Against the Heathen.* ANF, VI.

Athenagoras, *A Plea for the Christians.* ANF, II.

Commodianus, *Instructions for Christian Discipline.* ANF, IV.

Epistle to Diognetus. ANF, I.

Jerome, *Lives of Illustrious Men.* NPNF, 2nd ser., III.

Justin Martyr, *Apologies, Dialogue with Trypho.* ANF, I.

Melito, *Fragments.* ANF, VIII.

Minucius Felix, *The Octavius.* ANF, IV.

Tatian, *Address to the Greeks.* ANF, II.

Tertullian, *The Apology, Against Marcion.* ANF, III.

Theophilus, *Apology to Autolycus.* ANF, II.

III

Buonaniti, E., (ed.), *Gnostic Fragments.* Trans. Edith Cowell. London: Williams & Norgate, 1924.

Clement of Alexandria, *The Miscellanies.* ANF, II.

Hippolytus, *The Refutation of All Heresies.* ANF, V.

Irenaeus, *Against Heresies.* ANF, I.

Jerome, *Lives of Illustrious Men* (see Montanus). NPNF, 2nd ser., III.

Justin Martyr, *First Apology.* ANF, I.

Legge, F., *Forerunners and Rivals of Christianity.* London: Cambridge, 1915.

Mansel, *The Gnostic Heresies.* London: Murray, 1876.

Tertullian, *Against Marcion, A Treatise on the Soul, Against the Valentinians.* ANF, III.

IV

Irenaeus, *Against Heresies, Fragments.* ANF, I.

Rainy, R., *The Ancient Catholic Church.* Edinburgh: T. & T. Clark, 1902.

Robinson, J. A., *St. Irenaeus: The Demonstration of Apostolic Preaching.* London: S. P. C. K., 1920.

Tertullian, *The Prescription against Heresies, Against Marcion.* ANF, III.

V

Clement of Alexandria, *The Exhortation, The Instructor, The Miscellanies.* ANF, II.

Dionysius of Alexandria, *On the Promises.* ANF, VI.

Gregory Thaumaturgus, *The Panegyric*. ANF, VI.
Jerome, *Lives of Illustrious Men*. NPNF, 2nd ser., III.
Methodius, *On the Resurrection*. ANF, VI.
Origen, *De Principiis, Against Celsus*. ANF, IV.
Rufinus, *Apology*.

VI

Ambrose, *On the Holy Spirit*.
Athanasius, *Orations against Arius, On the Incarnation*.
Augustine, *On the Trinity*. NPNF, 1st ser., III.
Basil, *On the Holy Spirit*. NPNF, 2nd ser., VIII.
Burn, A. E., *The Athanasian Creed*. London: Rivingtons, 1918.
Calvin, *Institutes*. Trans. Henry Beveridge. Grand Rapids: Wm. B. Eerdmans Pub. Co.
Dionysius of Rome, *Against Sabellius*. ANF, VII.
Gregory of Nazianzen, *Orations, Sermons*. NPNF, 2nd ser., VII.
Gregory of Nyssa, *On the Holy Trinity*. NPNF, 2nd ser., V.
Hilary of Poitiers, *On the Trinity*. NPNF, 2nd ser., IX.
Hippolytus, *The Refutation of All Heresies, Against Noetus*. ANF, V.
Novatian, *On the Trinity*. ANF, V.
Tertullian, *Against Praxeas, The Prescription against Heresies*. ANF, III.

VII

Augustine, *The City of God, Commentary on St. John, Anti-Donatist Writings*. NPNF, 1st ser., II, IV, VII.
Bévénot, M., *The De Unitate of St. Cyprian*. Burns, Oates, 1938.
Chrysostom, *On the Priesthood*. NPNF, 1st ser., IX.
Cyprian, *Epistles, Treatises, Seventh Council of Carthage*. ANF, V.
Cyril of Jerusalem, *Catechetical Lectures*. NPNF, 2nd ser., VII.
Dionysius of Alexandria, *Epistles*. ANF, VI.
Dobschütz, E. von, *Church Life in the Primitive Church*. London: Williams & Norgate, 1904.
Duchesne, L., *The Origins of Christian Worship*. London: S. P. C. K., 1906.
Frend, W. H. C., *The Donatist Church*. New York: Oxford, 1952.
Harnack, A. von, *Constitution and Law of the Church*. London: Williams & Norgate, 1910.
Irenaeus, *Against Heresies*. ANF, I.
Lactantius, *The Divine Institutes*. ANF, VII.

Lindsay, T. M., *The Church and Ministry in the Early Centuries.* London: Hodder & Stoughton, 1902.

Mason, A. J., *Historic Martyrs of the Primitive Church.* London: Longmans, 1905.

———, *Persecution of Diocletian.* Deighton Bell, 1876.

Schroeder, H. J., *Disciplinary Decrees of the General Councils.* London, 1937.

Streeter, B. H., *The Primitive Church.* London: Macmillan, 1929.

Tertullian, *On Baptism, On the Resurrection of the Flesh.* ANF, III.

VIII

Augustine, *Confessions, On the Trinity, Christian Doctrine, Anti-Pelagian Writings, City of God.* NPNF, 1st ser., I-III, V.

Battenhouse, R. W., (ed.), *A Companion to the Study of Augustine.* New York: Oxford, 1955.

Burleigh, J. H. S., (ed.), *Augustine: Early Writings.* Philadelphia: Westminster Press, 1953.

Burnaby, J., (ed.), *Augustine: Later Works.* Philadelphia: Westminster Press, 1955.

Outler, A. C., (ed.), *Augustine: Confessions and Enchiridion.* Philadelphia: Westminster Press, 1955.

IX

Athanasius, *Life of Anthony.* NPNF, 2nd ser., IV.

Augustine, *City of God.* NPNF, 1st ser., II.

Baynes, N. H., *Constantine the Great and the Christian Church.* London, 1931.

Chrysostom, *Ascetic Treatises.* NPNF, 1st ser., IX.

Hardy, E. G., *Christianity and the Roman Government.* London: Longmans, 1894.

Harnack, A. von, *Monasticism: Its Ideals and History.* London: Williams & Norgate, 1901.

Jackson, F. J. Foakes, Articles: "The Empire Against the Church"; "Constantine, Patron of the Church"; "The First Monks" in *An Outline of Christianity.* London.

Lactantius, *The Deaths of Persecutors, On the Anger of God.* ANF, VII.

Mackean, W. H., *Christian Monasticism in Egypt.* London: S. P. C. K., 1920.

Nairne, A., Article, "The Ascetic Life" in *An Outline of Christianity.* London.

Setton, K. M., *Christian Attitude towards the Emperor in the Fourth Century.* New York: Columbia Univ. Press, 1941.
Socrates, *History of the Church.* NPNF, 2nd ser., II.
Sozomen, *History of the Church.* NPNF, 2nd ser., II.
Theodoret, *History of the Church.* NPNF, 2nd ser., III.

X

Alexander of Alexandria, *Epistle on the Arian Heresy and the Deposition of Arius.* ANF, VI.
Bindley, T. H., *Ecumenical Documents of the Faith.* London: Methuen, 1899.
Burn, A. E., *The Nicene Creed.* Rivingtons, 1913.
Clark, W. K. L., *St. Basil the Great.* Cambridge, 1913.
Decrees and Canons of the Seven Ecumenical Councils. NPNF, 2nd ser., XIV.
Du Bose, *The Ecumenical Councils.* Edinburgh: T. & T. Clark, 1897.
Gwatkin, H. M., *Studies of Arianism.* Deighton Bell, 1892.
Hefele, H. J., *A History of the Christian Councils.* Edinburgh: T. & T. Clark, 1874-1896.
Jalland, T. G., *The Life and Times of St. Leo the Great.* London: S. P. C. K., 1940.
Leo I, *Select Epistles.* NPNF, 2nd ser., XII.
Loofs, F., *Nestorius and His Place in Christian Doctrine.* Cambridge, 1914.
Miegge, G., *The Virgin Mary.* Trans. Waldo Smith. Philadelphia: Westminster Press, 1956.
Raven, C. E., *Apollinarianism.* Cambridge, 1923.
Socrates, *Church History.* NPNF, 2nd ser., II.
Sozomen, *Church History.* NPNF, 2nd ser., II.
Theodoret, *Church History.* NPNF, 2nd ser., III.

Articles of great value by well-known authorities are included in many of the Dictionaries, such as *Dictionary of Christian Biography*, London, 1877-1887; *Dictionary of Doctrinal and Historical Theology*, London, 1892; *Encyclopedia of Religion and Ethics*, Hastings, 1927; *The New Schaff-Herzog Encyclopedia of Religious Knowledge*, New York, 1908; *Catholic Encyclopedia*, New York, 1909.

GENERAL INDEX

Abel, 57, 81
Abraham, 38, 57, 89, 94, 172
Abraxas, 61
Acesius, 174
Acts, Book of, 75
Adam, 82f., 159, 161ff.
Aeons, 51ff., 62ff., 78, 107
Agape, 58
Ahab, 177
Alcibiades, 67
Alaric, 178
Alexander of Alexandria, 195
Alexander of Jerusalem, 93, 98, 144
Alexander Severus, 172
Alexandria, School of, 89
Alexandria, Cathechumen School of, 90
Allegorical method, 30, 35ff., 57, 89, 105ff.
Ambrose of Alexandria, 98f.
Ambrose of Milan, 139f., 155f., 160f., 165, 175, 180ff., 202
Ammoun. 188
Amos, 97
Anastasius, 203
Anaxagoras, 79
Angels, 58f., 80, 101, 104
Anicetus of Rome, 22, 25, 71
Anomoeans, 199, 201
Anomoion, 201
Anthony, 184ff.
Antioch, influence of, 89f., 196
Antiochus Epiphanes, 166
Antonius Pius, 25, 34, 36, 39, 171
Anulinus, 148
Apocryphal writings, 15
Apollinaris of Laodicea, 193, 204, 207
Apollinarians, 176, 208
Apollonius, 34, 171
Apologists, 33ff., 51, 56, 72, 74, 79, 89f., 92, 105, 113, 141, 153, 178, 185, 187
Apostasy, 131ff.
Apostles, 22, 38, 54, 58, 72, 74, 76, 91, 100, 106, 108, 132, 138, 145, 188, 197, 202
Apostles' Creed, *see* Creeds
Apostolic faith, 76
Apostolic Fathers, 15ff., 33
Apostolic Succession, 17, 74, 77
Apostolic writings, 74ff.

Aquinas, 97
Archons, 56, 58, 60ff.
Arianism, 175, 179, 196, 198ff., 209
Arian persecution, 201
Arians, 108, 132, 147, 175, 178ff., 188, 193f., 199, 201, 204
Arius, 48, 116, 126, 174ff., 184, 195ff., 205
Aristides, 36f.
Aristippus, 37
Aristotle, 37f., 58, 117
Arles, Council of, *see* Councils
Artemas or Artemon, 117, 120
Artemonites, 120
Athenagoras, 36, 40ff.
Athanasius of Alexandria, 27, 102, 118f., 125ff., 147, 147f., 177, 179f., 185, 187f., 195ff., 199f., 204
Athanasian Creed, 128
Atonement, 43, 82ff., 106f., 165, 206, 209
Augustine of Hippo, 37, 40, 82, 97, 126, 128, 134, 141f., 148, 153ff., 180, 183, 185
Aurelian, 120, 172
Autolycus, 36
Axionicus, 64

Babylus of Antioch, 144
Baptism, 138ff., 142, 160; dispute about Re-baptism, 145ff.
Baptismal Formula, 29
Bardesanes, 64
Basil of Caesarea, 126, 180, 185, 187, 198, 202, 204
Basilides, 60ff., 67
Basilides, Spanish bishop, 143, 147
Barnabas, 207
Barnabas, Epistle of, 15, 28ff., 35
Bartholomew, 90
Bassanius Antonius, 171
Bishops, authority of, 17, 20, 77, 138
Brisco, 198

Caecilian of Carthage, 148, 195
Caecilius, 35, 38
Caenobites, 187
Cain, 57, 81
Cainites, 51
Callistus of Rome, 34, 114, 117ff., 142, 209
Calvin, 97, 121, 186

General Index

Canon, 72, 75
Cappadocian Fathers, 128, 180, 202
Caracalla, 120, 171
Carpocrates, 58ff.
Carthage, councils of, see Councils
Carus, 173
Cassian, John, 166f.
Cathari, 143
Catholic Church, 20f., 27, 71, 118
Catholicism, 72ff., 132, 145
Catechumens, 90
Cecilius, 135
Celestine of Rome, 204
Celcus, 33, 35, 99f., 113, 161
Cerdo, 56ff.
Cerinthus, 65
Chalcedon, council of, see Councils
Chertus of Syracuse, 148
Christ, 93ff., 118f., 121, 179; see Logos, Son of God
Church, conceptions of the, 22, 133. 135, 188
Church and State, 175, 180ff., 195
Chrysostom, John, 166, 180, 187
City of God, 134, 157, 168, 183
Civitas Dei, civitas terrena, 157, 183
Claudius, 172
Cleanthes, 45
Clementina, Pseudo, 16
Clement of Alexandria, 25, 27, 29, 33, 54, 58, 72, 89ff., 105, 108f., 133, 136, 140f., 146, 153, 161
Clement of Rome, 16ff., 25
Cleomanes, 118
Coelistius, 158
Colossians, Ep. to the, 52
Commodus, 34, 37, 91, 171
Communio, externa, sanctorum, 134ff., 157ff.
Confessors, 136, 143
Constans, 174f., 177, 179, 200
Constantine the First, 148, 171, 173f., 176ff., 181f., 184, 194f., 199f.
Constantine the Second, 174f., 177, 179, 200
Constantinople, Council of (553 A.D.), 103, 164, 205
Constantine's vision, 177
Constantius I (Chlorus), 173
Constantius II, 174f.
Comunio, externa, sanctorum, 134, 157
Copernicus, 103
Corinthians, I Ep. to the, 16f., 159
Cornelius of Rome, 132, 135, 143
Councils:
 General: Chalcedon, 194, 204, 206f.
 Constantinople, 179, 194, 197, 199, 202, 204
 Ephesus, 159, 194, 202f., 206
 Nicea, 133, 147, 153, 174, 194ff., 202
 Antioch, 118, 120, 200, 204
 Regional:
 Ariminum, 201f.
 Arles, 146, 148
 Carthage, 143, 145
 Constantinople, 126, 207
 Lampsacus, 202
 Latrocinium, 207
 Philippopolis, 200
 Rome, 143, 204
 Sardica, 175, 200
 Seleucia, 201
 Sirmium, 201
Creationism, 164
Creeds: Apostles' Creed, 15, 76, 100, 105, 180; Athanasian Creed, 128; Creed of Antioch, 16; Creed of Eusebuis, 196; Nicene Creed, 42, 174f., 179, 182, 188, 193, 196ff., 208; Old Creed of Jerusalem, 16; Old Roman Creed, 16
Crispus, 176
Cynics, 37
Cyprian of Carthage, 134ff., 139f., 142ff., 147f., 153, 156
Cyril of Alexandria, 93, 180, 203f., 206
Cyril of Jerusalem, 133, 139f.

Deacons, 21, 23, 138
Deception of the devil, 106
Decius, 92, 135, 143f., 172
Definition of Chalcedon, 208
Demetrius of Alexandria, 92, 98
Demiurge, 57, 65, 86
Democritus, 79
Descent to hell, 15
Devil, 58ff., 82f., 104, 106, 165, 186
Diatessaron, 36
Didache, 27ff., 29
Diocletian, 147, 173, 184, 201
Diognetus, Ep. to, 33, 36, 38, 42, 56
Dionysius of Alexandria, 90, 92, 102, 143ff.
Dionysius of Rome, 119, 145
Dionysius of Corinth, 142
Dioscorus of Alexandria, 207f.
Discipline, 133, 136, 141ff., 153
Docetism, 65
Dogma of Papal Infallibility, 137, 145f.
Donatists, 147ff., 153, 158, 174, 182
Donatus, 148
Dynamic Monarchianism, 114, 120

General Index

Easter, observance of, 22, 71, 133
Ebionites, 65
Edicts, 172f., 176f., 181, 183f.
Eleutherus of Rome, 25, 56, 67, 71, 77
Elijah, 38, 177
Empedocles, 57, 79
Enoch, 57
Ephesians, Ep. to the, 52, 63, 153
Ephesus, General Council of, see Councils
Epigonos, 118, 120
Epiphanes, 66
Epiphanius of Salamis, 103, 119, 180
Episcopate, 17, 21, 136ff.
Erastianism, 178
Erminites, 187
Eschatology, 90
Eucharist, 20, 22, 29, 85ff., 137, 139ff., 142
Eunomians, 176
Eusebius of Caesarea, 25, 27, 29, 66f., 93, 97, 99, 102, 118ff., 132, 142ff., 176f., 180f., 194ff.
Eusebuis of Nicomedia, 174, 197ff.
Eustathius of Antioch, 199f.
Eutyches, 193, 207f.
Evil, the problem of, 158ff.
Extension of the Incarnation, 140
Externa communio, 134
Ezekiel, 160

Fabian of Rome, 144
Fabius of Antioch, 132, 143f.
Fall of man, 158ff., 167
Fausta, 176
Faustus of Rhegium, 166f.
Feet, washing of, 139
Felicissimus of Carthage, 135, 137, 143
Felix of Aptunga, 148
Firmilian of Caesarea, 145
Flavian of Constantinople, 207
Foreknowledge, 167
Forgiveness of sins, 141ff.
Formlessness, 60, 63
Fortunatus of Carthage, 143
Fourth Gospel, 23, 36, 41ff., 47, 153, 198
Free will, 103, 153ff., 160ff., 167f.

Galerius, 173, 184
Galileo, 103
Gallienus, 145, 172
Gallus, 135, 144, 172
Glover, T. R., 38
Gnosis, 53, 55, 61, 65

Gnostics, 35, 51ff., 67, 72, 74f., 78ff., 89ff., 95, 98, 105, 107, 116, 134, 142, 153, 166, 185, 194
Gnosticism, Christian, 90
God, conceptions of, 19, 40, 41, 56, 60, 64, 95, 104, 108ff., 113ff., 154f.
God-Man, 108, 139, 204
Gordian, 172
Grace, 162ff.
Gratian, 176f., 202
Gregory of Nazianzen, 126, 161, 180, 202
Gregory of Nyssa, 126, 140, 164f., 180, 202
Gregory Thaumaturgus, 98
Gregory VII, 146

Hadrian, 34, 36, 171
Harris, J. Rendel, 37
Hebrews, Ep. to the, 38, 75
Hegesippus, 25
Helen (Simon Magus), 55ff., 58
Helena (Constantine's mother), 177
Heliogabulus, 171
Heraclas of Alexandria, 92, 102, 146
Heraclitus, 38
Heracleon, 64
Heresies, 51ff., 65ff., 113ff., 117, 119, 126, 143, 158, 166, 193ff.
Hermas, 25ff.
Hilary of Poitiers, 126, 161, 164, 180
Hippolytus, 54, 56, 58, 61f., 71, 74, 117ff., 124ff., 142, 153
Holy Spirit, 21, 27, 55, 84ff., 113, 139, 157, 202; see Trinity
Homoeans, 199; see Semi-Arians
Homoiousios, 199
Homoousians, 199
Homoousios, 181, 197, 198, 199
Hosea, 55
Hosius of Cordova, 195
Hypomnemata, 25
Hyginus, 56
Hypostasis, 46, 114, 127, 128

Ignatius of Antioch, 16ff., 22f., 33, 92, 133, 137, 140, 263
Immersion, 139
Infant baptism, 139
Incarnation, 57, 66, 83, 107, 113, 120, 125f., 140, 204, 206, 209
Inspiration of the Bible, see Scriptures
Interpenetration of the Persons, 127
Invisible Church, 135, 157
Irenaeus, 17, 22, 24f., 33, 53f., 62, 71ff., 91, 106ff., 132, 139f., 160, 164, 166
Isis, 91

General Index

James the Just, 25
Jeroboam II, 91
Jerome, 66, 93, 98, 105, 123, 159. 164, 180, 185, 187
Jesus, Aeon, 63f.
Jewish religion, 89f.
Jezebel, 177
John the Apostle, 22ff., 41, 65, 75, 95, 99, 107, 109, 115, 124
John of Antioch, 203f.
John the Baptist, 41, 188
John of Constantinople, 198
John of Jerusalem, 159
John, Meletian bishop, 174
Josiah, 177
Jovian, 175, 201
Julian, 175, 177, 180ff., 198, 201
Justin Martyr, 33ff., 47ff., 54f., 62, 82, 90, 92, 105, 120, 140, 146, 155, 160, 171

Lactantius, 28, 37, 39, 134
Lapsi, 137, 141, 143ff., 146f.
Laurentius, 144
Laymen, their right to baptize, 139
Leo of Rome, 20, 180, 207
Leonidas, 92, 171
Liberius of Rome, 201
Licinius, 173f.
Linus of Rome, 77
Little Labyrinth, 119
Logos, 19, 40ff., 54, 65, 81, 93f., 103f., 108, 125, 194f., 200, 204f.
Lord's Day, 20
Lord's Supper, see Eucharist
Love, God is, 115
Lucian of Antioch, 126, 196
Lucius (Arian), 188
Lucius of Rome, 144
Luke, 57, 75
Luther, 156, 158, 198

Macedonius of Constantinople, 126, 202
Macedonians, 176, 202
Majorinus, 148
Mammaea, Julia, 98, 172
Man among men, 81
Man and the Fall, see Original Sin
Man and freedom, 158ff.
Manasseh, 177
Manhood of Christ, 205
Manichaeans, 155, 176, 185f.
Marcellina, 58
Marcellinus, 148
Marcellus of Ancyra, 103
Marcia, 34
Marcian, 208

Marcion, 22, 35ff., 56ff., 60, 75, 78ff., 204
Marcionites, 96, 132
Marcus Aurelius, 25, 34, 36, 43, 99, 171, 181
Marcurius, 187
Mardaura, 34
Mark, 23f., 75f., 89
Martialis, 143
Matthew, 23f., 28, 74, 76, 90, 99, 160, 178
Matthias, 61
Martyrdom, 19, 39, 135, 143
Martyrs, 19, 23, 34, 37, 43, 92, 102, 144
Mary, 53, 61, 64
Massilians, 167
Maxentius, 173, 176
Maximian, 173
Maximilla, 67
Maximin I, 172
Maximin II, 147, 173
Meletians, 174, 195
Meletius of Lycopolis, 147
Melito of Sardis, 36, 42ff.
Menander, 55ff.
Mensurius of Carthage, 147
Methodius of Olympus, 103
Merit versus grace, 158ff.
Milan, Edict of, 176f., 181ff.
Millennium, 24, 72
Millenarianism, 90
Miltiades of Rome, 67, 148
Milvian Bridge, battle of, 173, 176f., 180
Minucius Felix, 35, 38, 40, 46, 141
Mixed cup, 140
Modalism, 114
Monarchia, 114, 122ff., 127
Monarchians, 113ff., 122, 142f., 153
Monasticism, 166, 184ff.
Monica, 155
Montanism, 28, 66ff., 71, 77, 114, 122, 134f., 142, 158
Moses, 28, 36, 38, 40f., 53, 57, 80, 90, 94, 113, 116, 119, 142, 155, 208
Mother of God, 53, 202ff.

Muritorian Fragment, 15, 26
Natalius, 120
Natures of Christ, the two, 21, 44, 65, 90, 108; see Nestorius, Eutyches
Neo-Platonism, 91, 95, 108f., 131, 155, 157, 173, 185f.
Nestorius, 193, 203ff.
Nero, 91, 181
Nerva, 33
New Testament Canon, 15
Nicea, Council of, see Councils

General Index 223

Nicene Creed, *see* Creeds
Nicholas of Myra (Santa Claus), 195
Nitria, 186
Noah, 57, 138
Noetus, 117, 120, 124
Novatian, 119, 123, 135, 137, 142f., 212
Novatians, 147, 149, 153, 158, 174, 176, 182

Octavius, 38
Oikonomia, 122ff., 127
Ophites, 51
Orange, Council of, 158, 166f.
Origen, 15, 25, 29, 33, 35, 54, 72, 89ff., 97ff., 113ff., 124, 126, 128, 132, 134, 136, 139, 141ff., 154, 156, 158, 161, 162, 165f., 202f.
Original Sin, 139, 160, 162, 164
Ousia, 128, 193ff.

Pachomius, 187
Pamphilus of Caesarea, 97, 99, 102
Pantaenus of Alexandria, 90, 92
Papias of Hierapolis, 24ff.
Paraclete, 67f., 77, 134
Pastor of Hermas, The,, 15, 25ff.
Patripassians, 114, 117, 121, 142
Paul, the Apostle, 16, 19, 21, 23, 25, 28f., 35ff., 52, 54, 57f., 62, 65, 72ff., 82ff., 92, 103, 105, 107, 124, 153, 156, 162, 164ff., 188, 207
Paul of Neo-Caesarea, 195
Paul of Samosata, 117ff., 126, 172, 196, 205
Pelagius, 155, 158ff., 162, 165ff.
Penance, 142
Persecutions: (Decius) 135, 172; (Diocletian) 173; (Galerius) 173; (Gallus) 135; (Licinius) 173, 174; (Maximin) 173; (Septimius Severus) 91; (Valerian) 135
Person:
  God the Father, 78, 101, 114ff., 121ff., 126ff., 154
  God the Son, 65, 101, 114ff., 121ff., 126ff., 202ff., 133, 154, 206ff.
  God the Holy Spirit, 84ff., 102, 114ff., 121, 126ff., 154, 203
Peter, the Apostle, 16, 24, 41, 53, 58, 73ff., 92, 103, 137, 146
Peter of Alexandria, 146
Pharaoh, 146
Philemon, Ep. to, 75, 78
Philemon, Presbyter of Rome, 145
Philip, 172
Philip, the Evangelist, 24
Philo, 36, 40, 89, 124, 125

Photius, 98
Pierius, 102
Pilate, 58, 206
Pius, Bishop of Rome, 25
Plato, 37f., 53, 58, 72, 79, 89ff., 94, 108, 113, 122, 124
Pleroma, 51, 52f., 62ff., 79, 81, 194
Pliny, 34, 141
Polycarp of Smyrna, 16, 18f., 22ff., 24f., 33f., 71f., 92, 141, 171
Pontianus, 172
Pontifex Maximus, 176
Pope, 137, 146
Pothinus, 71
Praxeas, 117, 120f., 124
Predestination, 158, 165ff.
Pre-existence of the soul, 104, 164f., 204
Presbyters, 17, 21, 24, 77, 138
Prisca, 67
Probus, 173
Procession of the Holy Spirit, 127f.
Prophets, 28, 56f., 119
Ptolemais, 64
Pulcheria, Empress, 208
Pythagoras, 53, 58, 62, 64, 159
Pythagoreans, 79

Quadratus, 36, 37
Quicumque Vult, 188

Ransom to the devil, 82f., 106, 165
Resurrection, 17, 57, 83, 106
Revelation, Book of, 75, 90
Rhoda, 25
Roman Catholicism, 53
Romans, Ep. to the, 99, 153, 156, 162, 178
Rome, pre-eminence of the Church of, 17, 22, 96, 132
Rufinus of Aquileia, 98f., 102, 180
Rule of Faith, 72, 76ff., 84, 91, 100, 108, 122, 148

Sabbath, 20
Sabellius, 114, 116ff., 126
Sabellianism, 196, 199
Sacraments, 136, 138ff.
Sacrifice of Christ, 106f., *see* Atonement
Salvation only in the Church, 134
Satan's right over men, 82, 106, 107
Saturnilus or Saturninus, 59ff.
Scetis, 186
Schisms: Donatists, 147; Meletians, 146, 195; Montanists, 66; Novatians, 143
Scriptures, 57, 91, 100, 105f., 108, 118, 120

General Index

Second Coming, 29, 68, 90; see Millennium
Secundas of Ptolemais, 197
Secundus of Numidia, 147
Seed, cosmic, 61f.
Semi-Arians, 199f.
Semi-Augustinians, 166
Semi-Pelagians, 166
Septimius Severus, 91ff., 98, 120, 171
Serapio, 34
Seth, 81
Sethians, 51
Similitudes, 27
Simon of Cyrene, 60
Simon Magus, 54ff., 68
Sin, see Original Sin
Sinatic Manuscript, 15, 25, 29, 37
Sinlessness of Christ, 204
Socrates of Athens, 38, 53, 89, 94
Socrates (Church historian), 174, 176, 177, 180, 187f., 195, 198ff., 203
Solidarity of the race, 82, 164
Solomon, 177
Son of God, 47, 81ff., 94, 108, 196ff.
Sophia, 63f.
Sophroninus of Pompeiopolis, 199
Soul of Christ, 58, 104, 108, 204
Soul of man, 58, 60, 64, 104, 164
Sozomen, 176f., 180f., 186, 188, 199, 200f.
Stephan of Rome, 143, 145, 156
Stoics, 34, 37f., 40, 45, 89, 131
Substance, 128, 194, 196
Sufferings of Christ, 19, 43, 60, 66, 82, 96, 106, 117, 124, 165, 206
Symeon of Jerusalem, 25
Sylvester of Rome, 195

Tacitus, 173
Tatian, 33, 36f., 40, 46
Teaching of the Twelve Apostles, see *Didache*
Tertullian, 26, 33f., 36ff., 42, 44ff., 47f., 54, 56f., 66f., 71, 73ff., 91, 115, 117, 119ff., 126, 134, 136, 139f., 142, 146, 153, 156, 158, 161, 164, 193, 196
Theoctitus of Caesarea, 98
Theodas, 62
Theodore of Mopsuestia, 205f.
Theodoret of Cyrrhus, 180, 195, 197, 199f., 203ff.

Theodosius I, 176f., 181f., 197, 202
Theodosius II, 203, 207
Theodotus of Byzantium, 117
Theodutus of Rome, 117
Theodotians, 120
Theognis of Nicea, 174
Theonas of Marmarica, 197
Theophilus of Antioch, 36, 46
Theotokos, see Mother of God
Timothy, 72
Tischendorf, Count, 15, 37
Tome of Leo, 207f.
Traditores, 147
Traducianism, 164
Trajan, 33f., 141
Transmutation of souls, 79
Transubstantiation, 86, 139
Trent, Council of, 139
Trinitarian Formula, 55
Trinity, 43ff., 114ff., 121ff., 126ff., 135f., 153f.
Trypho, 35f., 39, 47
Two Ways, 28f.

Union of the two natures, see Nestorius, Eutyches
Unity of the Church, see Catholicism
Unity of the Godhead, see Trinity

Valens, 175, 180, 182, 185, 188, 201
Valentinian, 175, 182, 201
Valentinus, 62ff., 67, 98, 204
Valerian, 135, 144ff., 172
Victor of Rome, 67, 77, 114, 117, 120
Visible Church, 17, 21, 133ff., 157
Virgin birth, 19, 76, 82, 101

Wisdom, identified with Holy Spirit, 84
Wisdom, Queen of Philosophy, 91
Word, see Logos
Worship, 20, 34, 39, 40

Xystus of Rome, 144f.

Zeno, 45, 159
Zenobia, Empress, 120
Zephyrinus of Rome, 114, 117, 119f., 209
Zoroaster, 53
Zosimus of Rome, 159

www.ingramcontent.com/pod-product-compliance
Lightning Source LLC
Chambersburg PA
CBHW062026220426
43662CB00010B/1487